Microsoft System Center Data Protection Manager Cookbook

Maximize storage efficiency, performance, and security using System Center LTSC and SAC releases

Charbel Nemnom
Patrick Lownds

D1483507

BIRMINGHAM - MUMBAI

WITHDRAWN FROM
RAPIDES PARISH LIBRARY

RAPIDES PARISH LIBRARY
Alexandria, Louisiana HQ

Microsoft System Center Data Protection Manager Cookbook

Copyright © 2018 Packt Publishing

All rights reserved. No part of this book may be reproduced, stored in a retrieval system, or transmitted in any form or by any means, without the prior written permission of the publisher, except in the case of brief quotations embedded in critical articles or reviews.

Every effort has been made in the preparation of this book to ensure the accuracy of the information presented. However, the information contained in this book is sold without warranty, either express or implied. Neither the authors, nor Packt Publishing or its dealers and distributors, will be held liable for any damages caused or alleged to have been caused directly or indirectly by this book.

Packt Publishing has endeavored to provide trademark information about all of the companies and products mentioned in this book by the appropriate use of capitals. However, Packt Publishing cannot guarantee the accuracy of this information.

Commissioning Editor: Vijin Boricha
Acquisition Editor: Rahul Nair
Content Development Editor: Abhishek Jadhav
Technical Editor: Prachi Sawant
Copy Editor: Safis
Project Coordinator: Jagdish Prabhu
Proofreader: Safis Editing
Indexer: Tejal Daruwale Soni
Graphics: Tom Scaria
Production Coordinator: Arvindkumar Gupta

First published: December 2018

Production reference: 1211218

Published by Packt Publishing Ltd.
Livery Place
35 Livery Street
Birmingham
B3 2PB, UK.

ISBN 978-1-78728-928-4

www.packtpub.com

Nothing stops the man who desires to achieve. Every obstacle is simply a course to develop his achievement muscle. It's a strengthening of his powers of accomplishment.

– Charbel Nemnom

For Norman Callaghan who is always in my thoughts.

– Patrick Lownds

`mapt.io`

Mapt is an online digital library that gives you full access to over 5,000 books and videos, as well as industry leading tools to help you plan your personal development and advance your career. For more information, please visit our website.

Why subscribe?

- Spend less time learning and more time coding with practical eBooks and Videos from over 4,000 industry professionals

- Improve your learning with Skill Plans built especially for you

- Get a free eBook or video every month

- Mapt is fully searchable

- Copy and paste, print, and bookmark content

Packt.com

Did you know that Packt offers eBook versions of every book published, with PDF and ePub files available? You can upgrade to the eBook version at `www.packt.com` and as a print book customer, you are entitled to a discount on the eBook copy. Get in touch with us at `customercare@packtpub.com` for more details.

At `www.packt.com`, you can also read a collection of free technical articles, sign up for a range of free newsletters, and receive exclusive discounts and offers on Packt books and eBooks.

Contributors

About the authors

Charbel Nemnom is a Cloud Solutions Architect for itnetX (Switzerland) AG and a Microsoft Most Valuable Professional (MVP) for cloud and datacenter management. He has over 17 years of professional experience in IT. He works predominantly with the most recent versions of Windows Server, System Center, Microsoft Azure, and Azure Stack.

Charbel has previously contributed to several books, all of which were published by Packt. He is Microsoft-, Cisco-, and PMI- certified and holds the following credentials: MCP, MCSA, MCTS, MCITP, MCS, MCSE, CCNP, ITIL®, and PMP®. You can follow him on Twitter at @CharbelNemnom.

> *I would like to say a big thanks to my family and friends for their support and patience while I was busy than usual the last one and half year, and for always supporting the things I want to do. I thank my co-author and fellow MVP Patrick Lownds who offered great feedback, and support throughout this project. Also, I want to thank the Microsoft product group and give them the credit they deserve for helping me make this book as good as possible.*

Patrick Lownds is a master-level solution architect working for Pointnext Advisory & Professional Services, in the Hybrid IT COE, for Hewlett Packard Enterprise (HPE), and is based in London, UK.

He currently works with the most recent versions of Windows Server and System Center and has participated in the Windows Server, System Center, and Microsoft Azure Stack Early Adoption Program.

He is a community blogger for HPE and tweets in his spare time. He can be found on Twitter as @patricklownds.

About the reviewer

Michael Seidl is a senior consultant and team leader in service management and automation, working for Base-IT, a Gold Partner in Systems Management, located in Austria. He is a three-time System Center Cloud and Datacenter Management MVP and a well certified Microsoft engineer with MCSA and MCSE. His experience as an IT consultant has been growing since 2001 and is mainly focused on SCDPM, SCO, SCSM, and PowerShell. Working with some of the biggest companies in Austria gives him the opportunity to work on exciting projects with complex requirements. Michael is also the founder of au2mator, a self service portal for Microsoft Automation. Follow Michael on Twitter at @techguyat or @au2mator.

Packt is searching for authors like you

If you're interested in becoming an author for Packt, please visit authors.packtpub.com and apply today. We have worked with thousands of developers and tech professionals, just like you, to help them share their insight with the global tech community. You can make a general application, apply for a specific hot topic that we are recruiting an author for, or submit your own idea.

Table of Contents

Preface

System Center Data Protection Manager (SCDPM) is a robust enterprise backup and recovery system that contributes to your Business Continuity and Disaster Recovery (BCDR) strategy by facilitating the backup and recovery of enterprise data. With an increase in data recovery and protection problems faced in organizations, it has become important to keep data safe and recoverable. This book contains recipes that will help you upgrade to SCDPM and it covers the advanced features and functionality of SCDPM.

This book starts by helping you install SCDPM and then moves on to post-installation and management tasks. You will come across a lot of useful recipes that will help you recover your Hyper-V and VMware VMs. It will also walk you through tips for monitoring SCDPM in different scenarios. Next, the book will also offer insights into protecting windows workloads followed by best practices on SCDPM. You will also learn to back up your Azure Stack Infrastructure layer as well as the Tenant layer using SCDPM. You will also learn about recovering data from backup and implementing disaster recovery.

Lastly, the book will show you how to integrate SCDPM with Azure Backup service as well as how to enable protection groups for online protection, and finally how to centralize reports and monitor your backups using Power BI and Log Analytics.

Who this book is for

If you are a backup administrator and working with SCDPM, this book will help you verify your knowledge and provide you with everything you need to know about the latest release of System Center Data Protection Manager and Microsoft Azure Backup Server. This book will also cover the Long-Term Servicing Channel (LTSC) and Semi-Annual Channel (SAC) for SCDPM. No prior knowledge about System Center DPM is required, however, some experience of working with Windows Server and running backups will come in handy.

What this book covers

Chapter 1, *Installing and Upgrading DPM*, helps you to plan and prepare your DPM deployment. Then, you will learn how to install SQL Server for the DPM database. Also, we will cover how you can enable the Transport Layer Security 1.2 protocol for DPM. In the end, we will cover the installation and upgrading of DPM and DPM agents.

Chapter 2, *DPM Post-Installation and Management Tasks*, teaches you the techniques for dealing with the post-installation and management tasks of your Microsoft SCDPM. By the end of the chapter, you will have the knowledge to carry out common DPM management activities, such as using the DPM console, configuring modern backup storage, creating a dedicated backup network, creating custom reporting using SQL Server Reporting Services, and many more tasks besides.

Chapter 3, *Protecting Hyper-V VMs*, covers the protection and recovery of Hyper-V VMs at the private cloud scale using SCDPM. Different protection configurations that apply to Hyper-V VMs, and the different restore options that you can exercise, are covered in details.

Chapter 4, *Monitoring DPM and Configuring Role-Based Access*, provides you with the skills and techniques for dealing with post-deployment monitoring and management tasks of your Microsoft System Center DPM server. After reading this chapter, you will have the knowledge to carry out common DPM monitoring and management activities.

Chapter 5, *Protecting Microsoft Workloads with DPM*, describes how SCDPM orchestrates the backup of different Microsoft workloads. You will learn how to enable file server, SQL server protection, and Windows bare-metal protection with SCDPM.

Chapter 6, *Securing Windows Client with DPM*, helps you create a plan for backing up end-user data. Secondly, you will configure the SCDPM and Active Directory for end user protection. In the end, you will learn how to install agents automatically and manually on a client computer.

Chapter 7, *Protecting Microsoft Azure Stack with DPM*, gets into preparing backup tenant workloads in Azure Stack with SCDPM. Also, you will back up the infrastructure layer and Azure stack metadata.

Chapter 8, *Protecting Workgroups and Untrusted Domains*, explains NT LAN Manager (NTLM) and certificate-based authentication protection. Also, you will find out about how to protect workgroup machines using NTLM and certificate-based authentication.

Chapter 9, *Recovering Data from Backup*, describes how SCDPM orchestrates the recovery of different Microsoft workloads. You will learn how to recover file server, SQL databases using self-service recovery, and Windows bare metal recovery. In the end, you will learn about recovering from Azure Backup cloud recovery points as well as recover data from different DPM servers.

Chapter 10, *Integrating DPM with Azure Backup*, describes how Azure Backup and DPM provide a compelling, hybrid cloud backup solution for your organization. In the end, you will learn about monitoring and centralized reporting with Power BI and Log Analytics.

Chapter 11, *Protecting VMware VMs*, teaches you about DPM agentless VMware VM backup, and VMware credential management. Also, you will learn how you can create a new role in vCenter. In the end, you will learn how you can add, protect, back up, and recover VMware VMs. To go to this chapter refer to this link: https://www.packtpub.com/sites/default/files/downloads/Protecting_VMware_VMs.pdf

Chapter 12, *Implementing Disaster Recovery with DPM*, dives deep into how to protect the DPM database as well as how to recover your DPM server in case of disaster. In the end, you will implement DPM chaining and cyclic protection. To go to this chapter refer to this link: https://www.packtpub.com/sites/default/files/downloads/Implementing_Disaster_Recovery_with_DPM.pdf

Chapter 13, *Online Articles*, this chapter gives understanding about SCDPM concepts and what's new in DPM's latest release. It also covers prerequisites including what's new in DPM's latest release. To go to this chapter refer to this link: https://www.packtpub.com/sites/default/files/downloads/Online_Articles.pdf.

To get the most out of this book

In order to complete all the recipes in this book, you will require software such as DPM version 2016, DPM version 2019, DPM version 1801, DPM version 1807, and DPM version 1901. The operating systems that are used are Windows Server 2016 and Windows Server 2019. In terms of hardware, you will require physical or virtual machines with 8 GB RAM and 2 CPUs. All the installation steps and detailed information are given in the recipes of each chapter.

Download the color images

We also provide a PDF file that has color images of the screenshots/diagrams used in this book. You can download it here: https://www.packtpub.com/sites/default/files/downloads/9781787289284_ColorImages.pdf.

Conventions used

There are a number of text conventions used throughout this book.

`CodeInText`: Indicates code words in text, database table names, folder names, filenames, file extensions, pathnames, dummy URLs, user input, and Twitter handles. Here is an example: "On the protected server, use your preferred text editor to open the `c:\windows\system32\drivers\etc\hosts` file."

Any command-line input or output is written as follows:

```
Connect-DPMServer -DPMServerName $env:COMPUTERNAME
```

Bold: Indicates a new term, an important word, or words that you see on screen. For example, words in menus or dialog boxes appear in the text like this. Here is an example: "Click **OK** to confirm, and then click on **Next >** to continue."

Warnings or important notes appear like this.

Tips and tricks appear like this.

Sections

In this book, you will find several headings that appear frequently (*Getting ready*, *How to do it...*, *How it works...*, *There's more...*, and *See also*).

To give clear instructions on how to complete a recipe, use these sections as follows:

Getting ready

This section tells you what to expect in the recipe and describes how to set up any software or any preliminary settings required for the recipe.

How to do it...

This section contains the steps required to follow the recipe.

How it works...

This section usually consists of a detailed explanation of what happened in the previous section.

There's more...

This section consists of additional information about the recipe in order to make you more knowledgeable of it.

See also

This section provides helpful links to other useful information for the recipe.

Get in touch

Feedback from our readers is always welcome.

General feedback: If you have questions about any aspect of this book, mention the book title in the subject of your message and email us at customercare@packtpub.com.

Errata: Although we have taken every care to ensure the accuracy of our content, mistakes do happen. If you have found a mistake in this book, we would be grateful if you would report this to us. Please visit www.packt.com/submit-errata, selecting your book, clicking on the Errata Submission Form link, and entering the details.

Piracy: If you come across any illegal copies of our works in any form on the internet, we would be grateful if you would provide us with the location address or website name. Please contact us at copyright@packt.com with a link to the material.

If you are interested in becoming an author: If there is a topic that you have expertise in, and you are interested in either writing or contributing to a book, please visit authors.packtpub.com.

Reviews

Please leave a review. Once you have read and used this book, why not leave a review on the site that you purchased it from? Potential readers can then see and use your unbiased opinion to make purchase decisions, we at Packt can understand what you think about our products, and our authors can see your feedback on their book. Thank you!

For more information about Packt, please visit `packt.com`.

Installing and Upgrading DPM

1

In this chapter, we will cover the following recipes:

- Planning your DPM deployment
- Preparing your DPM deployment
- Installing SQL Server for the DPM database
- Enabling the Transport Layer Security 1.2 protocol for DPM
- Installing DPM
- Automating the installation of DPM
- Upgrading to the latest release of DPM
- Migrating legacy storage to Modern Backup Storage
- Installing the DPM agents
- Upgrading the DPM agents

Introduction

Data protection in today's world is becoming more critical than ever. With increasing amounts of data in this all-connected world comes more data that needs to be protected. As shown in the **Enterprise Strategy Group** (**ESG**) 2016 report, backup is one of the top five priorities that IT administrators continue to have in today's world:

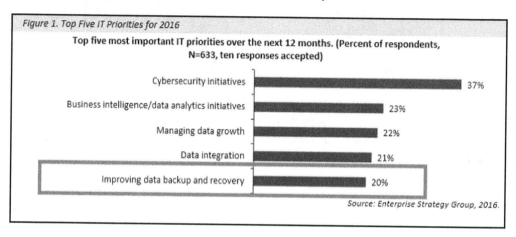

Figure 1. Top Five IT Priorities for 2016

System Center 2019's **Data Protection Manager** (**DPM**) is the latest release by Microsoft, and with it comes a lot of improvements and new features. DPM is well-recognized in the industry for protection of Microsoft workloads and VMware environments. With DPM 2019, you can back up the most common workloads that exist in any modern data center today.

The following diagram provides an overview of the DPM backup functionality:

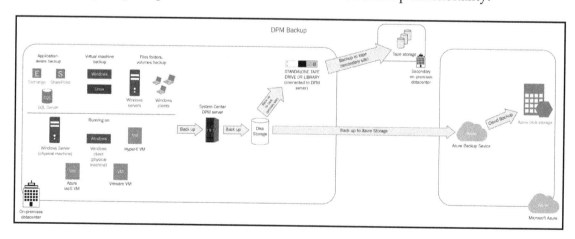

Typical malware attacks that happen today include ransomware, which is where target machines are forced to either re-encrypt their data or remove it permanently. If production data is impacted, then the backups that follow are impacted on too. Microsoft System Center DPM and Azure backup now provide security features that protect sensitive data. These security features ensure that you are able to secure your backups and recover your data if the production and backup servers are compromised. These features are built on three main principles—**Prevention**, **Alerting**, and **Recovery**—that help organizations to increase preparedness against attacks and equip them with a robust backup solution.

This chapter is designed to provide you with the necessary skills and techniques for dealing with installing and upgrading tasks for your Microsoft System Center DPM server. After reading this chapter, you will have the knowledge to carry out common DPM installation, migration, and planning activities, such as configuring the DPM firewall, calculating the storage requirements, preparing the SQL Server for the DPM database, installing and upgrading to the latest release of DPM, automating the installation of DPM, and much more.

Planning your DPM deployment

This recipe will cover the planning steps that you should consider before you start preparing to deploy your DPM servers.

Getting ready

Before you start planning your DPM server deployment, it's imperative that you start working on classifying the data sources that you would like to protect. A common strategy that I have observed that many companies still follow is to backup everything once a day. This is not a good approach.

There are, of course, several servers within your datacenter that need to be regularly backed up, but not all servers are the same. It is vital to adapt to your business continuity and disaster-recovery plan before you start any implementation. You can do this by identifying all of the services and working with all of the stakeholders in your company to develop more effective backup approaches, and then break down those services into smaller components to clearly see how or why they are of importance to your business.

How to do it...

From a more technical perspective, there are some considerations that need to be addressed during the planning phase, such as the following:

- The total amount of data that should be protected
- Firewall settings
- Network consideration
- Who can interact with DPM
- Untrusted domains/workgroup
- Backup repository

To start provisioning resources for the DPM server that you want to deploy, you must first take into consideration the following:

1. Starting with DPM 2016 onward, Microsoft removed the **Logical Disk Manager (LDM)** limits for protection groups. The absence of LDM limits allows the data sources to grow and shrink as many times as needed, without the need for manual intervention. DPM 2016 or later does not need to allocate storage to data sources beforehand compared to DPM 2012 R2. This will allow the backups to adjust dynamically as needed, thus achieving higher efficiency with less storage requirements. The snapshot limits do not apply to protection groups that have been created in DPM 2016, as DPM does not use disks anymore. Instead, it uses volumes. Please read Chapter 2, *DPM Post-Installation and Management Tasks*, for more information on this.

2. Here are the suggested data limits according to Microsoft for a single DPM server:
   - DPM can protect up to 600 volumes. The limit for each DPM is 120 TB, 80 TB ReplicaPoint Volume, and 40 TB RecoveryPoint.
   - The total amount of SQL DBs that can be protected by one DPM server is 2,000 and the total size is 80 TB.
   - The total amount of clients that can be protected with one DPM server is 3,000 and the total size is 80 TB.
   - The total amount of virtual machines that can be protected with one DPM server is 800 and the total size is 80 TB.

3. Firewall configuration for DPM deployment is required on the DPM server, on the machines that you want to protect, and on the SQL Server used for the DPM database (if you're hosting your DPM database on a remote SQL Server). If Windows Firewall is enabled when you install DPM, then DPM automatically configures the firewall settings on the DPM server.

The firewall settings, including the port numbers, are documented in the following link: https://docs.microsoft.com/en-us/system-center/dpm/plan-dpm-deployment?view=sc-dpm-1711#BKMK_Firewall.

4. The backup network for Hyper-V is not listed as a requirement by Microsoft. However, we strongly recommend isolating the backup traffic from the host Management OS by leveraging a converged network in Hyper-V where you combine multiple physical NICs with **Switch-Embedded Teaming** (**SET**) and **Quality of Service** (**QoS**) so that you can isolate all network traffic while maintaining resiliency. This implementation can be seen in following diagram:

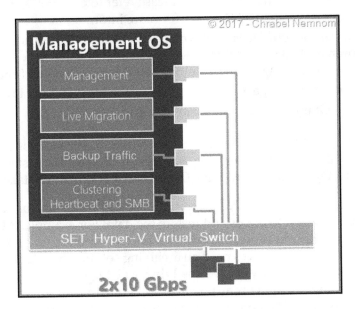

5. Before you begin with the deployment, you need to verify that the appropriate users have been granted the required privileges for performing various DPM tasks.

The required permissions needed are documented at the following link: https://docs.microsoft.com/en-us/system-center/dpm/plan-dpm-deployment?view=sc-dpm-1711#BKMK_Users.

6. If you want to protect multiple domains, you can create a two-way transitive trust between the domains. By doing this, the DPM server will work in both domains without any limitations. However, this approach comes with a security risk—please take into consideration that you need to create a two-way transitive trust between the untrusted domains.

7. Starting with System Center 2012 R2 Data Protection Manager, Microsoft added support for the protection of computers in workgroups and untrusted domains using NTLM with local accounts. However, in scenarios where an organization does not allow for the creation of local accounts, this solution does not work.

8. As an alternative, you can use certificate-based authentication for computers in workgroups or untrusted domains. Please refer to `Chapter 8`, *Protecting Workgroups and Untrusted Domains,* for more information.

9. A major part of your DPM deployment will be figuring out how to store data that's been backed up by DPM. There are currently three different solutions:

   - Disk storage using volumes with **Modern Backup Storage** (**MBS**)
   - Tape storage, such as Physical or the **Virtual Tape Library** (**VTL**)
   - Online storage with Azure Backup (off-site)

You should not just consider one of these three as an option. Instead, you need to focus on the requirements of the backup strategy in your organization by discussing the **Recovery Point Objective** (**RPO**) and **Recovery Time Objective** (**RTO**) with all stakeholders.

When you are planning for data source protection, you can choose the backup target based on how frequently you need to access and restore the data. For example, if the data sources will be used for archiving and need to be accessed once per month, you can go with Azure Backup. If the protected data sources need an archiving solution but should also be able to restore quickly, you can go with **Virtual Tape Library** (**VTL**) or Azure Backup. If you need to restore the data sources as quickly as possible, you go with disk storage on-premises. Finally, if the workloads need an off-site secure solution, you can go with Azure Backup.

 More information about the difference between RPO and RTO can be found here: `https://en.wikipedia.org/wiki/Recovery_point_objective`.

How it works...

Having all of the information we have just discussed and presented in an organized manner, you can now start designing the structure of the **Backup as a Service** (**BaaS**). A piece of advice here—make sure that you spend enough time on the planning phase and take small steps toward your goal and never rush an implementation. You will probably bump into a challenge or two, so it is of key importance to work using a well-defined structure.

See also

- Follow this blog post to learn more about how to set the firewall rules for DPM using Windows PowerShell: `https://charbelnemnom.com/2017/03/installing-system-center-data-protection-manager-2016-agent-on-windows-server-2016-core-scdpm-dpm-ws2016/`.
- Follow the following blog post to learn more on how to isolate DPM backup traffic: `https://charbelnemnom.com/2014/04/isolate-dpm-backup-traffic-in-hyper-v/`.

Preparing your DPM deployment

This recipe will cover the preparation steps that you must consider before you install the DPM server.

Getting ready

It's important to configure DPM properly and provide enough resources, or you will end up with quite a bad installation that could be part of the services you would like to provision within your data center. In the end, the DPM server can never work faster than what the underlying dependent architecture or technology allows.

There are certain requirements and considerations that you want to keep in mind when you deploy System Center DPM. By properly preparing a decent design, you can ensure that your DPM is scalable for future scenarios.

How to do it...

1. First things first, you want to decide how to deploy DPM server:
   - Virtual or physical deployment
   - Deduping DPM data
   - SQL Server consideration
   - DPM server requirement
   - Disks and storage consumption

   A common question that we have heard a lot is, can we deploy DPM in a virtual or physical machine? The DPM server can be deployed either in a physical deployment or via a virtual machine. However, running DPM in a virtual machine has more benefits, such as the following:

   - It is easier to move the DPM server to new hardware if needed (portability).
   - Easier to recover (protected DPM virtual machine).
   - You can enable de-duplication on the VHDXs attached to the DPM server. The VHDXs files could reside on a **Scale-Out File Server** (**SOFS**), on a **Storage Spaces Direct** (**S2D**) cluster, or any other type of storage, such as NAS or SAN.

2. Backup storage is one of the top consumers of storage infrastructure, so storage optimization techniques such as compression and de-duplication have always been priorities for backup IT administrators.

3. De-duplication involves locating duplicate blocks of storage and replacing them with a reference and a single instance of the duplicate block. Depending on the workload that is being written to the storage and the block sizes used to perform the de-duplication, storage savings can range anywhere from 50 to 90 percent.

4. With the introduction of S2D in Windows Server 2016 and Storage Spaces with SOFS in Windows Server 2012 R2, customers can create commodity storage that is built natively on a Windows-based server with local attached storage in S2D as well as Windows-based servers with JBODs, which can be a viable alternative to traditional SANs.

 In Windows Server 2016, Dedup is only supported on the NTFS filesystem and NOT on ReFS. However, in Windows Server 2019, Microsoft added Dedup support for ReFS volumes. Additionally, Dedup cannot be used for storing backups of volumes on physical DPM servers.

5. For DPM deployments, you need to have the following:

   - An instance of SQL Server installed and running to host the DPM database. The instance can be collocated on the DPM server or remotely.
   - A disk to be used as a dedicated space for DPM backup storage.
   - A DPM protection agent installed on the computers and servers you want to protect.

6. DPM uses SQL Server as a database to store backup information for the workloads, servers, and computers it protects. At the time of writing this book, the following SQL Server versions are supported with DPM Long-Term Servicing Channel (LTSC) and Semi-Annual Channel (SAC):

   - **SQL Server 2017**: Standard or Enterprise 64-bit (starting with DPM 2019 and DPM 1901 onward)
   - **SQL Server 2017**: Standard or Enterprise 64-bit (starting with DPM 1801 and DPM 1807 as upgrade only); you can upgrade SQL Server 2016 and SQL Server 2016 SP1/SP2, to SQL Server 2017
   - **SQL Server 2016**: Standard or Enterprise 64-bit (starting with DPM 2016 with Update Rollup 2 onward)
   - **SQL Server 2014**: Standard or Enterprise 64-bit with all service packs and updates
   - **SQL Server 2012 SP2 onward**: Standard or Enterprise 64-bit

 Please note that SQL Server 2016 SP1/SP2 or later is not a supported DPM database for DPM 2016.

7. DPM server is designed to run on a dedicated, single-purpose server. The following applications and roles are not supported to run side-by-side with DPM:

   - Application server role
   - Operations Manager Management server
   - Exchange server
   - A server running on a cluster node

8. The following Windows Server operating systems are supported with DPM 2016 or later:
    - Windows Server 2019, Datacenter and Standard editions
    - Windows Server 2016, Datacenter and Standard editions
    - Windows Server 2012 R2, Datacenter and Standard editions

Please note that if you install DPM 2016 or later on Windows Server 2012 R2, you will lose the benefit of using MBS. MBS technology uses ReFS block-cloning technology that was introduced in Windows Server 2016 to store incremental backups. Installing DPM on Windows Server 2016 or Windows Server 2019 dramatically improves storage utilization and performance.

9. **System Center Data Protection Manager (SC DPM)** can use any type of disk that is presented as local attached storage. DPM can use any of the following:

    - **Direct Attached Storage (DAS)**
    - **Fiber Channel Storage Area Network (FC SAN)**
    - **iSCSI Network Attached Storage (NAS)**
    - **Hyper-V Virtual Hard Disks (VHDX)**

A very important fact to be aware of is that the **internet Small Computer System Interface (iSCSI)** should not be considered as your primary choice for DPM backup storage due to some challenges that often occur when leveraging this technology. The most common challenge is that the initiation of the iSCSI target sometimes fails, and therefore the entire DPM disk volume fails.

iSCSI will work in smaller deployments with DPM, but if your main objective is to provide a more stable and performant solution, you should consider using Storage Spaces Direct (S2D). If your company does not provide S2D, you should use a Direct Attached Storage (DAS) solution and provision VHDX files to the virtual DPM servers. Microsoft recommendation moving forward is to create tiered volume using Storage Spaces with small SSD around 2 to 5% of total data disk to improve the ReFS cloning performance. As noted earlier, the recommendation is to deploy DPM as a virtual machine on top of Hyper-V.

As discussed earlier, DPM 2016 or later on Windows Server 2016 and Windows Server 2019 comes with MBS, which uses ReFS Block-Cloning technology for storing backup files. This leads to immense storage and performance savings. Furthermore, DPM uses incremental backups to store data. This means that it will transfer the complete data to be backed up initially. After that, it will transfer only the changed bits. Hence, the size of the data is determined by the initial size, the size of the changed bits (which depends on the churn percentage and the total size), the number of recovery points per day, and the retention period of the copies. Hence, small data, with a small churn, may take up more space if there are a large number of copies stored per day, and if they are retained for a long time.

 Please note that you must use volumes with MBS. A single DPM server can support up to 120 TB of storage.

How it works...

Calculating DPM storage is one of the biggest challenges, since we need to calculate the size of the disks for storage pools that are used for the protection of data sources. Microsoft recommends that you figure out the actual size of the DPM data storage by multiplying the total amount of protected data by 1.5. For instance, if you want to protect 10 TB of data, you need 15 TB of storage from a minimal perspective. However, from a maximum perspective, you need to multiply the total amount of protected data by 3.

 The best way to calculate data storage for specific workloads is to use the DPM storage calculator. To download the DPM storage calculator, go to `https://www.microsoft.com/en-us/download/details.aspx?id=54301`.

The DPM team released this calculator to help you provision storage for DPM by using storage savings and efficiency. Based on inputs, the calculator suggests the amount of storage that will be needed to store the backups to disk (on-premises) and to Azure Backup. For more information about Azure Backup, please refer to `Chapter 10`, *Integrating DPM with Azure Backup*.

You can plan the backup storage requirements by using the storage calculator in three simple steps, as follows:

1. Gather information about the size, type, number, and churn of workloads that have to be backed up. The churn is the amount of new data every day (that is, written or appended to existing backup files).
2. Calculate the number of DPM servers that would be required.
3. Decide on the policy you want to use, depending on the needs and resources available. This calculator may help you understand the resource requirements. If you expect the data to grow over time, you need to enter the maximum size expected for the workload, instead of the current size. Similarly, the churn values given are the average values. Please change the values if the workloads are expected to churn more or less. If you wish to remove a workload, simply set the **Total Size of workload** to 0.

You could also calculate the storage, including the growth rate. Note that this may change a bit depending on what you have for specific data types. With DPM, you can always add more storage later as needed. For monthly and yearly storage, this would need to be sent to tape and/or to Azure Backup. DPM cannot do long-term storage to disk.

 Please note that the maximum daily recovery points to a disk cannot exceed 48. The maximum number of recovery points for the entire retention period is 512 for applications and 64 for files and folders. For Azure Backup, the maximum number of recovery points per day is 2. Hence, the maximum number of weekly, monthly, and yearly backups is 14, 62, and 732.

There's more...

Planning for decent hardware to host the DPM disk volume is very important. You don't need a premium disk solution for the DPM disk volume, but you can use decent hardware that can easily scale out. Adding DPM volumes can be done via the DPM console or via PowerShell. For more information on this topic, please read the *Enabling Modern Backup Storage* recipe in Chapter 2, *DPM Post-Installation and Management Tasks*.

It's important to know the limitations of a DPM server that has been upgraded from DPM 2012 R2 and used a legacy storage pool:

- The disk that you want to add to the DPM storage pool must be dynamic in disk management.

- DPM cannot be installed on the disk that's used for the storage pool.
- You can attach or associate custom volumes with protected data sources. Custom volumes can be on basic or dynamic disks, but you can't manage the space on these volumes in the DPM Administrator Console.

See also

Follow this article to learn more on how to reduce DPM storage by enabling de-duplication on MBS: `https://charbelnemnom.com/2016/10/how-to-reduce-dpm-2016-storage-consumption-by-enabling-deduplication-on-modern-backup-storage/`.

Installing SQL Server for the DPM database

This recipe will cover the installation process in two scenarios:

- Local SQL Server instance
- Remote SQL Server instance

Getting ready

SQL Server is a core component and is required for the System Center Data Protection Manager database. It is of major importance that the installation and design of SQL Server is well-planned and implemented. If you have an undersized installation of SQL Server, it will provide you with a negative experience while operating the System Center Data Protection Manager.

Starting with DPM 2012 R2 and later, SQL Server is no longer a part of the installation media for DPM, which is a good thing. The majority of users need to understand SQL more and also understand that if you have a poorly set-up SQL Server, you will have a bad experience with the product hosting its database on that SQL Server. Remember to set up your SQL Server using domain service accounts, use a dedicated disk for the DPM database, and keep monitoring SQL's performance with a proactive monitoring approach.

The following requirements are recommended for a SQL Server database:

- **RAM**: 8 GB
- **Disk**: 3 GB
- **Required features**: Database Engine Services, Reporting Services
- **Collations**: `SQL_Latin1_General_CP1_CI_AS`
- **AlwaysOn**: Not Supported
- **Clustered SQL Server**: Supported

How to do it...

The following steps will cover the installation process of a local SQL Server that has been collocated with the DPM server on the same operating system.

Option 1 – local SQL Server instance

Make sure that your operating system is fully patched and that is has been rebooted before you start the installation of SQL Server 2016. Now, follow these steps:

1. Insert the SQL Server 2016 media and start the SQL server's setup. In the **SQL Server Installation Center**, click on **Installation** and click on **New SQL Server stand-alone installation...**
2. The **Setup Support Rules** will start and will identify any problems that might occur during the SQL server's installation. When the operation is complete, click on **OK** to continue.
3. In the **Product Key** step, enter the product key that ships with SQL server license and click on **Next** to continue.
4. The next step is the **License Terms** step, which is where you check the **I accept the license terms** checkbox if you agree with the license terms. Click on **Next** to continue.
5. The SQL Server installation will verify whether there are any product updates available from the Microsoft Update service. Check the **Use Microsoft Update to check for updates (recommended)** checkbox and click on **Next** to continue.
6. Select the **Include SQL Server product updates** checkbox and click on **Next** to continue:

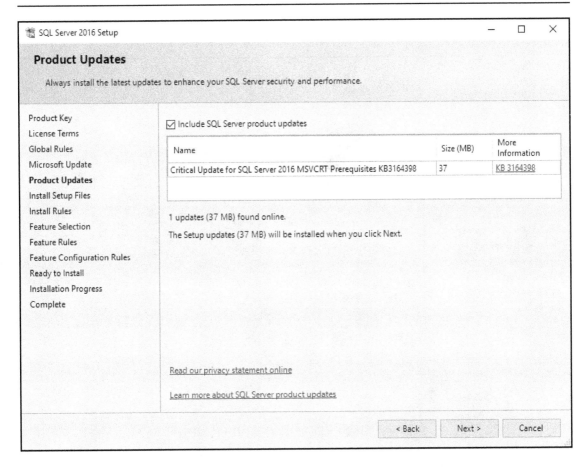

7. Next is the **Install Setup Files** step, which initializes the actual installation. When these tasks have finished, click on **Install** to continue.

8. Verify that all of the rules have passed in the **Install Rules** step of the SQL Server installation process. Resolve any warnings or errors and click the **Re-run** button to run the verification again. If all of the rules have passed, click on **Next** to continue.

9. In **Feature Selection**, choose the SQL Server features that you would like to install. System Center Data Protection Manager requires the following:
   - **Database Engine Service**
   - **Full-Text and Semantic Extractions for Search**
   - **Reporting Services – Native**

10. Click on **Next** to continue:

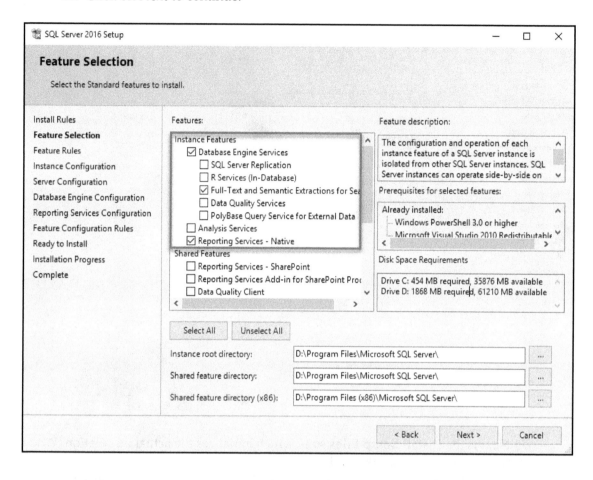

11. Verify the **Installation Rules** step, resolve any errors, and click on **Next** to continue.

12. In the **Instance Configuration** step, select **Named instance** and type in a suitable name for your SQL Server instance. Click on **Next** to continue:

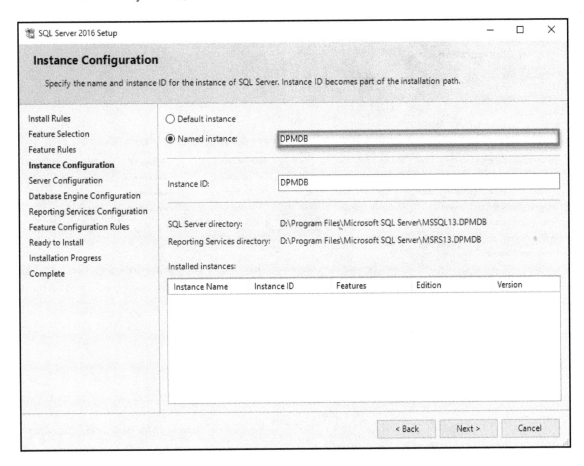

13. In the **Server Configuration** step, type in the credentials for the dedicated service account you would like to use for this SQL Server. Switch the **Startup Type** to **Automatic** for the **SQL Server Agent**. When all of the credentials have been filled in, click on the **Collation** tab:

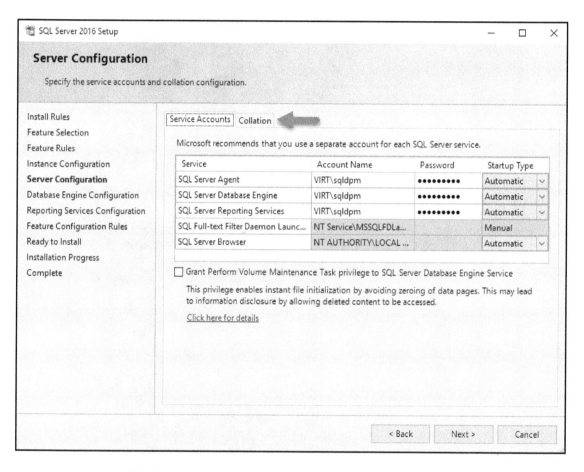

14. In the **Collation** tab, make sure that **SQL_Latin1_General_CP1_CI_AS** is listed in the **Database Engine Configuration**. If not, then click on the **Customize...** button to choose the correct collation and then click on **Next** to continue.

15. The next step is the **Database Engine Configuration** step. Enter the authentication security mode, administrators, and directories. In the **Authentication Mode** section, choose **Windows Authentication mode**. In the **Specify SQL Server administrators** section, click the **Add...** button and add the **DPM Admins** group into Active Directory:

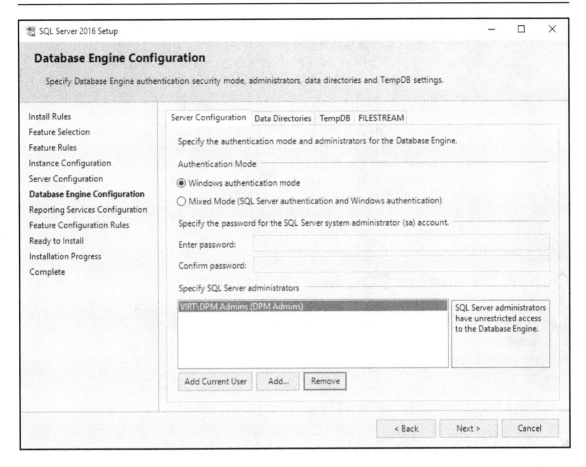

16. Click on the **Data Directories** tab as well as the **TempDB** tab to verify that all of your SQL Server configurations point to a dedicated disk. Click on **Next** to continue.

17. In the **Reporting Services Configuration** step, under the **Reporting Services Native Mode**, choose **Install and configure** and click on **Next** to continue.

18. Verify the configuration in the **Ready to Install** step and click on **Install** to start the installation.

19. The **Installation Progress** step will show you the current status of the installation process. When the installation has completed, **SQL Server 2016 Setup** will show you a summary of the **Complete** step. That is the final step page of the SQL Server Server 2016 installation wizard.

20. Click on the **Close** button to end **SQL Server 2016 Setup**.

After installing SQL Server, please make sure that you install an important update for SQL Server 2016 RTM (KB3210111). Please note that, starting with SQL Server 2014 and later, SQL **Server Management Studio** (**SSMS**) is not part of the installation media and you need to download it separately.

At the time of writing this book, SSMS version 17.8.1 is the latest generation of SQL Server Management Studio that supports SQL Server 2017. However, if you install SSMS version 17.X and later on the same OS, DPM installation will fail with the following error: *An unexpected error occurred during the installation – ID: 4387*. Alternatively, you can download SSMS version 16.5.3 from the following link, which will work side-by-side with DPM: `http://go.microsoft.com/fwlink/?LinkID=840946`.

Option 2 – remote SQL Server instance

When you need to build a large hosted DPM solution within your modern datacenter, you may want to use a dedicated backend SQL Server that is either a standalone SQL Server or a clustered one, for high availability. This step will cover the procedure to prepare a remote SQL server for hosting the DPM database.

After installing your backend SQL Server, you must prepare it for hosting the DPM database. Now look at the following steps:

1. Insert the DPM media on the SQL Server and run the setup. In the setup screen, click on the **DPM Remote SQL Prep** link:

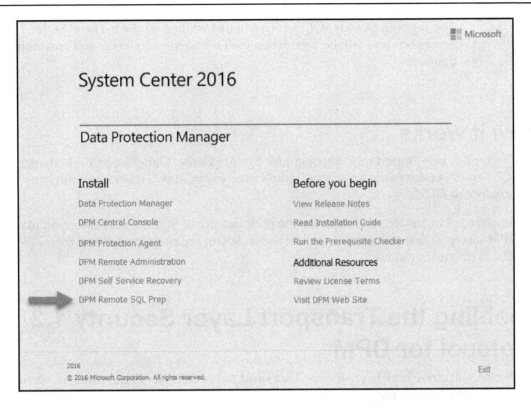

2. The next step is to go through the **Microsoft Software License Terms**, where you must check the **I accept the license terms and conditions** checkbox if you agree with the license terms. Click on **OK** to continue.

3. The installation wizard will start and install the **DPM Support Files**; this is a very quick installation.

4. When the installation has finished, a message box appears that informs you that the installation has finished and that the **System Center DPM Support Files** have been successfully installed:

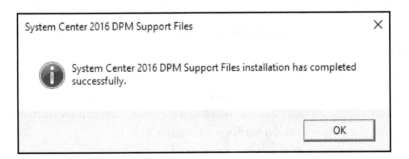

The support files for SQL Server will be installed on the backend SQL Server box and will be used when the DPM server connects and creates its database.

How it works...

SQL Server is a very important component for System Center Data Protection Manager. If the SQL Server is undersized or misconfigured in any way, it will reflect negatively on the performance of DPM.

It is crucial to plan, design, and measure the performance of SQL Server before you install the DPM server so that you know it will fit the scale you are planning for and the workloads that it should host.

Enabling the Transport Layer Security 1.2 protocol for DPM

This recipe will cover how to enable the **Transport Layer Security** (**TLS**) protocol version 1.2 for the DPM Management server.

Getting ready

TLS is a protocol that provides privacy and data integrity between two communicating applications. In this case, this is between DPM server and protected servers. TLS is the most widely deployed security protocol used today.

Several known vulnerabilities have been reported against SSL and earlier versions of TLS. Microsoft recommend that you upgrade to TLS 1.2 for secure communication.

To enable TLS protocol version 1.2 in your DPM environment, you need to perform the following steps:

1. Install all of the required updates.
2. Make sure that the DPM setup is functional as it was before applying the updates (for example, you can check if you are able to launch the DPM console).
3. Change the configuration settings to enable TLS 1.2.

4. Ensure that all required SQL Server services are up and running.

5. Finally, validate the protection and recovery process.

How to do it...

To enable TLS protocol version 1.2, follow these steps:

1. Make sure that you are running Windows Server 2012 R2, Windows Server 2016, or Windows Server 2019 and that it is up-to-date with the latest security fixes.

2. Make sure that .NET version 4.6 is installed on all of your machines (DPM server, protected servers) .NET version 4.7 is supported on Windows Server 2019. You can use the following PowerShell command to determine whether .NET has been installed: `Get-WindowsFeature NET*`:

```
CharbelNemnom.com #> Get-WindowsFeature NET*

Display Name                                          Name                      Install State
------------                                          ----                      -------------
[X] .NET Framework 3.5 Features                       NET-Framework-Features        Installed
    [X] .NET Framework 3.5 (includes .NET 2.0 and 3.0) NET-Framework-Core            Installed
    [ ] HTTP Activation                               NET-HTTP-Activation           Available
    [ ] Non-HTTP Activation                           NET-Non-HTTP-Activ            Available
[X] .NET Framework 4.6 Features                       NET-Framework-45-Fea...       Installed
    [X] .NET Framework 4.6                            NET-Framework-45-Core         Installed
    [ ] ASP.NET 4.6                                   NET-Framework-45-ASPNET       Available
    [X] WCF Services                                  NET-WCF-Services45            Installed
        [ ] HTTP Activation                           NET-WCF-HTTP-Activat...       Available
        [ ] Message Queuing (MSMQ) Activation         NET-WCF-MSMQ-Activat...       Available
        [ ] Named Pipe Activation                     NET-WCF-Pipe-Activat...       Available
        [ ] TCP Activation                            NET-WCF-TCP-Activati...       Available
        [X] TCP Port Sharing                          NET-WCF-TCP-PortShar...       Installed
```

3. For the DPM database and for all SQL Servers that you intend to protect with DPM, you need to make sure that you are running a SQL Server that supports TLS 1.2. You can follow the instructions described here to find out whether you need this update: https://support.microsoft.com/en-in/help/3135244/tls-1-2-support-for-microsoft-sql-server.

4. You need to make sure that SQL Server 2012 Native client 11.0 is installed on the DPM Management Server. You can verify whether SQL Native client 11.0 is installed by running the following PowerShell command on SQL Server: **Get-odbcdriver -name "SQL Server Native Client*"**. You can download Microsoft SQL Server 2012 Native client 11.0 from the following link: https://www.microsoft.com/en-us/download/details.aspx?id=50402.

5. Make sure that you are running a DPM server that supports TLS 1.2. Starting with DPM 2012 R2 Update Rollup 14, DPM 2016 Update Rollup 4 including DPM 1801, DPM 1807, DPM 2019, and DPM 1901, the DPM team added TLS version 1.2 support.

6. System Center components now generate both SHA1 and SHA2 self-signed certificates. This is a requirement for enabling TLS1.2. If case CA signed certificates are used for workgroup machines or untrusted domains, please ensure that they are either SHA1 or SHA2. In other words, TLS 1.2 supports only SHA1 and SHA2 certificates. Hence, all of the certificates must be updated to be SHA1 or SHA2.

7. You need to implement these settings on all of the Windows machines in the environment on which System Center Data Protection agent is installed, including the DPM management server. Follow these steps to disable all of the SCHANNEL protocols except TLS 1.2 system-wide so that only TLS 1.2 protocol is used for communication. Making these registry changes does not affect the use of Kerberos or NTLM protocols:

    1. Open the registry on your server(s) by running `regedit` in the run window and navigate to the following location: `HKEY_LOCAL_MACHINE\SYSTEM\CurrentControlSet\Control\Sec urityProviders\SCHANNEL\Protocols`

    2. Add the SSL 2.0, SSL 3.0, TLS 1.0, TLS 1.1, and TLS 1.2 keys under **Protocol**.

    3. Now, create two keys called `Client` and `Server` under the SSL 2.0, SSL 3.0, TLS 1.0, TLS 1.1, and TLS 1.2 keys.

8. Now create two `REG_DWORD` values under the `Server` and `Client` keys if you want to enable the TLS 1.2 protocol: set the `DisabledByDefault` value to `0` and the `Enabled` value to `1`. You will now have something that looks as follows:

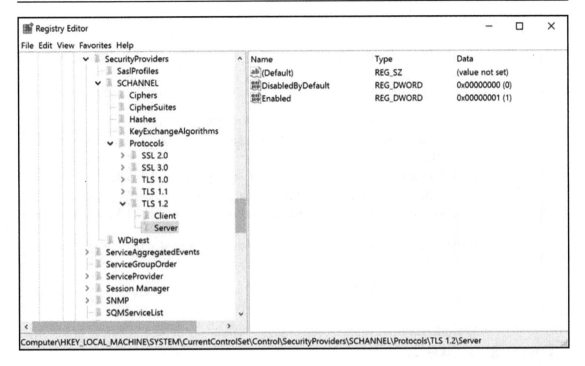

9. If you want to disable the protocol, you can set the `DisabledByDefault` value to `1` and the `Enabled` value to `0`.

10. After we have enabled the TLS 1.2 protocol on all systems, we need to set DPM to use only TLS 1.2. The following settings should be implemented on the DPM management server and all other servers on which DPM agents are installed, that is, Hyper-V hosts, File Server, SQL, Exchange, SharePoint, and so on. Follow these steps to create these settings:

    1. Open the registry on your server by running `regedit` in the run window and navigate to the following location:
       `HKEY_LOCAL_MACHINE\SOFTWARE\Microsoft\.NETFramework\v4.0.3031`.

    2. Now, create the `REG_DWORD` value under the registry:
       `SchUseStrongCrypto [Value = 1]`.

    3. Navigate to the following registry location:
       `HKEY_LOCAL_MACHINE\SOFTWARE\WOW6432Node\Microsoft\.NETFramework\v4.0.30319`.

    4. Now, create the same `REG_DWORD` value under the preceding registry as well: `SchUseStrongCrypto [Value = 1]`.

11. Finally, you need to restart the system (DPM server and the protected server).

How it works...

For all kinds of workloads backed up by DPM TLS 1.2 enabled (that is, SQL, SharePoint, Exchange, File Servers, Hyper-V hosts, Hyper-V VMs, VMWare VMs, Clients, System State, and BMR), you can do the following:

1. **Attach the Protected Server** in the workgroup/untrusted domain to DPM.
2. While **Creating Protection Groups**, all data sources on the protected server will be displayed.
3. **Protect** different kinds of workloads to disk, to tape, and to the cloud.
4. **Recover** the different kinds of workloads at the Original Location, Alternate Location, recover cloud recovery points, and use an External DPM server.

 Please note that VMware VM backup is not supported when DPM TLS 1.2 is enabled.

There's more...

There are two scenarios that are impacted when using TLS 1.2 with DPM:

Using certificate-based authentication to protect servers in a workgroup or untrusted domain

The DPM agent can be installed on the protected server either directly from the DPM server for the servers in the domain, or using certificate-based authentication for computers in a workgroup or untrusted domain. Please refer to Chapter 8, *Protecting Workgroups and Untrusted Domains*. DPM uses elements of the .NET Framework on the protected server to communicate if certificate-based authentication is used. TLS 1.2 needs .NET 4.5 or above. Since DPM is built with .NET 4.0—which does not support TLS 1.2 directly—when DPM tries to communicate with the protected servers, establishing the connection will fail.

Protecting workloads on the cloud using DPM

DPM requires a MARS agent to back up data to the cloud. The MARS agent also leverages the .NET Framework, and changes need to be made on the DPM server to ensure that the backups continue smoothly when TLS 1.2 is enabled. Check out `https://support.microsoft.com/en-ie/help/4022913/how-to-resolve-azure-backup-agent-issues-when-disabling-tls-1-0-for-pc` to resolve Azure Backup agent issues when enabling TLS 1.2.

For more information about Azure Backup, please check `Chapter 10`, *Integrating DPM with Azure Backup.*

See also

Check out the following article to learn more about how to automate and enable TLS 1.2 in System Center Data Protection Manager: `https://charbelnemnom.com/2018/08/how-to-enable-tls-1-2-protocol-in-system-center-data-protection-manager-dpm-scdpm-tls1-2`.

Installing DPM

This recipe will cover two installation scenarios:

- Installing DPM using a local SQL Server
- Installing DPM using a remote SQL Server

Getting ready

Before you start installing System Center Data Protection Manager, it is recommended that you read the *Planning your DPM deployment* and *Preparing your DPM deployment* recipes in this chapter.

How to do it...

This step will cover the installation process of DPM using a local SQL Server on the same operating system as DPM.

Option 1 – installing DPM using a local SQL Server

Make sure that your operating system is fully patched and rebooted before you start the installation. Now follow these steps:

1. Insert the DPM media and start the setup for System Center Data Protection Manager. When the installation list is presented, click on **Data Protection Manager** to start the installation:

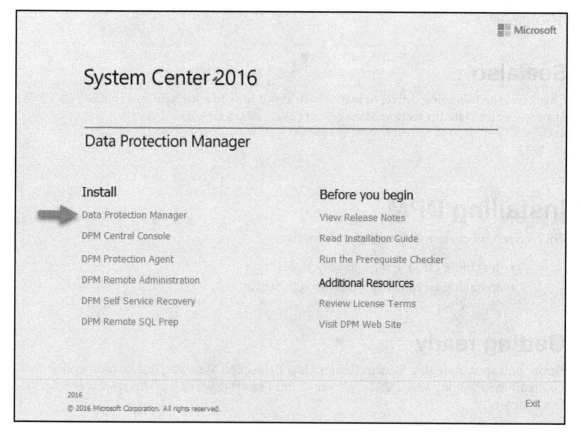

2. The installation wizard will start and prompt you with the **Microsoft Software License Terms**. Accept the license terms by checking the **I accept the license terms and conditions** checkbox, which will continue the installation.

3. Please wait while the setup starts copying the temporary files.

4. The installation wizard will now prompt you with eight different installation steps. Currently, you are on the **Welcome** step. To continue with the installation, click on **Next**.

5. The next step is the **Prerequisites Check**, where you can choose to install the DPM database by using a standalone or a clustered SQL Server.

 Please read the *Installing DPM using a remote SQL Server* scenario in this recipe.

6. In the **Instance of SQL Server** box, type in your server name and the instance name that should host your DPM database. In this example, the server name and SQL instance is `WS16-SQL16-01\DPMDB`:

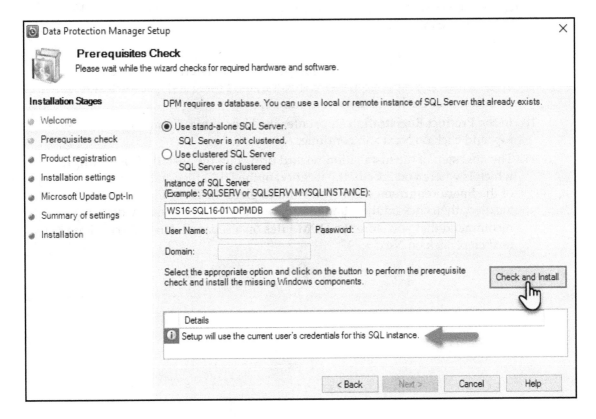

Please note that when you install DPM and use a local SQL Server installation, the setup will use the current user's credentials for the SQL Server instance. If the domain account that is logged on and performing the installation is not a member of the DPM Admin group in the Active Directory, the installation will fail.

7. Click on the **Check and Install** button to run a verification that all of the prerequisites have been met before the installation can continue.

8. In this step, there are some prerequisites that will be installed as part of the required Windows components by DPM. The Hyper-V role and Hyper-V PowerShell module will be installed as well during this step. You will be required to restart afterward.

The Hyper-V role needs to be installed on the DPM server for **Item-Level Recovery** (**ILR**) support. Please read Chapter 3, *Protecting Hyper-V VMs*, for more information on this.

9. Simply restart the DPM server and start the installation wizard one more time. When you run the prerequisites checker in the **Prerequisites Check** step, it will be successful. Click on **Next >** to continue.

10. In the **Product Registration** step, enter the **User name**, **Company**, and **Product key** and click on **Next >** to continue.

11. The next step of the installation wizard brings up the **Installation Settings**, which is where you specify the location of the DPM files and read the summary of the **Space requirements**. If you want to place the DPM files in a specific location, then click on the **Change...** button and specify the new destination. We recommend that you store the **DPM Files** on a separate drive. To continue to the next step, click on **Next >**:

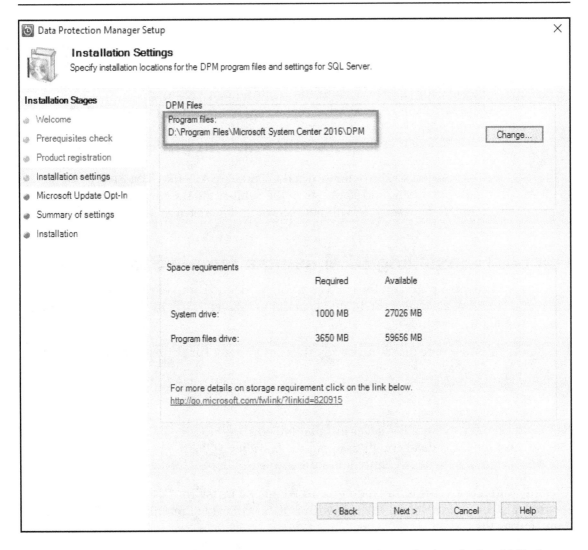

12. You can specify in the **Microsoft Update Opt-In** box whether the local Windows Update should be redirected so that you can use Microsoft Updates instead.

13. Choose the most appropriate option for your implementation and click on **Next >** to continue.

14. In the **Summary of settings** section, you can verify your installation's configuration. If everything looks good, click on the **Install** button to start the installation.

15. The last step is the **Installation**. Here, you can keep a watch on the installation progress in real time. When the installation has finished, click on the **Close** button.

 Finally, you need to install and update DPM server to the latest **Update Rollup** (**UR**) if you are using the **Long-Term Servicing Channel** (**LTSC**). At the time of writing this book, DPM 2016 Update Rollup 6 has been released and is available for download. You can download it at `https://www.catalog.update.microsoft.com/Search.aspx?q=4456327`. If you are using the **Semi-Annual Channel** (**SAC**) for DPM (that is, DPM 1801, 1807, 1901, and so on), then the Semi-Annual Channel, with its more frequent release cycle, will not receive update releases.

Option 2 – installing DPM using a remote SQL Server

This step will cover and explain the configuration needed to complete a DPM installation when you are using a backend, dedicated, standalone server or a SQL cluster for achieving a high-availability scenario.

 Please note that SQL Server Always-On is not supported to host the DPM database.

Before you can start your DPM sever installation, you need to prepare SQL Server so that you can host the DPM database. Please read the *Installing SQL Server for DPM Database* recipe in this chapter, since it is a prerequisite.

The only difference in the installation wizard when you install the DPM server on a separate machine or on the same server with SQL Server is the **Prerequisites Check** step. Now, follow these steps:

1. Insert the DPM media on a separate machine and start the setup for System Center Data Protection Manager. When the installation list is presented, click on **Data Protection Manager** to start the installation.

2. In the **Prerequisites Check** step of the installation wizard, you have the option to choose whether you would like to place the DPM database on a remote standalone SQL Server or a SQL cluster.

3. For a standalone backend remote SQL Server hosting your DPM database, enter SQLSERVER\INSTANCE in the **Instance of SQL Server** field:

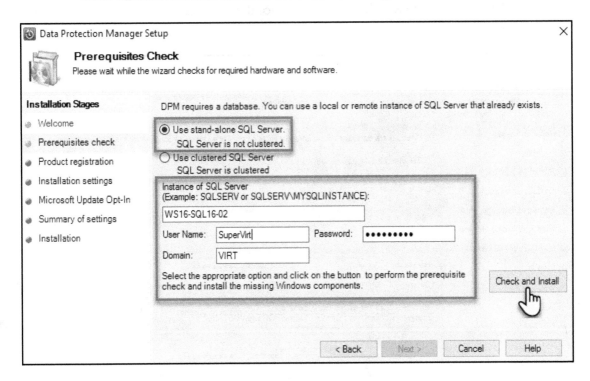

4. Enter the **User Name**, **Password**, and **Domain** for the account that has the appropriate rights for the SQL configuration. Click on the **Check and Install** button to verify these prerequisites.

   The account that's used for this configuration must be a member of the DPM Admin group in the Active Directory.

5. In the case of a SQL clustered environment, you must specify both the **SQL Server Instance** for the DPM database and also where the **Instance of SQL Server Reporting Service** is located, since the SQL Server Reporting Service does not support being clustered:

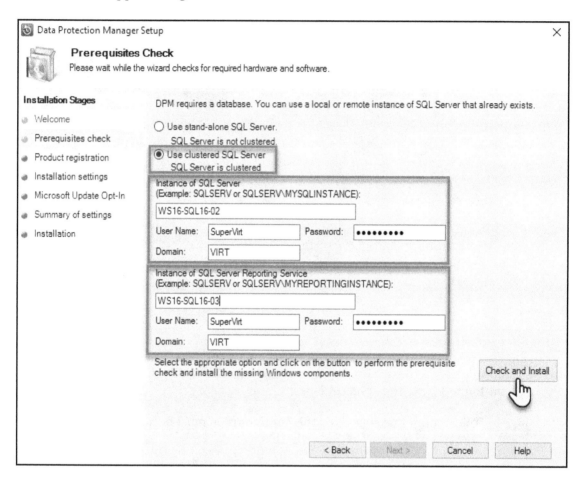

6. Enter the **Instance of SQL Server** for the DPMDB and also provide information for the **Instance of SQL Server Reporting Service** that will host the reporting for the DPM server.

7. Provide the credentials that have rights in the SQL Server configuration; the accounts should be members of the DPM Admin group in the Active Directory. Click on the **Check** button to check the prerequisites.

8. Click on **Next >** to continue with the installation wizard.

How it works...

The installation media for System Center Data Protection Manager will provide you with the installation bits for the DPM software. Since the 2012 R2 release of DPM, the SQL media is no longer included on the DPM media, so you need to consider how you design and install the SQL Server that will host the DPM server software.

The DPM server installation wizard will provide you with the right configuration that's needed regarding the **SQL Server Reporting Services** (**SSRS**) configuration for the DPM reports. The SSRS does not support being clustered.

When System Center Data Protection Manager's installation has completed successfully, DPM's setup will create the following firewall exceptions for you:

- Exception for DCOM communication on port 135 (TCP and UDP) in all profiles
- Exception for Msdpm.exe in all profiles
- Exception for DPMRA.exe in all profiles
- Exception for AMSvcHost.exe in all profiles
- Exception for DPMAM Service communication on port 6075 (TCP and UDP) in all profiles

There's more...

When System Center Data Protection Manager has been installed, you need to perform a number of post-installation tasks before your DPM servers are able to start protecting your production environment.

Automating the installation of DPM

This recipe will cover how to automate the installation of DPM Server.

Getting ready

In the *Installing DPM* recipe in this chapter, we showed you how to install DPM using a local SQL Server and using a remote SQL Server. However, this was a manual installation.

Automating the installation of DPM consists of two steps:

1. Installing the SQL Server instance
2. Installing the DPM server

You can disregard the first step if you already have SQL Server deployed locally or on a remote server in your environment.

In this recipe, we will cover the installation of SQL Server and DPM in an automated fashion.

How to do it...

Make sure that your operating system is fully patched and rebooted before you start the installation. Now follow these steps:

1. **Install the SQL Server instance**:
    1. Mount the SQL Server 2016 media and then open the **Command Prompt (cmd)**.
    2. Browse to the drive letter where SQL Server is mounted.
    3. Type in the following command to automate the installation of SQL Server and add all of the required features:

 Please make sure to update the domain name and SQL Service accounts in the following command so that they match your environment.

```
Setup.exe /Q /ACTION=install /IACCEPTSQLSERVERLICENSETERMS
/FEATURES=SQLEngine,RS /INSTANCENAME=DPMINSTANCE
/INSTANCEDIR="D:\Program Files\Microsoft SQL Server"
/INSTALLSHAREDWOWDIR="D:\Program Files (x86)\Microsoft SQL
Server" /INSTALLSHAREDDIR="D:\Program Files\Microsoft SQL
Server" /SQLSVCACCOUNT="VIRT\sqldpm"
/SQLSYSADMINACCOUNTS="VIRT\sqldpm"
/SQLSVCPASSWORD="dpm2016+1" /RSSVCACCOUNT="VIRT\sqldpm"
/RSSVCPASSWORD="dpm2016+1" /AGTSVCACCOUNT="VIRT\sqldpm"
/AGTSVCPASSWORD="dpm2016+1" /SECURITYMODE=SQL
/SAPWD="dpm2016+1" /SQLTEMPDBDIR="D:\Program
Files\Microsoft SQL Server\TempDB\\"
/SQLUSERDBDIR="D:\Program Files\Microsoft SQL
Server\SQLData\\" /SQLUSERDBLOGDIR="D:\Program
Files\Microsoft SQL Server\SQLLog\\"
```

Please refer to the following screenshot for its output:

```
Administrator: C:\Windows\system32\cmd.exe                                      —    □    ✕

E:\>Setup.exe /Q /ACTION=install /IACCEPTSQLSERVERLICENSETERMS /FEATURES=SQLEngine,RS /INSTANCENAME=DPMINSTANC
E /INSTANCEDIR="D:\Program Files\Microsoft SQL Server" /INSTALLSHAREDWOWDIR="D:\Program Files (x86)\Microsoft
SQL Server" /INSTALLSHAREDDIR="D:\Program Files\Microsoft SQL Server" /SQLSVCACCOUNT="VIRT\sqldpm" /SQLSYSADMI
NACCOUNTS="VIRT\sqldpm" /SQLSVCPASSWORD="dpm2016+1" /RSSVCACCOUNT="VIRT\sqldpm" /RSSVCPASSWORD="dpm2016+1" /AG
TSVCACCOUNT="VIRT\sqldpm" /AGTSVCPASSWORD="dpm2016+1" /SECURITYMODE=SQL /SAPWD="dpm2016+1" /SQLTEMPDBDIR="D:\P
rogram Files\Microsoft SQL Server\TempDB\\" /SQLUSERDBDIR="D:\Program Files\Microsoft SQL Server\SQLData\\" /S
QLUSERDBLOGDIR="D:\Program Files\Microsoft SQL Server\SQLLog\\"_


Microsoft (R) SQL Server 2016 13.00.1601.05
Copyright (c) 2016 Microsoft Corporation.  All rights reserved.

Microsoft .NET Framework CasPol 4.6.1586.0
for Microsoft .NET Framework version 4.6.1586.0
Copyright (C) Microsoft Corporation.  All rights reserved.

WARNING: The .NET Framework does not apply CAS policy by default. Any settings shown or modified by CasPol
will only affect applications that opt into using CAS policy.

Please see http://go.microsoft.com/fwlink/?LinkId=131738 for more information.


Success
Microsoft .NET Framework CasPol 4.6.1586.0
for Microsoft .NET Framework version 4.6.1586.0
Copyright (C) Microsoft Corporation.  All rights reserved.

WARNING: The .NET Framework does not apply CAS policy by default. Any settings shown or modified by CasPol
will only affect applications that opt into using CAS policy.

Please see http://go.microsoft.com/fwlink/?LinkId=131738 for more information.


Success
```

4. Make sure that you have downloaded **SQL Server Management Studio** (**SSMS**) version 16.5.3 and that you have copied it to the server: `http://go.microsoft.com/fwlink/?LinkID=840946`.

5. Open the `cmd.exe` window and type in the following command:

> **SSMS-Setup-ENU.exe /install /quiet /norestart**

Please note that the SSMS installation may take some time to finish.

2. **Install the DPM server**:

1. Open a command-line prompt in elevated mode and type in the following command:

> **dism.exe /Online /Enable-feature /All**
> **/FeatureName:Microsoft-Hyper-V /FeatureName:Microsoft-**
> **Hyper-V-Management-PowerShell /quiet /norestart**

DPM supports **Item-Level Recovery** (**ILR**), which allows you to perform a granular recovery of files, folders, volumes, and **virtual hard disks** (**VHDXs**) from a host-level backup of Hyper-V virtual machines. The Hyper-V Role and PowerShell Management Tools features are required by the DPM server. Please read `Chapter 3`, *Protecting Hyper-V VMs*, for more information.

2. Once the Hyper-V role is installed, you need to restart the DPM server before you move on to the next step.

3. Once the DPM server has been restarted, open Notepad, copy the following scripts into it, and then save the file as DPMSetup.ini:

 Please note that you can use the same script that follows, regardless of whether the SQL Server instance has been installed on the DPM server or on a remote SQL Server.

```
[OPTIONS]
 UserName=<Domain-name\Username>
 CompanyName=<Ur-Company>
 ProductKey=XXXX-XXXX-XXXX-XXXX-XXXX
 SqlAccountPassword=<The password for the SQL sa account>
 ProgramFiles = <Location path where you want to install
DPM>
 DatabaseFiles = <Location path where you want to install
DPMDB>
 IntegratedInstallSource = <Location path where the DPM
media is extracted>
 SQLMachineName=<Name of the SQL Server Computer> OR <SQL
Cluster Name>
 SQLInstanceName=<Name of the SQL Server instance>
 SQLMachineUserName=<Domain-name\Username>
SQLMachinePassword=<Password for the user name Setup must
use>
 SQLMachineDomainName=<Domain name to which the SQL Server
computer is attached to>
 ReportingMachineName=<Name of the SQL Server Computer> OR
<SQL Cluster Name>
 ReportingInstanceName=<Name of the SQL Server instance>
 ReportingMachineUserName=<Domain-name\Username>
 ReportingMachinePassword=<Password for the user name Setup
must use>
 ReportingMachineDomainName=<Domain name to which the SQL
Server computer is attached to>
```

4. The following screenshot shows you what the DPMSetup.ini file will look like:

5. After saving the DPMSetup.ini file, in an elevated command prompt on the DPM server, type in the following command and press *Enter*:

```
start /wait D:\SCDPM2016\setup.exe /i /f
D:\DPMSetup.ini /l D:\dpmlog.txt
```

 The D:\SCDPM2016\ path indicates the media in the DPM location where you'll run setup.exe. D:\DPMSetup.ini is the location path where you saved the DPMSetup.ini file.

6. In just a few minutes, DPM will be installed automatically, as shown in the following screenshot:

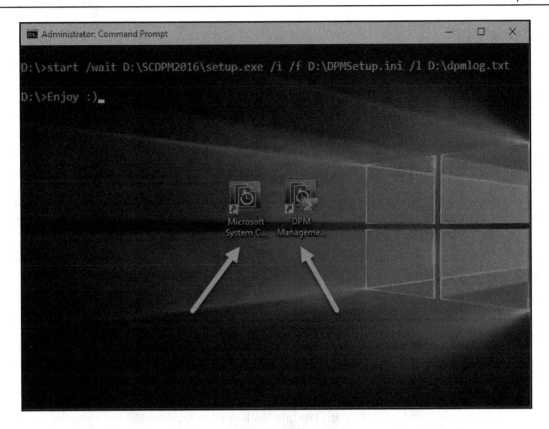

Finally, you need to install and update the DPM server to the latest
Update Rollup (UR) if you are using the **Long-Term Servicing Channel**

(LTSC). At the time of writing this book, DPM 2016 Update Rollup 6 has
been released, and you can download it from the following link: `https://`
`www.catalog.update.microsoft.com/Search.aspx?q=4456327`.
If you are using the **Semi-Annual Channel (SAC)** for DPM (that is, DPM
1801, 1807, 1901, and so on), then the Semi-Annual Channel, with its more
frequent release cycle, does not receive update releases.

How it works...

The final result of an automated installation will be better than a manual implementation.
Thus, this will ensure that you have a consistent deployment across your environment.

See also

Check out the following blog post to learn more about how to automate the installation of DPM using System Center Virtual Machine Manager: `https://charbelnemnom.com/2017/01/how-to-deploy-dpm-2016-using-vmm-2016-on-ws2016-scdpm-scvmm-sysctr-hyperv-ws2016/`.

Upgrading to the latest release of DPM

This recipe will cover the supported upgrade scenarios from the previous version of DPM to the latest release of DPM.

Getting ready

Before you get started with the upgrade, make sure that your existing installation has the necessary updates by following the upgrade path:

- As a minimum requirement, upgrade your existing DPM 2012 R2 to DPM 2012 R2 Update Rollup 10. At the time of writing this book, Update Rollup 14 is also available for DPM 2012 R2. You can download UR 10 from the following link: `http://www.catalog.update.microsoft.com/Search.aspx?q=4043315`.
- Upgrade DPM 2012 R2 with Update Rollup 10 or Update Rollup 14 to the latest DPM version.
- Update the DPM agents on the protected servers.
- Upgrade Windows Server 2012 R2 to Windows Server 2016 or Windows Server 2019.

 Please note that it is possible to upgrade DPM 2016 or later from DPM 2012 R2, which is running on Windows Server 2012 R2. However, if you want to use the latest features that come with DPM 2016 or later, such as MBS, Microsoft recommends installing DPM 2016 or later on a new installation of Windows Server 2016 or Windows Server 2019. Please check the *Installing DPM* recipe in this chapter for more information.

How to do it...

The following steps will illustrate the upgrade process:

1. Mount the latest DPM media on the DPM 2012 R2 server and double-click **Setup.exe** to open the System Center Wizard.

2. Under **Install**, click **Data Protection Manager**. This starts the setup. Select **I accept the license terms and conditions** and follow the setup wizard.

3. The last step in the wizard is the **Installation** process. Here, you can keep an eye on the upgrade progress in real time. When the upgrade has finished, click on the **Close** button:

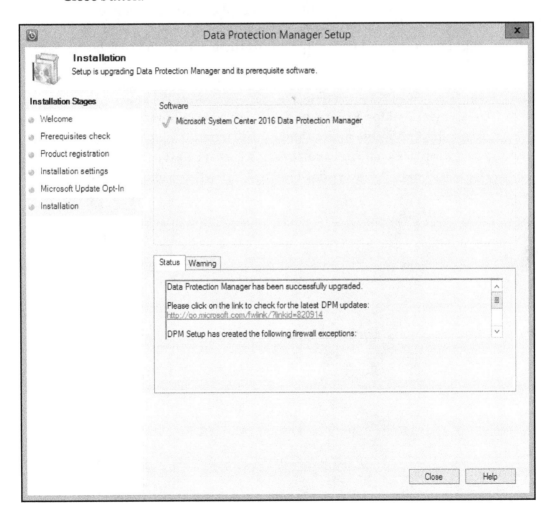

Finally, you need to install and update DPM server to the latest UR if you are using the LTSC. At the time of writing this book, DPM 2016 Update Rollup 6 has been released. You can download it from the following link: `http://www.catalog.update.microsoft.com/Search.aspx?q=4456327`. If you are using the **Semi-Annual Channel** (**SAC**) for DPM (that is, DPM 1801, 1807, 1901, and so on), then the Semi-Annual Channel, with its more frequent release cycle, does not receive update releases.

4. Update the DPM agents on the protected servers. Please check out the *Installation of DPM Agents* recipe in this chapter for more information on this.

5. The last step is to upgrade Windows Server 2012 R2 to Windows Server 2016. Mount the Windows Server 2016 media on the DPM server and double-click **Setup.exe** to open the Windows Server 2016 Setup Wizard.

6. Select **Download and install updates (recommended)** and click on **Next** to continue.

7. Select the image you want to install. If your exiting DPM server is installed on Windows Server 2012 R2 Datacenter, and then select **Windows Server 2016 Datacenter (Desktop Experience)**. Click on **Next** to continue.

8. Accept the **Applicable notices and license terms**. Click **Accept** to continue.

9. Select **Keep personal files and apps** and click on **Next** to continue.

10. Please wait until Windows finishes checking updates, and then click on **Next** to continue.

11. Click **Confirm** next to the information note:

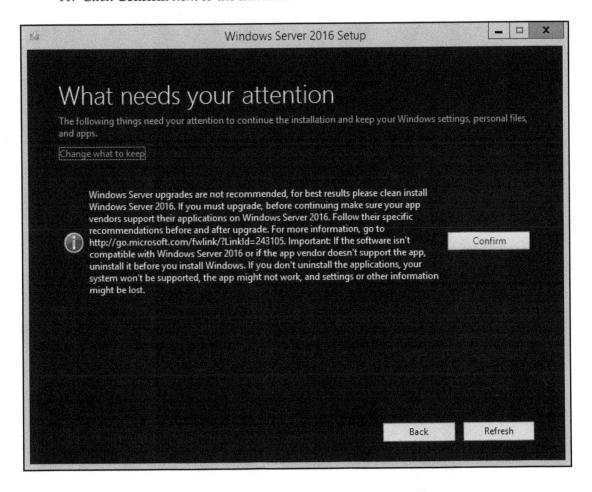

12. In the last step in the installation wizard, click **Install**:

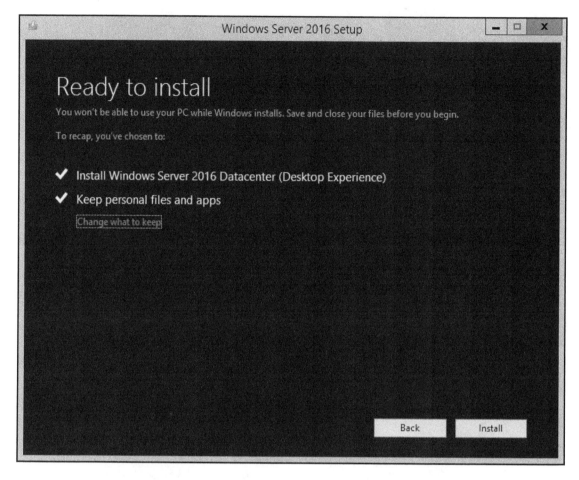

13. DPM server will restart several times during the Windows upgrade. This might take a while.
14. When the upgrade has completed, click on **Accept** for the license terms.
15. The final step is to make sure that you run and install the latest Windows Update.

How it works...

Upgrading DPM 2012 R2 to the latest DPM release is a straightforward process. In this example, we are running SQL Server 2012 with SP3 as a local instance on the same OS.

As a part of your upgrade, you may also want to move the DPM database if you ever encounter the following scenarios:

- You are merging instances of SQL Server.
- You are moving to a remote SQL Server that's more powerful than SQL Server.
- You want to add fault tolerance by using a SQL Server cluster.
- You want to move from a remote SQL Server to a local SQL server or vice versa.

The DPM setup allows you to migrate the DPM database to different SQL Servers during the upgrade process.

There's more...

In the upgrade scenario where you have a primary and a secondary DPM server, the preceding recommended strategies apply. However, it is recommended that you always start the upgrade process with your secondary DPM server and then upgrade your primary DPM server; this is to avoid any unnecessary disturbance.

If you are going to upgrade from DPM 2012 R2 or DPM 2016 (LTSC), to DPM 1801 or DPM 1807 (SAC), then make sure to follow this path:

- If you are upgrading from DPM 2012 R2, **then first upgrade to DPM 2012 R2 Update Rollup 14**.
- If you are upgrading from DPM 2016, **then first upgrade to DPM 2016 Update Rollup 4**.
- Upgrade to DPM 1801, and then apply DPM 1807 update. You can download 1807 update from the following link: `http://catalog.update.microsoft.com/v7/site/Search.aspx?q=4339950`.
- Update the agents on the protected servers.
- Upgrade the DPM Remote Administrator on all production servers.
- Backups continue without rebooting your production server.

See also

For more information about the supported upgrade scenarios, please check the following article:

`https://docs.microsoft.com/en-us/system-center/dpm/upgrade-dpm?view=sc-dpm-1801`

Migrating legacy storage to Modern Backup Storage

This recipe will cover how to migrate legacy storage to MBS.

Getting ready

After upgrading DPM 2012 R2 to DPM 2016 and the operating system to Windows Server 2016, as described in the *Upgrading to the latest release of DPM* recipe in this chapter, you can update your existing protection groups to the new DPM features. By default, the protection groups haven't been changed, and continue to function as they were configured in DPM 2012 R2.

After upgrading to Windows Server 2016 and DPM 2016 or later, you can no longer create new protection groups using legacy storage. All newly created protection groups will leverage MBS. We strongly recommend moving existing protection groups to MBS to take advantage of the new storage space-saving improvements.

You also need to make sure that you have added a new volume to DPM by using Modern Backup Storage technology. Please refer to the *Enabling Modern Backup Storage (MBS)* recipe in `Chapter 2`, *DPM Post-Installation and Management Tasks*:

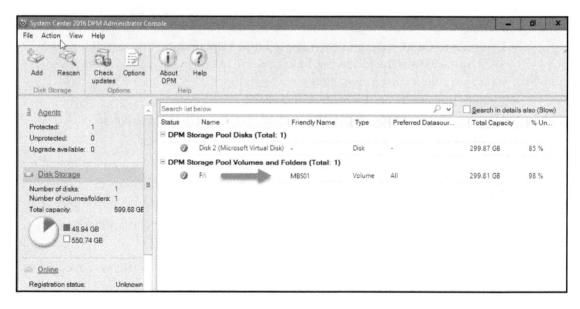

How to do it...

To update the protection group, you need to stop the protection of all data sources with **Retain Data**, and then add the data sources to a new protection group. DPM will begin protecting these data sources using MBS:

1. Open the Administrator Console, select the **Protection** feature, and in the **Protection Group Member** list, right-click the member and select **Stop protection of member...**:

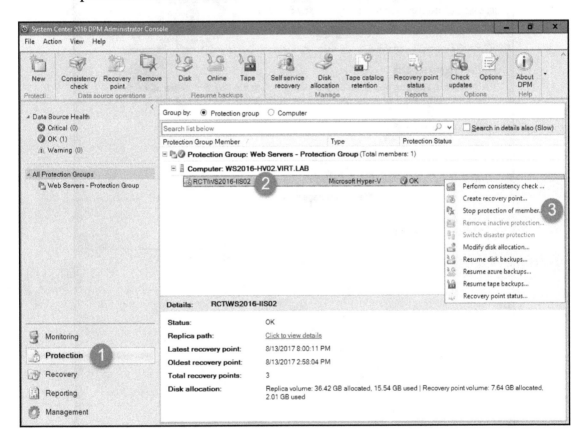

2. In the **Stop Protection** dialog, review the used **Disk space** and the **Current free disk space in the DPM storage pool**. The default is to **Retain protected data**, leave the recovery points on the disk, and allow them to expire per their associated retention policy. Click **Stop Protection**:

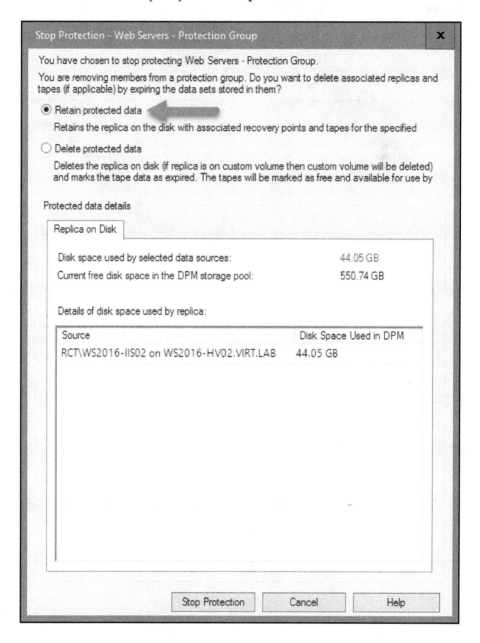

If you want to immediately return the used disk space to the free storage pool, select **Delete protected data**. This will delete the backup data (and recovery points) associated with that member.

3. In the last step, you need to create a new protection group that uses MBS, and include the **same unprotected** data sources.

How it works...

The end result is that you will have a single new protection group that uses MBS. The previous protection group that was created in DPM 2012 R2 will be removed. The old recovery points will be maintained since we did not delete the protected data:

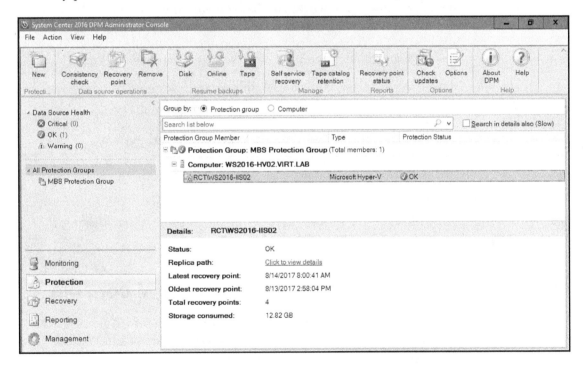

You might need to perform a **Consistency Check** (**CC**) after the initial replica is created for the new protection group so that the protection status will be in a healthy state.

Installing the DPM agents

This recipe will cover the installation of a DPM agent from the DPM console as well as a manual-based installation.

Getting ready

Before you can start protecting a workload within your datacenter, you must install a DPM agent on the server hosting the workload that you would like to protect (that is, Hyper-V, SQL Server, Exchange, and so on).

You can install the DPM agent via the DPM Administrator Console in push mode; however, there are some scenarios where you will not able to perform a push installation of the DPM agent to the server hosting the workload that you would like to protect. On the DPM server, you can find two executables for the DPM agent that you can share or download to a removable media. Then, you can install the agent manually. The DPM agent is also available on the DPM installation media. There are two different executables here:

- `DpmAgentInstaller_x86.exe` is for 32-bit operating systems
- `DpmAgentInstaller_x64.exe` is for 64-bit operating systems

Both are applicable for Windows server and Windows client operating systems.

How to do it...

The following steps will illustrate the process of installing DPM agent in two different ways.

Option 1 – installing the agent from the DPM console

1. Open the DPM Administrator Console and click **Management** | **Agents**. Click **Install** on the tool ribbon to open the **Protection Agent Installation Wizard**.
2. On the **Select Agent Deployment Method** page, click **Install agents** | **Next**.
3. On the **Select Computers** page, DPM will display a list of available computers that are in the same domain as the DPM server. Add the required computer.

4. The **Advanced** button page is enabled only when there is more than one version of a protection agent available for installation on the computers. You can use this option to install a previous version of the protection agent that was installed before you upgraded DPM server to a more recent version. However, it's recommended that you always keep the protection agent updated.

5. Click **Next >** to continue.

6. On the **Enter Credentials** page, type the username and password for a domain account that is a member of the local administrators group on the selected computer(s).

7. If you select a node in a cluster, DPM detects all of the additional nodes in the cluster and displays the **Select Cluster Nodes** page. On the **Select Cluster Nodes** page, select an option that you want DPM to use for installing agents on additional nodes in the cluster. Then, click **Next**.

8. In the **Choose Restart Method** step, select the method that you want to use to restart the selected computers after the protection agent has been installed.

For greenfield agent installation, the computer must be restarted before you can start protecting data. A restart is necessary to load the volume filter that DPM uses to track and transfer block-level changes between the DPM server and the protected computers.

9. If any of the computers that you have selected are members of a cluster, an additional **Choose Restart Method** page will appear that you can use so that you can select the method to restart the clustered computers.

Please note that you need to install a protection agent on all of the nodes in a cluster to successfully protect the clustered data.

10. Choose an appropriate option and click on **Next >** to continue.

11. In the **Summary** page, you can verify the information you have chosen and then click on **Install** to initialize the installation and configuration process of the DPM agent.

12. After a short period of time, the **Agent** will appear in the DPM console and report back with status **OK**.

Option 2 – installing the agent manually

You can perform a manual installation in two different ways:

- By providing the FQDN of the DPM server when running the `DpmAgentInstaller` executable
- By providing the NetBIOS name of the DPM server using `setdpmserver.exe` if the DPM agent is already installed but not configured

Now follow these steps:

1. On the computer that you want to protect, open an elevated command window, and then run `net use Z: \\<DPMServerName>\d$`, where `Z` is the local drive letter that you want to assign and `<DPMServerName>` is the name of the DPM server that will protect the computer. `d$` is where DPM software is installed.

2. For a 64-bit computer, type the following:

   ```
   cd /d <assigned drive letter>:\Program Files\Microsoft System
   Center 2019\DPM\DPM\ProtectionAgents\RA\5.0.<build number>.0\amd64
   ```

   Here, `<assigned drive letter>` is the drive letter that you assigned in the previous step and `<build number>` is the latest DPM build number. For example:

   ```
   cd /d "Z:\Program Files\Microsoft System Center
   2019\DPM\DPM\ProtectionAgents\RA\5.0.158.0\amd64"
   ```

3. For a 32-bit computer, type the following:

   ```
   cd /d <assigned drive letter>:\Program Files\Microsoft System
   Center 2019\DPM\DPM\ProtectionAgents\RA\5.0.<build number>.0\i386
   ```

   Here, `<assigned drive letter>` is the drive that you mapped in the previous step and `<build number>` is the latest DPM build number.

4. To install the protection agent for a 64-bit computer, run the following command:

   ```
   DPMAgentInstaller_x64.exe <DPMServerName>
   ```

   Here, `<DPMServerName>` is the **fully qualified domain name (FQDN)** of the DPM server.

5. To install the protection agent for a 32-bit computer, run the following command:

```
DPMAgentInstaller_x86.exe <DPMServerName>
```

Here, <DPMServerName> is the FQDN of the DPM server.

6. Select **I accept the license terms and conditions** for the Microsoft Software License Terms, and click **OK**.

7. The installation will start and you will receive a confirmation message that states **Agent installation completed successfully**. The DPM agent has now been configured and the appropriate firewall exceptions have been made in the domain profile of the Windows Firewall. Press *Enter* key to close the window.

To perform a silent installation and to accept the EULA license in a silent installation , you can use the /q and /IAcceptEULA options after the command. For example: DPMAgentInstaller_x64.exe /q <DPMServerName> /IAcceptEULA.

8. If the DPM agent is already installed, you should run the setdpmserver.exe executable with the –dpmservername switch to configure the DPM server that the DPM agent should report to as follows:

```
Setdpmserver –dpmservername DPM2019
```

When using the SetDpmServer executable, you only need the NetBIOS name of the DPM server.

After installing the agent manually, you must attach the DPM agent to the DPM server. You can do this via the DPM Administrator console or via the DPM PowerShell cmdlet.

9. Open the DPM console and go to **Management**. Click on **Production Servers** and, at the top-left corner of the console, click on the **Add** button to start the **Production Server Addition Wizard**.

10. Under the **Select Agent Deployment Method** page, click **Attach agents**, followed by **Computer on trusted domain**. Click the **Next >** button to continue:

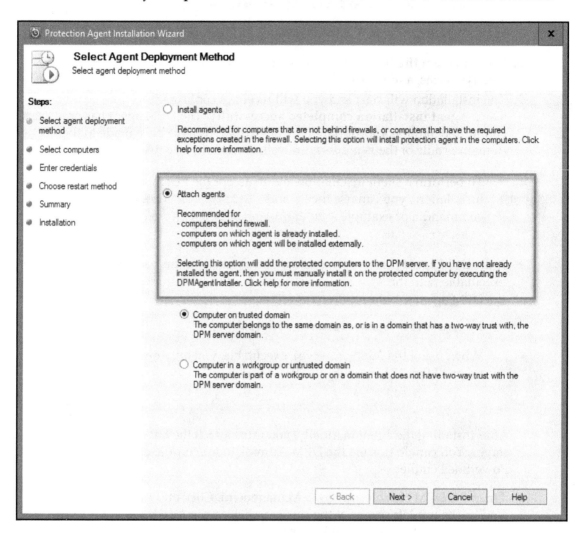

 If you want to attach a DPM agent in a workgroup or untrusted domain, please refer to Chapter 8, *Protecting Workgroups and Untrusted Domains*, for more information.

11. In the **Select Computers** page, choose the server that you would like to attach to the DPM server and click on **Next >** to continue.

You can also provide a list of servers that you would like to have attached. The list should have all of the FQDN of every server per row in a simple text file. Click on the **Add From File...** button to import the files' data.

12. In the **Enter Credentials** page, enter the credentials that should be used to execute this process. Keep in mind that the credentials you provide must have administrative rights on the server that you are trying to attach. Provide the credentials and click on **Next >** to continue.
13. In the **Summary** page, verify the configuration and click on **Attach** to start.
14. Verify that the **Attach protected computer** task has been successful. Click **Close** to close the **Protection Agent Installation Wizard**.
15. The **Agent** will appear in the DPM console and report back with status **OK**.

How it works...

The DPM agent is the core component for the DPM so that it's able to provide restore capabilities for your data. The DPM relies on the DCOM object of the protected server which is mapped to the DPMRA service so that the SQL job on the DPM server starts. System Center Data Protection Manager stores all protection group configurations as **SQL Jobs,** and the **SQL Server Agent** initializes the DPM agent to start creating snapshots by using the underlying architecture of the **Volume Shadow Copy Service** (also known as **Volume Snapshot Service** or **VSS**) within the operating system.

The setdpmserver.exe executable command has the ability to configure the DPM agent to set which DPM server the DPM agent reports to. It also provides the configuration needed for the local Windows Firewall so that the DPM agent can start reporting to the DPM server.

There's more...

System Center Data Protection Manager manages data replication and provides management of the DPM agents using two different TCP ports:

- 5718
- 5719

TCP port 5718 is used for data replication and TCP port 5719 is used by the DPM agent **coordinator**. The **coordinator** is the function within the DPM agent architecture that manages the installation, uninstallation, and updates of the DPM agent. For more information regarding firewall ports and configuration, please read the *Planning your DPM deployment* recipe in this chapter.

Upgrading the DPM agents

This recipe covers how you can upgrade DPM agents from the DPM console and also provides information about other scenarios.

Getting ready

Microsoft keeps releasing updates that are critical to apply, since they contain new enhancements that will provide you with optimization of the DPM software. They also enable new restore capability features for your workload.

How to do it...

After you have upgraded DPM 2012 R2 to the latest DPM release, you must upgrade all of the DPM agents that are attached to the DPM server before protection can continue. This is something you need to do manually:

1. Open the DPM console, select **Management** and, on the left-hand side of the console, click on **Agents**. In the display pane, you will see DPM agents reporting **Update Available**.
2. Right-click the agents that you want to update and choose **Update** from the drop-down list.

 Starting with DPM 2016 or later, once the agent has been updated, no reboot is required. DPM will continue to protect your workloads. However, we have seen some servers reboot automatically, even if the option to automatically reboot is not checked, so make sure to upgrade the agent during a maintenance window.

How it works...

The DPM agent coordinator is the function within the DPM agent architecture that provides you with the ability to upgrade your DPM agents via the DPM console.

Some Update Rollups require a restart if the file filter drivers, or any DLL in the change-tracking process, has been updated. It is recommended that you read the release notes for the update before applying it to the production environment.

There's more...

You can also apply the updates manually via Microsoft Update, local **Windows Server Update Services (WSUS)**, or **System Center Configuration Manager (SCCM)**.

2
DPM Post-Installation and Management Tasks

In this chapter, we will cover the following recipes:

- Using the **Data Protection Manager** (**DPM**) UI
- Enabling **Modern Backup Storage** (**MBS**)
- Configuring DPM agent throttling
- Optimizing the protection group
- Working with filters
- Configuring email notifications
- Applying **Update Rollups** (**UR**) to the DPM server
- Configuring a dedicated backup network
- Configuring Workload-Aware Storage
- Backup Storage Migration
- Preventing unexpected data loss
- Creating a manual initial replica
- Creating custom reports

Introduction

This chapter is designed to provide you with skills and techniques for dealing with post-installation and management tasks for your Microsoft **System Center Data Protection Manager** (**SCDPM**) server. After reading this chapter, you will have the knowledge to carry out common DPM management activities, such as using the DPM console, configuring storage, creating custom reporting, working with SQL self service, and many more tasks.

To follow the recipes in this chapter, you need to have successfully installed Microsoft System Center DPM and also have a second instance of SQL Server that has been prepared for a remote DPM database installation.

Using the DPM UI

The following recipe provides an overview of the Microsoft System Center DPM Administrator Console; it includes a tour of the console, describes the console layout, and explains where you can find the controls for performing general administrative tasks. This recipe also includes an overview of the five task areas of the Administrator Console and their associated functions.

How to do it...

The DPM Administrative Console is the central management tool for DPM. It provides a consolidated interface that gives you immediate access to the **Monitoring**, **Protection**, **Recovery**, **Reporting**, and **Management** task areas. The task areas themselves are a set of logically related functions and actions that have been grouped together in the Administrator Console. Each task area consists of two panes: the display pane, which is unlabeled, and the details pane. The following steps will guide you through the layout and usage of the DPM Administrative Console:

1. From the **Start** screen, select the **Microsoft System Center Data Protection Manager**. The DPM Administrator Console loads and the **Monitoring** task area is highlighted.
2. The **Monitoring** task area is used to monitor the status of the **Protection**, **Recovery**, **Reporting**, and **Management** operation tasks.
3. The **Monitoring** task area contains **Alerts** and **Jobs**. **Alerts** display critical errors, warnings, and information messages, and **Jobs** displays the status of jobs initiated by DPM and their operational status, for example, completed, running, failed, canceled, or scheduled.
4. Click on the **Protection** task. Here, you can create protection groups, rename and manage members of that protection group, configure self service recovery for SQL Server, and specify tape catalog retention.

5. Click on the **Recovery** task. The **Recovery** task area allows you to find and recover data from your recovery points. You can **Browse** for available recovery points by protected computer or use **Search**, which enables you to search for available recovery points based on data type, location, origin, and recovery point date.

6. Click on the **Reporting** task. Here, you can generate and view reports on your DPM operations, plus schedule automatic report generation.

7. Finally, click on the **Management** task. Here, you can manage protection agents and disk storage, integrate DPM with public Azure and Azure Backup, and manage tape libraries:

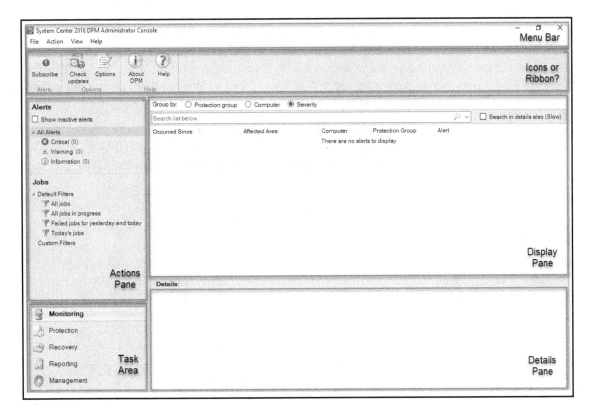

How it works...

The initial management of Microsoft SCDPM focuses on the use of the DPM Administrative Console. The console allows administrators to manage every aspect of their backup and recovery from within a single user interface.

Once DPM has been installed and configured successfully, typically an administrator will spend the majority of their time in the **Monitoring, Recovery**, and **Reporting** task areas.

You must be a member of the local Administrators group on your DPM server to be able to access the DPM Administrator Console.

Enabling Modern Backup Storage (MBS)

Starting with Microsoft System Center 2016 DPM, Microsoft introduced a new feature called **Modern Backup Storage** (**MBS**). MBS is supported when DPM is installed on Windows Server 2016 or later. MBS helps to reduce the overall backup storage space, and Microsoft claims this is by a factor of around 50%. It also reduces the amount of I/O and the load placed on the backup server by using **Resilient File System** (**ReFS**) technology, which is available in Windows Server 2016 and Windows Server 2019.

To be able to configure Modern Backup Storage, you will need to have some primordial storage (unallocated storage capacity) available and connected to the DPM server that you are currently managing.

Getting ready

Microsoft System Center DPM uses, by default, the new backup option, Modern Backup Storage. Once a volume is added in the Admin Console, DPM will automatically format that volume with the ReFS. There are four steps to setting up MBS:

1. Provide a new storage pool
2. Create a new virtual disk and define its properties
3. Create a new volume and define its storage layout and provisioning scheme
4. Add the this new volume to DPM

How to do it...

The following steps will guide you through configuring storage in Windows Server 2016 and Server Manager, and adding that storage in the Microsoft System Center Data Protection Manager Administrative Console, so that you can take advantage of MBS:

1. From the **Start** screen, select **Server Manager**. When the Windows Server 2016 **Server Manager** console loads, select **File and Storage Services** and then select **Storage Pools**:

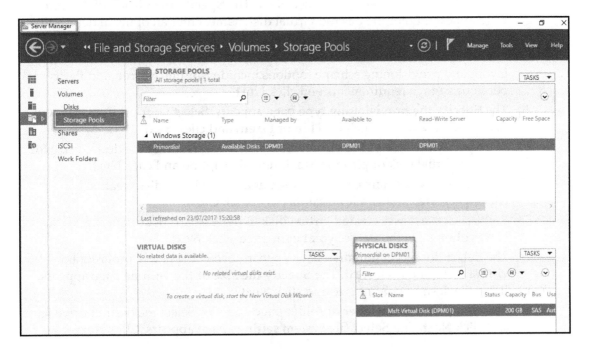

2. In the **PHYSICAL DISKS** pane, right-click your primordial storage and select **New Storage Pool**; the **New Storage Pool Wizard** appears.
3. On the **Before you begin** page, click **Next**. The **Specify a storage pool name and subsystem** page appears.
4. Enter the desired storage pool name and an optional description. Make sure that you have selected the primordial storage pool that you want to use (if there is more than one option) and click **Next**.

5. The **Select physical disks for the storage pool** page appears. Select the number of physical disks needed for pool creation (if there is more than one option) and click **Next**.

6. The **Confirm selections** page appears. Initiate the storage pool creation by clicking **Create**. The **View results** page appears. Click **Close**.

7. Highlight the newly created storage pool and in the **Virtual disks** pane click **Tasks** and select **New virtual disk**. Ensure the correct storage pool is selected and click **OK**.

8. On the **Before you begin** page, click **Next**. The **Specify the virtual disk name** page appears. Enter the desired virtual disk name, enter an optional description, and click **Next**.

9. On the **Specify enclosure resiliency** page, click **Next**. Select the desired storage layout and provisioning scheme (options include **Simple**, **Mirror**, and **Parity**) as per your storage requirements and click **Next**.

10. The **Specify the provisioning type** page appears. Select your provisioning type requirements (options include **Thin** or **Fixed**) and click **Next**.

11. The **Specify the size of the virtual disk** page appears. Enter the desired size for the new virtual disk or pick the **Maximum size** option and click **Next**.

12. The **Confirm selections** page appears. Initiate the virtual disk creation by clicking **Create**. On the **View results** page, click **Close**.

13. Right-click the newly created virtual disk in the **Virtual disks** pane and click **New volume**. On the **Before you begin** page, click **Next**.

14. The **Select the server and disk** page appears. Select the newly provisioned virtual disks and click **Next**. The **Specify the size of the volume** page appears. Enter the desired volume size and click **Next**.

15. The **Assign to a drive letter or folder** page appears. Select the desired drive letter and click **Next**. The **Select file system settings** page appears. Click **Next**.

16. The **Enable data duplication** page appears. Click **Next**. The **Confirm selections** page appears. Initiate the volume creation by clicking **Create**. On the **Completion** page click **Close**:

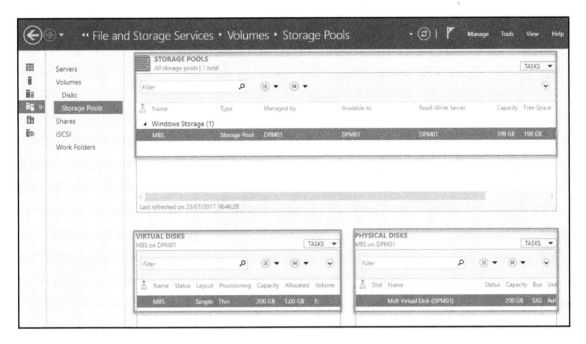

17. From the **Start** screen, select **Microsoft System Center Data Protection Manager**. The DPM Administrator Console loads and the **Monitoring** task area is highlighted.

18. Select the **Management** task area. Click **Disk Storage**, then click the Rescan icon and finally click the Add icon. The **Add Disk Storage** page appears.

19. Select the available volume and click **Add**. DPM will then format the volume before adding it to the DPM storage pool. Click **Yes** to continue. Optionally, give the volume a friendly name and click **OK**:

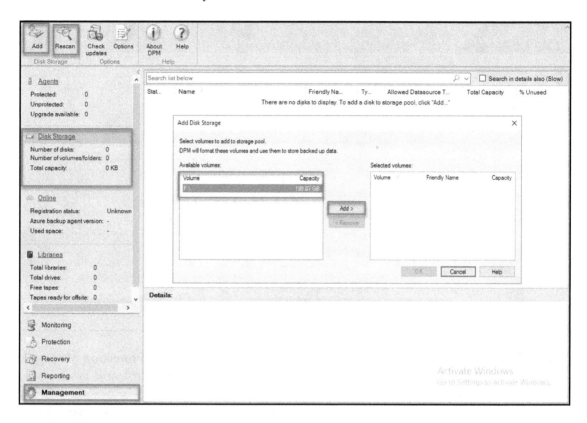

How it works...

DPM leverages Windows Server 2016 and ReFS to provide support for MBS. To add a volume to DPM as a MBS volume, simply configure your volume with a drive letter identifier. When you add an volume under management, DPM will format that volume using ReFS and add that volume to the DPM storage pool. The new MBS utilizes VHDX files to store its backup data and remove the use of physical disks, over-allocation, and the need for collocation of workloads.

To use the MBS (which is enabled by default) the following prerequisites must be met:

- You must be using Microsoft System Center 2016 DPM or later
- DPM itself must be installed on Windows Server 2016 or later
- The underlying physical disk must not be a dynamic disk (only basic disks are supported)

There's more...

When adding a new ReFS volume to DPM, the system requires a drive letter to be associated with that volume. However, if you run out of drive letters on your system, you can also use a mount point instead of a drive letter as backup target storage.

See also

Read this article to learn more about how to use mount points with MBS: `https://charbelnemnom.com/2017/09/using-volume-mount-points-with-modern-backup-storage-in-dpm-2016-dpm-mbs-scdpm-mabs/`.

Configuring DPM agent throttling

Configuring DPM agent throttling in Microsoft System Center DPM allows you to restrict the amount of network bandwidth consumed by DPM during the execution of a backup synchronization job. Managing network bandwidth helps to ensure that DPM is not using all the available bandwidth and there is sufficient bandwidth available to support other applications. However, there is an impact when you start to manage bandwidth usage and that is that the backup synchronization jobs themselves will take longer to execute.

Getting ready

Microsoft System Center DPM manages network bandwidth at the agent level. When managing network bandwidth usage, start to think about limiting the amount of bandwidth used, in terms of the maximum amount of data to be transferred on a per-second basis. To be able to enable network bandwidth throttling, you must have the DPM protection agent deployed.

How to do it...

The following steps will guide you through configuring network bandwidth throttling:

1. From the **Start** screen, select **Microsoft System Center Data Protection Manager**. The DPM Administrator Console loads and the **Monitoring** task area is highlighted.

2. Select the **Management** task area. In the **Display** pane, select a server where you want to enable network bandwidth throttling and click the Throttle Computer icon on the Ribbon bar.

3. Click **Enable network bandwidth usage throttling** and configure your network bandwidth throttling based on the day and time period of your working and non-working windows of operation. Note that you can set your working hours and non-working days separately. Once you are finished, click **OK**:

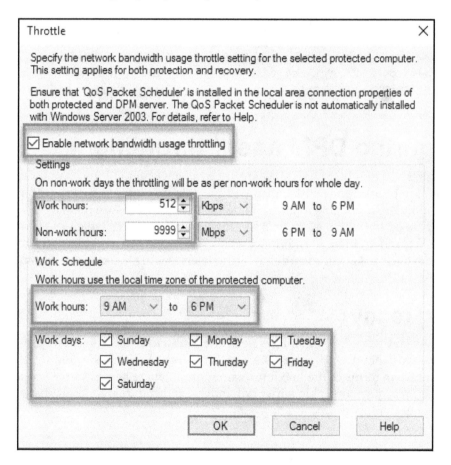

How it works...

The Microsoft System Center DPM agent relies on the underlying architecture of the Windows operating system and the **Quality of Service** (**QoS**) packet scheduler, which is a Windows feature that is enabled by default. The QoS packet scheduler is designed to control the IP traffic of various networking services within the operating system. If this feature is not enabled—for example, if it is disabled via Group Policy hardening on the DPM server or the server that is hosting the protected workload—then network bandwidth throttling will not be function.

Optimizing the protection group

Optimizing the protection group in Microsoft System Center DPM allows you to reduce the amount of data being transferred over the wire during replica creation, backup synchronization, consistency check operations, and recovery jobs, through the use of compression. This has the advantage of allowing more data throughput with less overall impact to your network's performance. However, enabling this option will add additional CPU load to both your DPM server and the server you are protecting.

Getting ready

Compression is enabled at the protection group level and here you can define what the backup settings are for your protected data source. To be able to optimize your protection group, you must have a protection group defined.

How to do it...

The following steps will guide you through how to optimize the protection group:

1. From the **Start** screen, select **Microsoft System Center Data Protection Manager**. The DPM Administrator Console loads and the **Monitoring** task area is highlighted.
2. Select the **Protection** task area. Select the protection group that you want to optimize and click the Optimize icon on the Ribbon bar.

3. On the **Network** tab, check **Enable on-the-wire compression.** You can further optimize the performance of the protection group by offsetting the start time of synchronization jobs across your different protection groups. Select the hours and minutes to offset the start of the synchronization job and click **OK**:

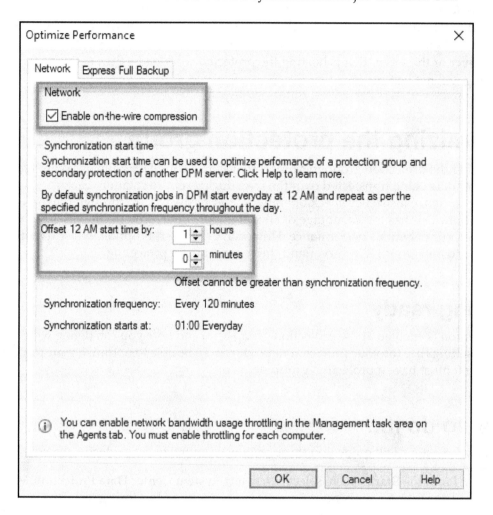

How it works...

When you create a protection group, you can optimize it by doing the following:

- Enabling compression on the protection group
- Offsetting the start time of synchronization jobs across your various protection groups

Launch the Microsoft System Center Data Protection Manager Administration Console. Go to the **Protection** task area and select the protection group that you want to optimize. Here, you can enable compression and offset the start time of your synchronization job for that particular protection group. Be aware that the maximum allowed value for the scheduled offset is the same as the synchronization frequency.

Working with filters

Filters in Microsoft System Center DPM allow you to query the result of jobs executed or scheduled in a number of varying ways. Filters are simply SQL queries that present the results of the fetched data to the DPM Admin Console. You can also go ahead and define your own custom filters, and these results appear under the custom filters option in the **Action** pane of the Admin Console.

Getting ready

You can filter jobs by using the following criteria by default:

- All jobs
- All jobs in progress
- Failed jobs for yesterday and today
- Today's jobs

How to do it...

The following steps will guide you through how to use the default filters and build your own custom filters:

1. From the **Start** screen, select **Microsoft System Center Data Protection Manager**. The DPM Administrator Console loads and the **Monitoring** task area is highlighted.

2. Select the **Monitoring** task area. Select one of the default filters in the **Action** pane to retrieve the associated data:

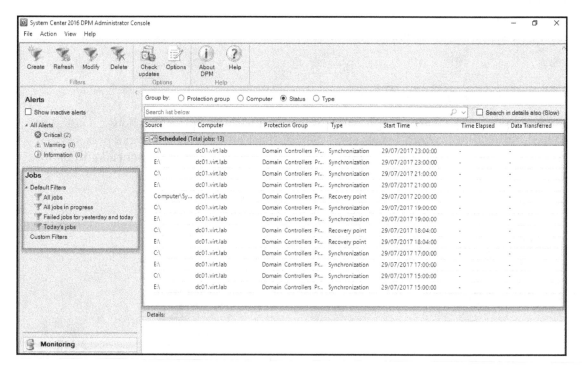

3. To create a custom filter, click the Create icon on the Ribbon bar. Enter a filter name, select the **Time from** option from the drop-down menu, and select a **time from** value.

4. Select the **Time to** option from the drop-down menu and select a **time to** value.

5. On the **Jobs** tab, select one or more of the job types and the job status—for example, completed, failed, in progress, or scheduled—and click on the **Protection** tab.

6. Select whether to group the jobs by protection group or by computer group and then select the protection group and members of that protection group that you want information displayed on. If you want DPM to filter external media, select **External tape jobs**.

7. Click on the **Others** tab, specify the **Time elapsed** in either minutes or hours, the **Data transferred** in MB, and clear or leave enabled the option for libraries, if you want to apply the filter here.

8. Click **Preview** to preview the filtered jobs or **Save** to save the custom filter. Click the Refresh icon on the Ribbon bar. In the **Display** pane, you will see the results of your custom query:

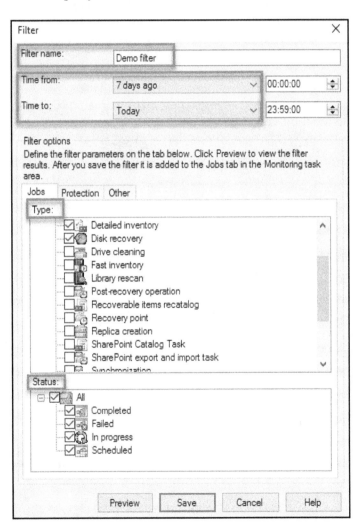

How it works...

Creating custom filters in Microsoft System Center DPM allows you to easily query the DPM SQL database, via the DPM Admin Console, without the need to be an SQL DBA. Custom filters consist of varying job types and statuses.

Configuring email notifications

You can configure Microsoft System Center DPM to subscribe to notifications and reports via email. If you decide to enable either of these features, you will need to configure a **Simple Mail Transfer Protocol** (**SMTP**) server that you want DPM to use to send email.

Getting ready

You can subscribe to alert notifications and to reports by email. If you plan to enable either of these features, do the following:

1. Set up the SMTP server
2. Subscribe to email notifications

How to do it...

The following steps will guide you through how to configure email notifications:

1. From the **Start** screen, select **Microsoft System Center Data Protection Manager**. The DPM Administrator Console will load and the **Monitoring** task area will be highlighted.
2. Select the **Management** task area, click the Options icon on the Ribbon bar, and click the **SMTP servers** tab. Specify values for the **SMTP server name**, **Port**, and **From email address**. Click **Send Test E-mail...** and specify where you want to send the test email:

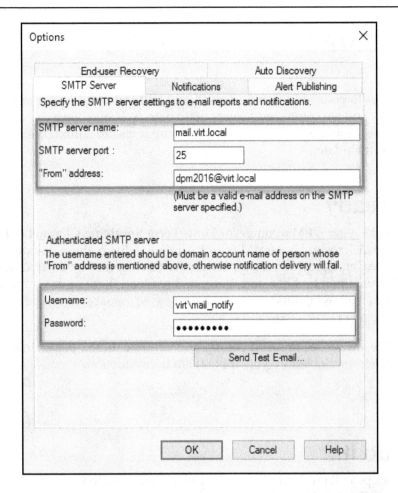

3. Click the **Notifications** tab. Select the types of alerts that you want to be notified about—that is, **Critical**, **Warning**, and **Informational**—and the email recipients. Use commas to separate individual email addresses and click **OK**.

How it works...

Microsoft System Center DPM provides you with the capability to subscribe to notifications and reports via email. You need to configure the SMTP server that you want DPM to use to send email.

For added security, the SMTP server is configured to use authenticated SMTP. Finally, you can subscribe to specific types of alerts, that is, **Critical**, **Warning**, and **Informational**.

Applying Update Rollups (UR) to the DPM server

Applying updates to your Microsoft System Center DPM server is important: updates keep your DPM server and any protected servers up to date. You may have a preferred mechanism for deploying updates; however, DPM updates are automatically available through Microsoft Update.

Getting ready

Microsoft System Center DPM updates for **Long-Term Servicing Channel** (**LTSC**) are available through Microsoft Update. Microsoft Update delivers these updates from the Microsoft Update Catalog, which is a repository for Microsoft software updates that is managed and maintained by Microsoft. You can download these updates automatically or manually from the following link: `https://www.catalog.update.microsoft.com/Search.aspx?q=Data+Protection+Manager`.

We always recommend you try and validate these updates in a test environment before you apply them in production.

How to do it...

The following steps will guide you through applying updates to your Microsoft System Center DPM server, while installed on Windows Server 2016:

1. Click **Start**, then click **Settings**, then click **Updates & security**. On the **Windows Update** tab, click **Check for updates** and click **Install now**:

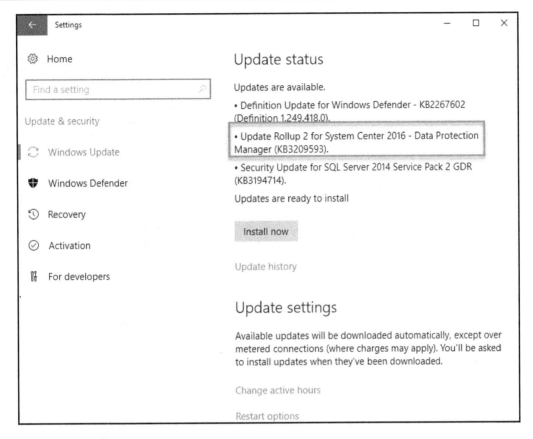

2. Alternatively, manually download the update by going to the Microsoft Update Catalog at `https://www.catalog.update.microsoft.com/Home.aspx`, entering the KB article related to the update, and manually downloading the update by specifying a location locally to store the required update.

3. From the **Start** screen, select **Microsoft System Center Data Protection Manager**. The DPM Administrator Console loads and the **Monitoring** task area is highlighted.

4. Select the **Management** task area, and then click on **Production** Servers; you will notice that the updates are available. In the **Display** pane, highlight the protected server that you want to update and click **Update** on the **Ribbon** bar. Click **Yes** when prompted to update the agent.

5. Click the **Management** task area, select the protected server, and in the **Details** pane verify that the protection agent version value has been updated to reflect the new version.

How it works...

You can obtain and install update packages from Microsoft Update or you can manually download these updates from Microsoft Update Catalog. Once downloaded and installed, you need to update the agents running on the protected servers within your environment. To update the agents, you can carry out a push install from the Microsoft System Center DPM Administrator console.

Configuring a dedicated backup network

Providing a dedicated backup network for your backup traffic is a sensible strategy. It isolates backup-specific traffic away from other more common production-based traffic in your data center and can often remove dependencies from the production network.

Getting ready

There are a number of prerequisites to enabling a backup network with Microsoft System Center DPM, for example, the availability of a secondary **network interface card (NIC)**, which can be either a **physical NIC (pNIC)** or a **virtual NIC (vNIC: converged network in Hyper-V)**.

The name resolution can be done either through DNS or the hosts file, since the backup network may not have a DNS server, and this will ensure that you have network connectivity through the backup NIC for both the DPM server and protected servers.

How to do it...

The following steps will guide you through configuring a backup network:

1. On your DPM server, from the Windows desktop, right-click on the DPM Management Shell icon and select **Run as administrator**.
2. In the PowerShell cmdlet window, run the following cmdlet:

   ```
   Get-DPMBackupNetworkAddress
   ```

3. This cmdlet runs and doesn't return a value. Here, we can see that a backup network is not configured as of yet and by default DPM is using the production network.

4. On the protected server, use your preferred text editor to open the `c:\windows\system32\drivers\etc\hosts` file. Add an entry using the **fully qualified domain name** (**FQDN**) notation of the DPM server backup NIC.

5. On the DPM server, open the `c:\windows\system32\drivers\etc\hosts` file. Add an entry using the FQDN notation of the backup NIC of the protected servers.

6. In the PowerShell window, run the following cmdlet:

   ```
   Add-BackupNetworkAddress -DPMServerName <Your_DPM_Server_Name>
   <Your_Backup_IP_Address_CIDR_Notation> -SequenceNumber 1
   Add-BackupNetworkAddress -DPMServerName <Your_DPM_Server_Name>
   <Your_Production_IP_Address_CIDR_Notation> -SequenceNumber 2
   ```

7. Finally, you need to restart the DPM agents on both the DPM server and the protected servers connected to the backup network. To do this, click **Start**, type cmd, then right-click the **Command Prompt** option and select **Run as administrator**. The Command Prompt window appears.

8. In the command window, run the following command:

   ```
   Net Stop DPMRA / Net Start DPMRA
   ```

9. In the **DPM Management Shell**, run the following cmdlet to ensure that both the backup and production networks are now listed:

   ```
   Get-DPMBackupNetworkAddress
   ```

You need to configure the production network as a second backup network to act as a fallback and so that protected servers that are not configured can use the backup network.

How it works...

Microsoft System Center DPM doesn't by default have a dedicated backup network configured to use out of the box. To configure the backup network, you need to use PowerShell instead of using the DPM Administrator Console. The PowerShell cmdlet that is used to configure the backup network is `Get-DPMBackupNetworkAddress`. Multiple networks can be configured and the priority is controlled with a sequence number where the lowest sequence number has priority.

Configuring Workload-Aware Storage

Starting with System Center 2016 Data Protection Manager, Microsoft introduced a new feature called **Workload-Aware Storage** (**WAS**). With WAS, you can create storage based on performance efficiency to back up designated workloads to specific volumes; thus you will improve DPM performance and reduce I/O requirements. In this recipe, we will show you how to configure Workload-Aware Storage.

Getting ready

Before you start configuring WAS, you need to enable MBS by adding volume(s) as backup disk storage. DPM will automatically format each volume with ReFS. For more information, please check the *Enabling Modern Backup Storage (MBS)* recipe in this chapter.

How to do it...

After adding the volume to DPM, the next step is to configure WAS; this feature can only be configured using PowerShell. Open a Windows PowerShell session on your DPM server and follow these steps:

1. Query all disk storage volumes that are attached to DPM using the `$vol = Get-DPMDiskStorage -Volumes` command:

```
CharbelNemnom.com #> $vol = Get-DPMDiskStorage -Volumes
CharbelNemnom.com #> $vol

Name AccessPath Tag TotalSpace      LogicalUsedSpace
---- ---------- --- ----------      ----------------
     G:\        All 107307073536
     F:\        All 107307073536
     E:\        All 107307073536


CharbelNemnom.com #>
```

2. Next, you need to specify the data source type for the desired volume by using the `Update-DPMDiskStorge` cmdlet, followed by the `-Volume` parameter, space bar, then we are going to refer to our previous variable, `$vol`. We are specifically interested in the `G:\` drive—you can make that reference in this case with square brackets, `[0]`, then you need to specify the `-DataSourceType`. In this example, we need to back up Hyper-V and VMware virtual machines, SQL Server, and the file server. The `-DataSourceType` parameter can be set using any of the following, or a combination of more than one type: **FileSystem**, **SystemProtection**, **Client**, **Exchange**, **SharePoint**, **SQL**, **VMware**, **All**, **HyperV**, **Other**, or **NotOwnedByDPM**. The full syntax for the command is `Update-DPMDiskStorage -Volume $vol[0] -DatasourceType HyperV, VMware -FriendlyName "Hyper-V & VMware Storage"`:

```
CharbelNemnom.com #> Update-DPMDiskStorage -Volume $vol[0] -DatasourceType HyperV, VMware -FriendlyName "Hyper-V & VMwar
e Storage"
CharbelNemnom.com #> Update-DPMDiskStorage -Volume $vol[1] -DatasourceType SQL -FriendlyName "SQL Storage"
CharbelNemnom.com #> Update-DPMDiskStorage -Volume $vol[2] -DatasourceType FileSystem -FriendlyName "File System"
CharbelNemnom.com #> Get-DPMDiskStorage -Volumes

Name                     AccessPath Tag             TotalSpace    LogicalUsedSpace
----                     ---------- ---             ----------    ----------------
Hyper-V & VMware Storage G:\        HyperV, VMware  107307073536
SQL Storage              F:\        SQL             107307073536
File System              E:\        FileSystem      107307073536
```

3. The changes made using the PowerShell cmdlet are reflected in the DPM Administrator Console.

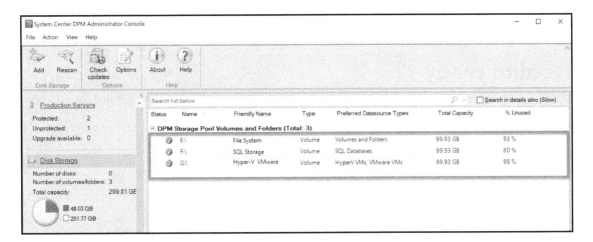

How it works...

When you configure WAS on multiple volumes, DPM will proactively select these volumes to store the associated workloads; you can also manually select **Target Storage** for each data source using **Disk Storage Allocation** during the creation of the protection group. For example, the SSD volumes that support high IOPS can be configured to store workloads that need frequent, high-volume backups such as SQL Server with transaction logs. Workloads that are backed up less frequently, such as Hyper-V or VMware VMs, can be backed up to low-cost HDD volumes. Additionally, DPM will also filter out any storage that currently doesn't have enough space to accommodate what you're trying to protect.

Backup Storage Migration

One of the most common requests to Microsoft in earlier DPM versions was the ability to move data backups from one volume to another volume. Starting with DPM 2016 Update Rollup 4 and later, you can move data backups from one volume to another; this is useful in scenarios where you want to upgrade your storage from a low-performant volume to a high-performant volume, or you want to move data sources to other volumes when an existing volume is getting full and cannot be extended.

Please note that this feature is only supported for Modern Backup Storage volumes. DPM Classic Storage to Modern Backup Storage is not supported, and DPM Classic Storage to DPM Classic Storage is not supported either. DPM Classic Storage is what we had in DPM 2012 R2 and earlier versions.

Getting ready

Make sure your DPM server is in a healthy state and is running any of the following versions:

- DPM 2016 with minimum Update Rollup 4, DPM 2019 or a later version
- DPM 1801, DPM 1807, DPM 1901, or a later version
- Microsoft Azure Backup Server version 3 or later

How to do it...

1. Open your **DPM Administrator Console**, go to the **Protection** workspace, and then select the desired **Protection Group**.

2. Under the **Protection Group**, select the workload that you wish to move, right-click, and then select **Move disk storage...**:

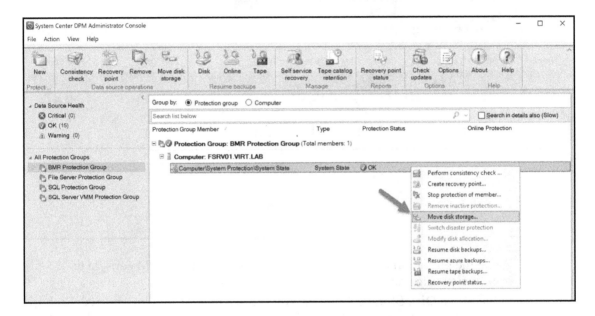

3. A new window will open, where you can see the **Current disk storage** for the data source, and the available volume(s) that can be migrated to. Select the **target disk storage** you want to migrate to and then click **OK**:

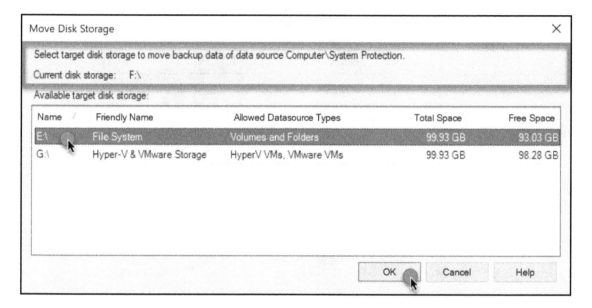

4. While the migration is in progress, you can open another DPM console to continue monitoring progress for any ongoing jobs.
5. In the **Move Disk Storage** window, you can see that it's moving the disk backup storage of the data source. The moving operation will take some time depending on the amount of data you are migrating. After a moment, you'll see that the move completed successfully. Click **Close**:

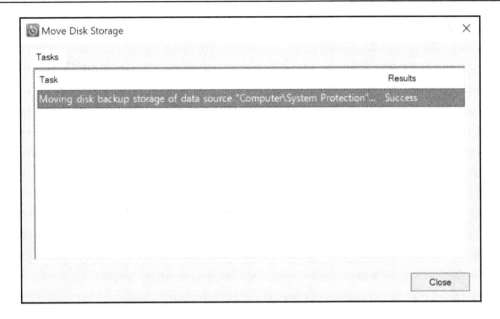

How it works...

Once you start moving the disk backup storage, DPM begins copying (reading) the data from the source and then writing to the target storage. Once the migration is completed, the backup and the source are deleted, and any new recovery points will hence be created on the target storage source. This is a lot like modifying a protection group; you cannot revert any ad hoc jobs while the migration is in progress. Also, when the migration is completed, any job that is running for that particular protection group will be pre-empted.

See also

Please check this article to see how you can migrate the backup storage using Windows PowerShell: https://charbelnemnom.com/2017/10/how-to-move-backup-storage-in-dpm-2016-modern-backup-storage-scdpm-dpm/.

Preventing unexpected data loss

DPM servers may be managed by a team of IT administrators. Assigning the wrong volumes for backup storage can cause critical data loss. Starting with DPM 2016 Update Rollup 4 and later, you can disable volumes or mount points from being used as backup storage. In this recipe, we will show you how to exclude volume and mount points from being available for DPM.

Getting ready

Make sure your DPM server is in a healthy state and is running any of the following versions:

- DPM 2016 with minimum Update Rollup 4, DPM 2019, or a later version
- DPM 1801, DPM 1807, DPM 1901, or a later version
- Microsoft Azure Backup Server version 3 or later

How to do it...

The volume exclusion feature can only be configured using PowerShell. In this example, we will exclude the `H:\` drive and `D:\MountPoints\MountPoint01` from being available to the DPM as disk storage:

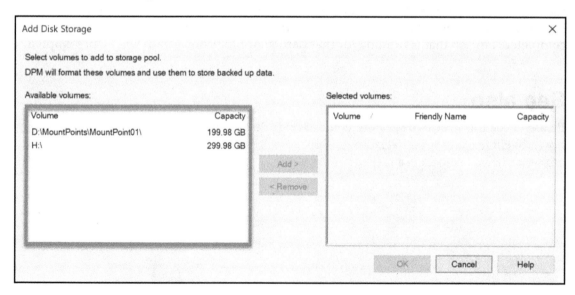

Open a Windows PowerShell session on your DPM server and follow these steps:

1. Run the `Set-DPMGlobalProperty` cmdlet followed by the – `DPMStorageVolumeExclusion` parameter. The full syntax based on our example is the following: `Set-DPMGlobalProperty -DPMStorageVolumeExclusion "H:,D:\MountPoints\MountPoint01"`.

2. Next, **Rescan** the storage using the **DPM Administrator Console**, or use the **Start-DPMDiskRescan** PowerShell cmdlet. When you try to **Add** a volume as disk storage, you will see that none of the previous available volumes will show:

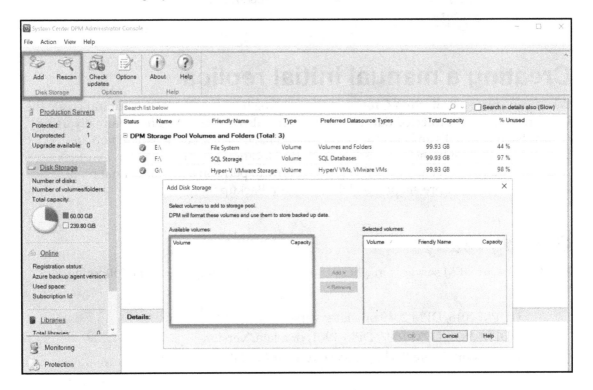

3. If you want to remove the volume exclusion, open Windows PowerShell and type the `Set-DPMGlobalProperty` cmdlet followed by the parameter – `DPMStorageVolumeExclusion`, without specifying any value. The full syntax will look like this: `Set-DPMGlobalProperty -DPMStorageVolumeExclusion ""`.

4. After removing volume exclusion, **Rescan** the storage again. All volumes and mount points that were previously removed, except for System Volumes, will be available to DPM as backup storage.

See also

Read this article to learn more about how to use mount points with MBS: `https://charbelnemnom.com/2017/09/using-volume-mount-points-with-modern-backup-storage-in-dpm-2016-dpm-mbs-scdpm-mabs/`.

Please check this guide to learn more about the `Set-DPMGlobalProperty` cmdlet, which can also be used to set exclusions for Exchange, and Hyper-V virtual hard disks from backup jobs for a System Center DPM installation: `https://docs.microsoft.com/en-us/powershell/module/dataprotectionmanager/set-dpmglobalproperty?view=systemcenter-ps-2016`.

Creating a manual initial replica

When you create a **Protection Group**, you can define how the DPM sever should create the initial replica of the protected data source. You can also create the replica manually using removable media if it's an enormous amount of data, or in a scenario where you are backing up different branch offices from a central location and you don't have a quick network link. In this recipe, we will show you how to perform a manual initial replica, also called pre-seeding or pre-staging on DPM Modern Backup Storage.

Getting ready

Make sure your DPM server is in a healthy state and is running any of the following versions:

- DPM 2016, DPM 2019 or a later version
- DPM 1801, DPM 1807, DPM 1901, or a later version
- Microsoft Azure Backup Server version 2 or later

How to do it...

Before you enable protection, you should always verify that the targeted server is accessible and that the DPM agent is reporting **OK** in the DPM console. Now, take the following steps:

1. When you create or modify a protection group, in the **Choose Replica Creation Method** step, select **Manually** as the replica option. This operation is faster when creating the replica across a slow WAN link:

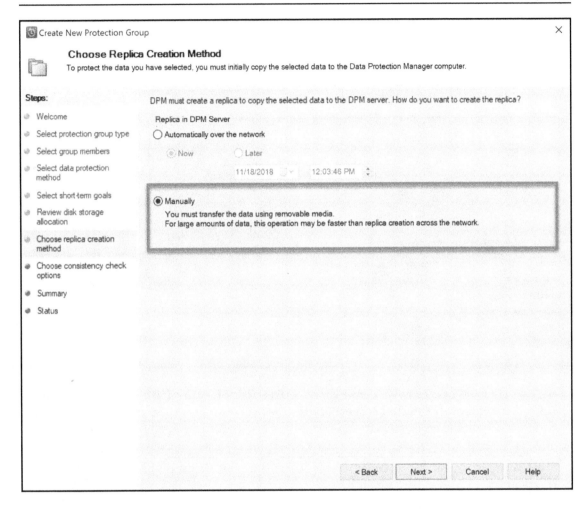

2. Once you complete the creation or modification of the Protection Group, you will end up with the status **Manual replica creation pending**:

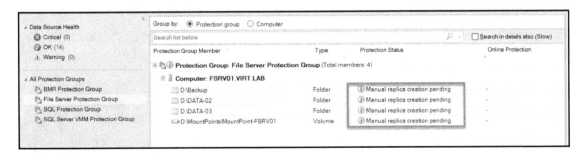

3. To check the **Replica Path**, you can select any protected member, and in the following screenshot you can see the details; there's a link you can click on to view the details of where the replica is stored on the DPM server:

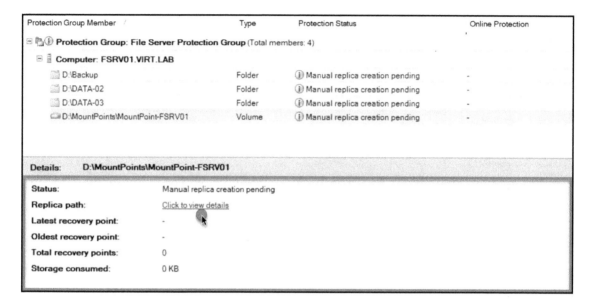

4. This will open a new window for the **Details of Replica Path**, where you'll find the **Source (Protected server)**; in this case, its our file server, and the destination path on the DPM server:

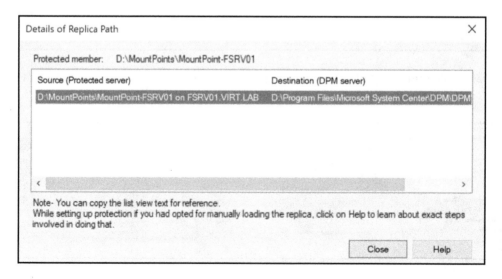

5. Next, you need to copy the path and save it in Notepad. Right-click and select **Copy**:

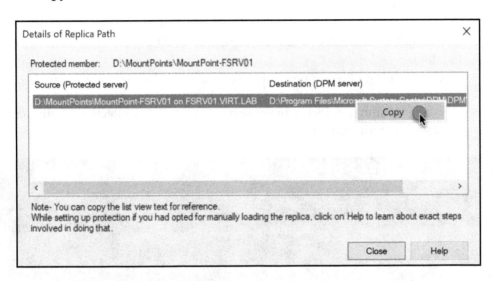

6. The first part of the copied string is the protected source server. The second part, separated by a space, is the destination path on the DPM server. In our example, the destination path contains the following information:

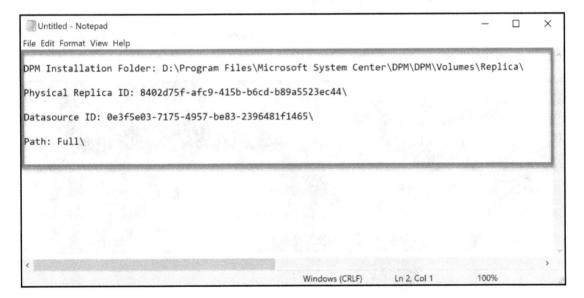

7. In this step, the replica is not mounted yet. If you look at the mount point in File Explorer, you will see it's empty. In our example, the replica path is under `D:\Program Files\Microsoft System Center\DPM\DPM\Volumes\Replica`. To mount this replica, you'll need to use PowerShell to manually mount the replica as VHDX before you're able to copy the data.

8. Open a Windows PowerShell session on your DPM server and run the `$PG = Get-DPMProtectionGroup | Where-Object Name -like "*File Server*"` command. Please make sure to change the Protection Group name to match your environment:

```
CharbelNemnom.com #> $PG = Get-DPMProtectionGroup | Where-Object Name -like "*File Server*"
CharbelNemnom.com #> $PG

Name                           ProtectionMethod
----                           ----------------
File Server Protection Group   Short-term using disk


CharbelNemnom.com #>
```

9. The next step is to select the correct data source in your Protection Group by running the following command: `$DS = Get-DPMDatasource -ProtectionGroup $PG | Where-Object Name -Like "*MountPoints*"`. As shown in the next screenshot, we are interested in selecting the first data source called `D:\MountPoints\MountPoint-FSRV01`.

```
CharbelNemnom.com #> Get-DPMDatasource -ProtectionGroup $PG

Computer Name                                ObjectType
-------- ----                                ----------
FSRV01   D:\MountPoints\MountPoint-FSRV01    Volume
FSRV01   D:\                                 Volume

CharbelNemnom.com #> $DS = Get-DPMDatasource -ProtectionGroup $PG | Where-Object Name -Like "*MountPoints*"
CharbelNemnom.com #> $DS

Computer Name                                ObjectType
-------- ----                                ----------
FSRV01   D:\MountPoints\MountPoint-FSRV01    Volume
```

10. Now, you are able to mount the replica volume by running the `Start-DPMManualReplicaCreation` cmdlet, followed by the `-Datasource`. `Start-DPMManualReplicaCreation -Datasource $DS`. This command will mount the Replica VHDX file so the initial replica data can be copied to it:

```
CharbelNemnom.com #> Start-DPMManualReplicaCreation -Datasource $DS
Replica volume for datasource D:\MountPoints\MountPoint-FSRV01 has been mounted at D:\Program Files\Microsoft System Cen
ter\DPM\DPM\Volumes\Replica\8402d75f-afc9-415b-b6cd-b89a5523ec44. Copy the datasource's data on the volume and then run
Stop-DPMManualReplicaCreation cmdlet.
CharbelNemnom.com #>
```

11. Keep your Windows PowerShell session open so you can use the same variable later to dismount the VHDX file. Now, if you browse back to the replica path in File Explorer, you can see the mounted drive:

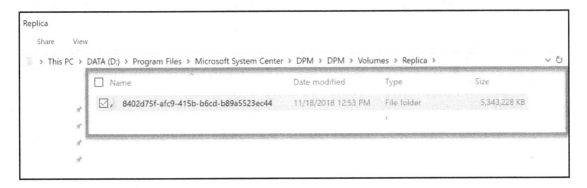

12. Open the Command Prompt window and navigate to the replica path, and then type **Tree**; you can see the expected full folder structure:

```
Administrator: Command Prompt

D:\Program Files\Microsoft System Center\DPM\DPM\Volumes\Replica>tree
Folder PATH listing for volume DATA
Volume serial number is 902A-21E4
D:.
└───8402d75f-afc9-415b-b6cd-b89a5523ec44
    └───0e3f5e03-7175-4957-be83-2396481f1465
        └───Full

D:\Program Files\Microsoft System Center\DPM\DPM\Volumes\Replica>
```

13. Now, you can start copying your workload data to the mounted replica volume. In our example, these are files and folders stored in our file server. If it's an SQL Server, then you have to set the database(s) in offline mode to be able to copy the .mdf and .ldf files. Before you start copying the files, you need to keep the original folder structure as it is. In our example, the files and folders that we need to copy are stored on the protected file server under the following path:

```
CharbelNemnom.com #> Get-ChildItem -Recurse -Path D:\MountPoints\MountPoint-FSRV01\  | FT FullName

FullName
--------
D:\MountPoints\MountPoint-FSRV01\Sub-mountpoint
D:\MountPoints\MountPoint-FSRV01\BRK1000 - What's new in Microsoft Project.mp4
D:\MountPoints\MountPoint-FSRV01\BRK1001 - Driving success with Project Online.mp4
D:\MountPoints\MountPoint-FSRV01\BRK1025 - Preparing for IoT in IT- Microsoft's IoT Vision and Roadmap.mp4
D:\MountPoints\MountPoint-FSRV01\BRK1026 - Getting started with Microsoft Azure and Azure Portal.mp4


CharbelNemnom.com #> _
```

14. This means that we've to copy all the data to the D:\Program Files\Microsoft System Center\DPM\DPM\Volumes\Replica\8402d75f-afc9-415b-b6cd-b89a5523ec44\0e3f5e03-7175-4957-be83-2396481f1465\Full\MountPoints\MountPoint-FSRV01\ path on our DPM server:

Name	Date modified	Type	Size
Sub-mountpoint	11/18/2018 1:28 PM	File folder	
BRK1000 - What's new in Microsoft Project.mp4	9/28/2018 9:33 PM	MP4 Video	217,266 KB
BRK1001 - Driving success with Project Online.mp4	9/28/2018 7:09 PM	MP4 Video	291,939 KB
BRK1025 - Preparing for IoT in IT- Microsoft's IoT Vision and Roadmap.mp4	10/5/2018 10:14 PM	MP4 Video	149,791 KB
BRK1026 - Getting started with Microsoft Azure and Azure Portal.mp4	9/28/2018 7:12 PM	MP4 Video	368,733 KB

/olumes\Replica\8402d75f-afc9-415b-b6cd-b89a5523ec44\0e3f5e03-7175-4957-be83-2396481f1465\Full\MountPoints\MountPoint-FSRV01

15. Once you finish copying all the data, you need to dismount the VHDX file replica volume by running the `Stop-DPMManualReplicaCreation -Datasource $DS` command:

```
CharbelNemnom.com #> Stop-DPMManualReplicaCreation -Datasource $DS
Replica volume for datasource D:\MountPoints\MountPoint-FSRV01 dismounted successfully. Run a consistency check job to s
tart scheduled backups.
CharbelNemnom.com #>
```

16. The final step is to **Perform consistency check** for the protected member from the **Protection** workspace in the **DPM Administrator Console**, or run the following PowerShell command: `Start-DPMDatasourceConsistencyCheck -Datasource $DS`.

17. After a moment, the **Protection Status** in the **DPM Administrator Console** will report **OK**, and the backups will continue to run normally afterwards:

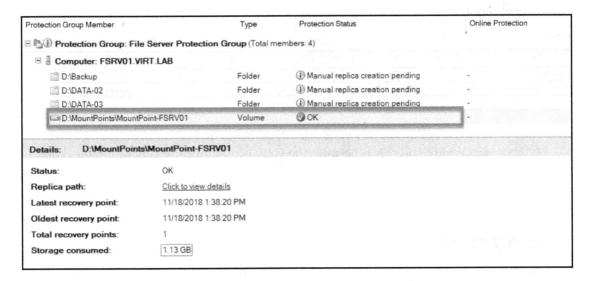

18. Last but not least, you need to repeat the same steps described here for the remaining protection members in this Protection Group.

How it works...

Starting with System Center 2016 Data Protection Manager, Microsoft changed the whole architecture with the introduction of MBS, in terms of how DPM stores its backup data. MBS utilizes VHDX files to store its backup data. This new architecture changed the procedure for manually creating initial replicas as well. DPM no longer creates *real* replica volumes similar to what we had in DPM 2012 R2 and earlier versions that were always accessible; instead, you need to mount the VHDX replica volume in PowerShell, then copy all the data, and finally dismount the volume.

Creating custom reports

Microsoft System Center DPM integrates into SQL Server Reporting Services to create custom reports. In the **Reporting** task area of the Administration Console, you can generate and view custom reports, schedule report generation, manage report settings, and subscribe to reports.

DPM includes a number of SQL Server views that can be used to create custom reports. SQL Server views provide a much simpler way to query SQL tables directly, by populating columns of data collected from multiple tables stored in the SQL database. Here, you don't need in-depth knowledge about the entire SQL Server database or the underlying relationship between tables and keys.

 The use of SQL Server views can degrade the overall performance if used frequently and this is because the view is dynamically generating the data each time the view is queried.

Getting ready

In order to generate a custom report, you will need to access the reporting service on your Microsoft System Center DPM server. To be able to determine the URL for your reporting service, you can use the **Reporting Services Configuration Manager** tool, which is part of your SQL Server installation.

How to do it...

The following steps will guide you through creating a custom report in the Microsoft System Center DPM server:

1. From the **Start** screen, select the **Reporting Services Configuration Manager** tool under your SQL Server folder. The Reporting Services Configuration Manager console loads.

2. Connect to your local report server instance, then click the **Report Manager** URL to observe the default URL. Your URL will be similar to `http://ServerName/Reports/`:

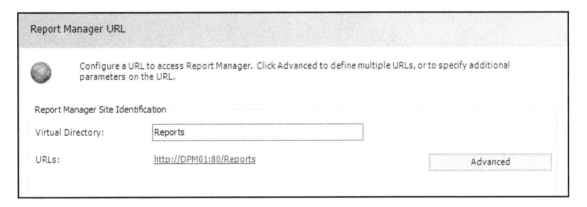

3. Launch **Internet Explorer** and specify the Reports URL. Then, **SQL Server Reporting Services**, **Home** page loads. Click on **New Folder** in the SQL Server Reporting Services site, create a folder for your custom reports, add an optional description, and click **OK**.

4. Click on the newly created folder and click **New Data Source**. Enter a name for this new data source, enter an optional description, enter a valid connection string, specify your connection string credentials, and click **OK**:

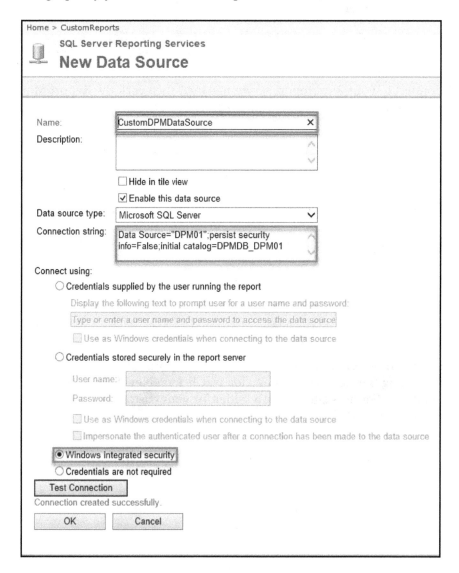

5. Now, click on **Report Builder** and this launches the Report Builder application. If prompted by a security warning, just click **Run**. Report Builder is downloaded and after a short period of time the Microsoft SQL Server Report Builder is loaded.

6. In the **Getting started** wizard, click on **Chart Wizard** and click **Next**. In the **Choose a connection to a data source** window click **Browse**, select the data source you created earlier, click **Open** and select the data source again, and click **Open** again. If you didn't previously test the data connection source, you now have the option to validate the connection; otherwise, click **Next**.

7. After selecting the relevant SQL Server Views to include in your custom report, click **Run Query**. When the query results are returned successfully, click **Next**:

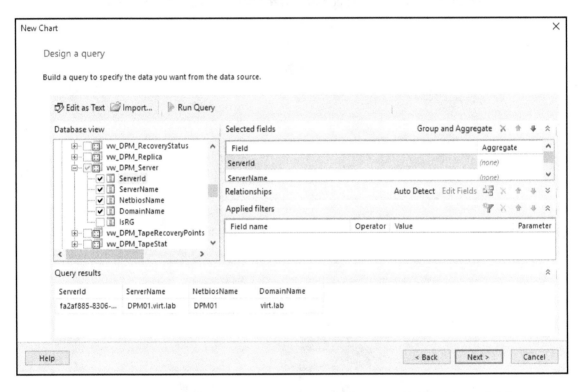

8. Then, choose your chart type and click **Next**. The **Available Chart Fields** page contains the data that you can add to your chart. To add a field, just drag a field from the **Available fields** area to **Categories**, **Series**, or **Values**, and then click on **Next**.

9. Then, choose your chart style. Click **Finish** and then **Run** to generate your custom report. You will then see the completed report with the actual data presented. In order to reuse this report, you need to make sure you save the report to the custom report folder that you created earlier by using the Save button.

How it works...

SQL Server views are similar to tables in SQL. Views can be considered virtual tables that aggregate data from multiple tables. They dynamically generate their data when the view is referenced. Microsoft System Center DPM includes a number of SQL views in the DPM database by default. This allows the DPM administrator to generate custom reports. SQL Reporting Services and Report Builder are used to generate these custom DPM reports. Once the custom DPM reports have been generated, they can be saved and reused.

Protecting Hyper-V VMs 3

In this chapter, we will cover the following recipes:

- Configuring Hyper-V protection with DPM
- Protecting Hyper-V VMs with Resilient Change Tracking
- Protecting Hyper-V clusters over SMB and Hyper-V replica
- Protecting Hyper-V clusters over Clustered Shared Volumes
- Protecting Hyper-V shielded VMs
- Enabling DPM for scale-out Hyper-V protection
- Recovering a Hyper-V virtual machine
- Recovering a Hyper-V virtual hard disk
- Recovering a single file using Item-Level Recovery

Introduction

Virtualized servers have already surpassed physical servers in terms of the number of their deployed instances, and this is primarily due to the cost savings achieved with server virtualization. With virtualized servers becoming first-class citizens of any modern datacenter today, building a virtualized private cloud is the next step in the cloud computing journey to get all the benefits of the cloud while keeping control within an IT department. Whether the private cloud is built on Hyper-V or VMware, Microsoft System Center **Data Protection Manager** (**DPM**) protects both deployments.

This chapter covers the protection and recovery of Hyper-V VMs at the private cloud scale using SCDPM. Different protection configurations that apply to Hyper-V VMs and the different restore options that you can exercise are covered in detail. For protection and recovery of VMware VMs, please check Chapter 11, *Protecting VMware VMs*.

Configuring Hyper-V protection with DPM

This recipe covers how to configure Hyper-V protection with DPM.

Getting ready

Before you start configuring protection for Hyper-V, you need to make sure that the latest DPM agent is installed on all Hyper-V nodes that will be part of the Hyper-V protection. Please check the *Installing the DPM Agents* recipe in `Chapter 1`, *Installing and Upgrading DPM*.

How to do it...

To configure protection for Hyper-V, take the following steps:

1. Open the DPM Administrator Console, and go to the **Protection** workspace. Click on **New** in the ribbon tab. This will trigger the **Create New Protection Group** wizard.
2. In the **Select Protection Group Type** step, select **Servers** and click on **Next >.**
3. In the **Select Group Members** step, expand your Hyper-V server(s) and select which virtual machine you want to protect. Click on **Next >** to continue.
4. In the **Select Data Protection Method** step, provide the following information:
    - Protection group name
    - Select the protection method that you want:
        - Short-term protection using **Disk**
        - Online protection using **Microsoft Azure Backup**
        - Long-term protection using **Tape**
5. Note the following screenshot. For DPM to be able to protect your Hyper-V server workload using **Microsoft Azure** or **Tape**, this must be configured before you create or modify the protection group. Select the option(s) that you would like to use and click on **Next >** to continue:

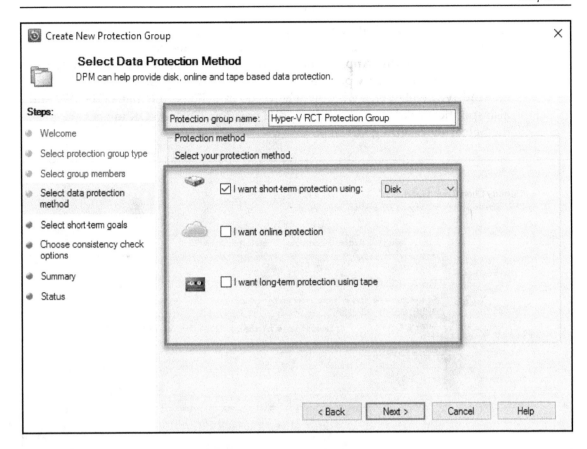

 You can also use **Tape** for short-term protection, but this will disable online protection to Microsoft Azure. For more information regarding online protection, please read `Chapter 10`, *Integrating DPM with Azure Backup*.

6. In the **Specify Short-Term Goals** step, you will specify the retention range, that is, the number of days you would like to keep the protected data in the DPM storage volume. In the **Application recovery points** section, you can specify when to create a recovery point for the protected Hyper-V data sources. Clicking on **Modify...** will open a window where you can choose the time of the day and also specific weekdays for recovery point creation. Click on **OK** to get back to the **Select short-term goals** step:

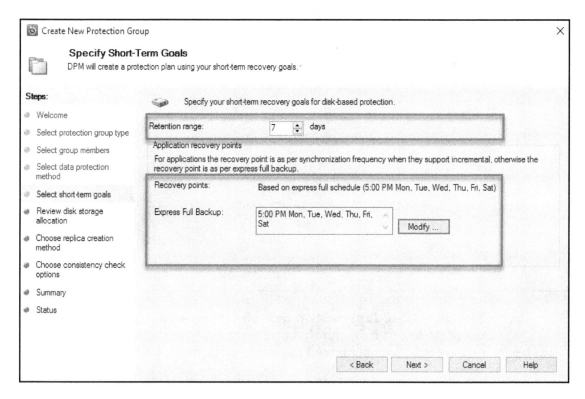

7. In the **Review Disk Storage Allocation** step, review the target storage assigned for each data source and change it if needs be. When you are finished with your disk storage allocation, click on **Next >** to continue:

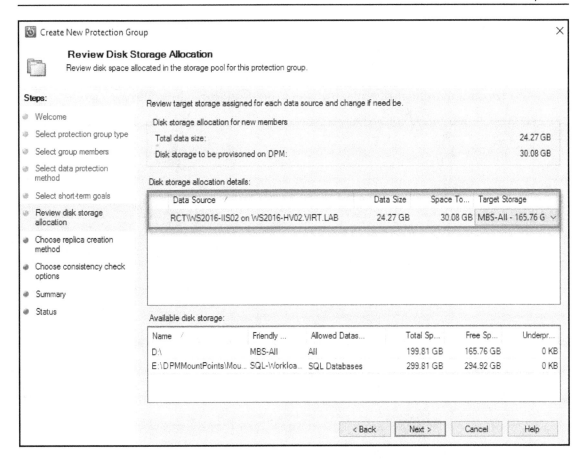

8. In the **Choose replica creation method** step, you can define how the DPM server should create the replica of the protected data source. You can create the replica now or you can schedule the creation of the replica. You can also create the replica manually; this is covered in the *Creating a replica manually* recipe in `Chapter 2`, *DPM Post-Installation and Management Tasks*. Click on **Next >** to continue.

9. In the **Choose consistency check options** step, you can specify whether DPM should run a consistency check if a replica becomes inconsistent; this is an auto-heal function within the DPM server technology. You can also specify whether you want it to run a daily consistency check, where you set the start time and the maximum number of hours the task should run for. Click on **Next >** to continue:

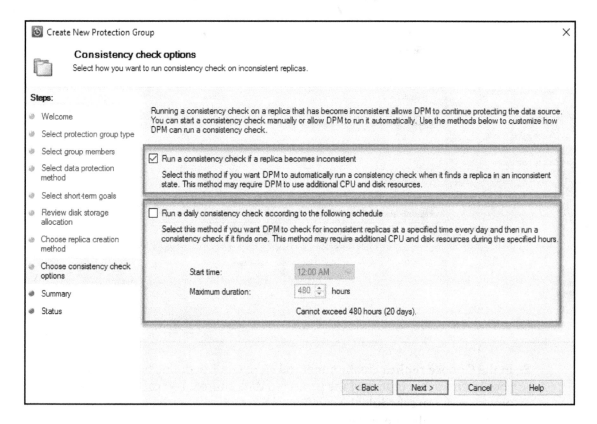

10. In the **Summary** step, review the summary for the protection group and click on the **Create Group** button to create the protection group:

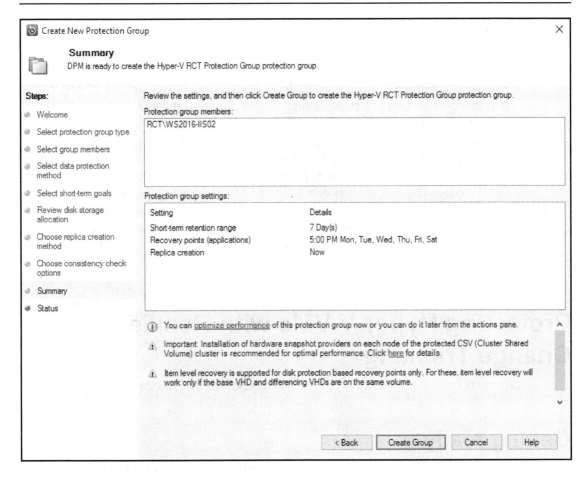

11. In the **Status** step, you can see the actual status of the protection group creation.

How it works...

System Center Data Protection Manager is able to provide online snapshots of a virtual machine, making it possible to eliminate the scheduled backup windows. However, the Hyper-V **Volume Shadow Copy Service** (**VSS**) must be in a stable state and, most importantly, the virtual machine must have its own VSS stable. If the guest operating system is facing an internal VSS error, System Center Data Protection Manager will not able to provide a consistent data snapshot.

There's more...

SCDPM can be used to protect virtual machines hosted on the following:

- Stand-alone Hyper-V hosts that use local or **direct-attached storage** (**DAS**). Note that this option does not provide high availability and it is not recommended for production deployments.
- Hyper-V cluster with **Storage Spaces Direct** and on **Server Message Block** (**SMB**) shares backed by ReFS-based **Scale-Out File Server** (**SOFS**) clusters. This deployment type is referred to as *Hyper-V over SOFS*; more on that in the *Protecting Hyper-V clusters over SMB and Hyper-V replica* recipe.
- Hyper-V clusters with the virtual hard disks stored on **Clustered Shared Volumes** (**CSV**). This deployment type is referred to as *Hyper-V over CSV*; there is more on that in the *Protecting Hyper-V clusters over Clustered Shared Volumes* recipe.

Protecting Hyper-V VMs with Resilient Change Tracking

This recipe covers how to protect a Hyper-V VM with **Resilient Change Tracking** (**RCT**).

Getting ready

Starting with Windows Server 2016, Microsoft introduced built-in change tracking for Hyper-V virtual hard disks known as RCT. As a result, in the case of a Hyper-V host outage, or VM migration, change tracking is automatically preserved.

System Center 2016 Data Protection Manager or later will take the benefit of this feature when protecting Hyper-V VMs running on Windows Server 2016 with configuration version 8.0 and later.

With RCT, DPM backups benefit as follows:

- **More reliable**: **Consistency Checks** (**CC**) aren't required after a VM migration
- **Scalable**: More parallel backups and less storage overhead
- **Improved performance**: Lower impact on the production fabric and faster backup

How to do it...

Hyper-V VMs, deployed on Windows Server 2016 or Windows Server 2019 and protected using DPM 2016 or later, have RCT by default. VMs deployed on Windows Server 2012 R2 or earlier do not support RCT. However, you can upgrade older virtual machines.

To upgrade older VMs and use RCT, please take the following steps:

1. In Hyper-V Manager, shut down the desired virtual machine, and once the VM is shut down, select **Action** | **Upgrade Configuration Version...**:

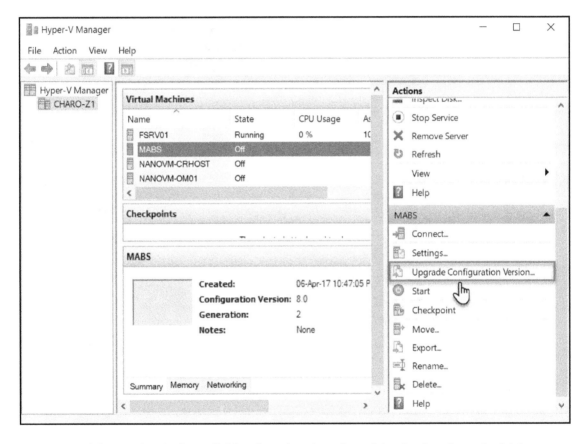

2. If this option isn't available, then the virtual machine is already at the highest configuration version supported by the Hyper-V host.

3. You can also use Windows PowerShell to upgrade the virtual machine configuration version. Open **Windows PowerShell** as administrator and run the following command, where <VMName> is the name of the virtual machine:

```
Update-VMVersion <VMName>
```

For additional information about checking or upgrading the virtual machine configuration version, see the article here: https://docs. microsoft.com/en-us/windows-server/virtualization/hyper-v/ deploy/Upgrade-virtual-machine-version-in-Hyper-V-on-Windows-or-Windows-Server.

4. To back up virtual machines with RCT support, please follow the steps described in the previous recipe, *Configuring Hyper-V protection with DPM*. The only difference that you will see when protecting a VM with RCT support is that you will see **RCT** before the VM name, as shown in the following screenshot:

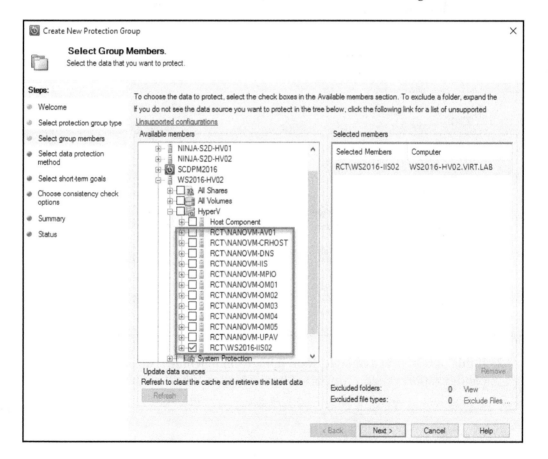

The remaining steps in the wizard will remain the same.

How it works...

With RCT technology, the changed blocks tracking has moved from the backup products to the hypervisor level, since Hyper-V has the information about the changed blocks in a virtual machine. DPM 2016 or later rely now on RCT technology to check the blocks that have changed, and only read the changed blocks instead of tracking the VM changes using the file system filter, which significantly simplifies the backup and recovery process of Hyper-V VMs.

DPM 2016 or later still installs the file system filter on each Hyper-V host, similar to what System Center 2012 R2 Data Protection Manager used to do; this gives you the flexibility to migrate VMs from Windows Server 2012 R2 to Windows Server 2016, or to Windows Server 2019, and vice versa, while protecting those VMs seamlessly. However, VMs deployed on Windows Server 2012 R2 or earlier do not support RCT. You need to upgrade the configuration version for the VMs, but as soon as you upgrade your virtual machine configuration version to 8.0, DPM will detect that and switch automatically, and start using RCT technology instead of the old changing tracking mechanism.

Best of all, DPM and RCT technology is transparent and does not need any configuration or management from your side.

There's more...

With RCT, DPM 2016 or later does not need to go through **Consistency Check** (**CC**) in case of sudden power loss or VM storage migration, because when you move a VM between different types of storage, DPM will keep track of these changes by leveraging RCT technology.

See also

To know more about RCT and **Modified Region Table** (**MRT**) files in Windows Server 2016 Hyper-V, including backup architecture and the difference between different versions, we highly recommend to check our recently published book, *Windows Server 2016 Hyper-V Cookbook - Second Edition* (`https://www.packtpub.com/virtualization-and-cloud/windows-server-2016-hyper-v-cookbook-second-edition`).

For more information about the auto-heal function in DPM, please check the following article: https://charbelnemnom.com/2017/09/powershell-script-for-consistency-check-when-replica-is-inconsistent-dpm-scdpm-powershell/.

Check this article on how to automate the upgrade of virtual machine configuration version in Hyper-V: https://charbelnemnom.com/2015/06/how-to-automate-the-upgrade-of-virtual-machine-configuration-version-in-hyper-v-2016-hyperv-ws2016/

Protecting Hyper-V clusters over SMB and Hyper-V replica

This recipe covers how to protect a Hyper-V cluster over SMB and Hyper-V replica.

Getting ready

Hyper-V over Storage Spaces Direct clusters, and ReFS-based SOFS clusters, enable cost-effective, highly available, scalable, and flexible storage solutions for business-critical virtual deployments. They leverage industry-standard commodity servers and allow you to use Windows Server 2019 for highly available software-defined storage that can cost-effectively grow on demand.

How to do it...

DPM protects Hyper-V VMs that use Storage Spaces Direct, including the backup of VMs using Storage Spaces Direct hyper-converged scenarios with the Hyper-V (compute) and Storage Spaces Direct (storage) components on the same cluster.

To protect VMs on SOFS clusters, there are some considerations that you need to be aware of, such as adding the machine accounts to the backup operator groups and share permissions.

To add the machine accounts to the backup operator groups, run the following steps on each node in the SOFS cluster:

1. Open the Command Prompt window, and type `lusrmgr.msc` to open **Local Users** and **Groups**.

2. In the **Local Users and Groups** dialog, click **Groups**. In the list of groups, right-click **Backup Operators** and select **Properties**. The **Backup Operators Properties** dialog opens:

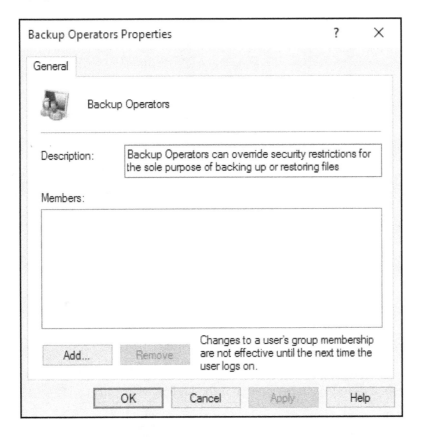

3. In the **Backup Operators Properties** dialog, click **Add**.

4. In the **Select Users**, **Computers**, **Services Accounts**, or **Groups** dialog, click **Object Types**. The **Object Types** dialog opens:

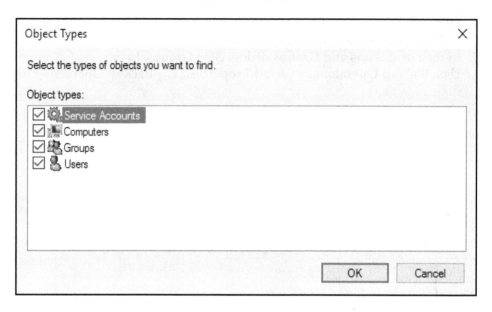

5. In the **Object Types** dialog, select **Computers** and click **OK**. The **Object Types** dialog closes.

6. In the **Select Users**, **Computers**, **Service Accounts**, or **Groups** dialog, enter the name of the server or cluster, and click **Check Names** to resolve the name, then click **OK** and restart the node.

If you are protecting a highly available virtual machine, you need to provide the machine account name of the host cluster and cluster nodes, and the DPM server.

If you are protecting a non-HA VM, you need to provide the machine name of the Hyper-V host and the DPM server only.

To give share permissions on the server where the SOFS/SMB share is hosted, take the following steps:

1. Open **Server Manager**, select **File and Storage Services**, and then click on **Shares**.
2. Right-click on the VM storage share name, and then click **Properties**.
3. In the **Properties** dialog, on the left navigation menu, click **Permissions**.
4. Click **Customize permissions** to open the **Advanced Security Settings** for permissions dialog:

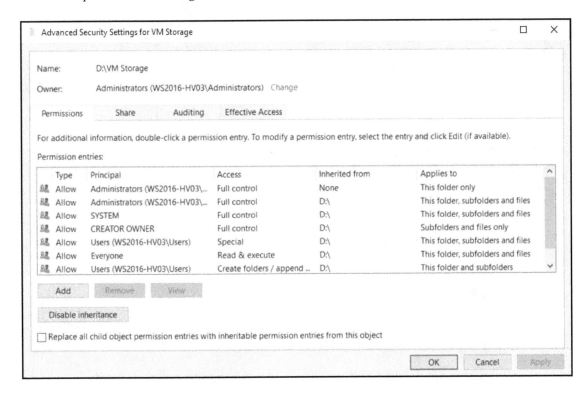

5. On the **Permissions** tab, click **Add**.
6. Click **Select a Principal**.
7. In the **Select User, Computer, Services Account**, or **Group** dialog, click **Object Types**.

8. In the **Object Types** dialog, select **Computers**, and click **OK**.
9. In the **Select User, Computer, Service Account,** or **Group** dialog, enter the name of the Hyper-V node or cluster name to which you want to give permission.
10. Click **Check Names** to resolve the name, and click **OK**.
11. In the **Advanced Security Settings** for share dialog, click the **Share** tab instead of the **Permissions** tab, and then repeat *Steps 2-8*:

12. When you are finished adding permissions for the servers, click **Apply**.

Please note that DPM agents should be installed on the Hyper-V cluster nodes and on all the storage nodes (since the storage server is also clustered). You'll need full-share and folder-level permissions for the `local $` account of the storage node on the SMB share.

How it works...

In this configuration, compute (Hyper-V) and Storage Spaces Direct (storage) can run on the same set of hardware known as hyper-converged, or compute and storage can be decoupled running on a separate hardware known as disaggregated; with the disaggregated model, you can independently scale one without the need to scale the other. This configuration provides the lowest acquisition and operations cost. It allows highly available VMs, and fault-tolerant storage.

There's more...

When protecting virtual machines using Hyper-V replica, the first question that comes to mind is whether you should protect the replica VMs or the primary VMs. From what we have seen in the real world, three scenarios are found to be useful when protecting replica VMs:

- **Reduce the impact of backup on the production workloads**: In today's world, workloads need to run 24 hours a day, 7 days a week with high performance. If the workload will run on differencing virtual disks for a long period of time, this will impact the system during backup operations.
- **Limited network bandwidth between the branch office and primary office**: Network bandwidth is expensive, and it is redundant to send data to the head office twice, one for disaster recovery and a second for backup. A more efficient way is to support backup from a replica DR site so that you can manage the backup infrastructure from a single location.
- **Enterprise to hoster scenario**: Many customers do not want to build a second datacenter for disaster recovery and prefer to leverage a hosting service provider. Hosting service providers offer SLAs as a way around backing up VMs on a regular basis (for example, daily), and this can be easily achieved using Hyper-V replica VM backups.

There is some limitation with backing up replica VMs: you can only get crash-consistent backups. However, most customers are comfortable with this. Remember, crash-consistency doesn't mean inconsistency. It's equivalent to the state when the power plug is pulled. Applications know how to recover from this state.

 For more information about the backing up of replica VMs using DPM, please check the following article: https://blogs.technet.microsoft.com/dpm/2014/04/24/backing-up-of-replica-vms-using-dpm/.

See also

- For more information about **Windows Server Software-Defined (WSSD)** storage solutions, please check the WSSD partner program: `https://www.microsoft.com/en-us/cloud-platform/software-defined-datacenter`
- For more information about Storage Spaces Direct, check the article on Storage Spaces Direct in Windows Server: `https://docs.microsoft.com/en-us/windows-server/storage/storage-spaces/storage-spaces-direct-overview`

Protecting Hyper-V clusters over Clustered Shared Volumes

This recipe covers how to protect Hyper-V clusters over CSV.

Getting ready

Hyper-V over CSV (connected by SAN) is the traditional deployment where virtual machines are hosted on a Hyper-V cluster with CSV storage. There is no limit to the number of disks a Hyper-V cluster can be configured to use, which allows much flexibility in designing the storage architecture of Hyper-V clusters.

How to do it...

For backing up the VMs, the DPM agent should be installed on each cluster node, and you can get reliable backups at scale with the latest version of DPM.

Starting with DPM 2012 R2 and later, there are no more host-level volume snapshots; it calls guest-level VSS (Volume Shadow Copy Service inside the VM) to get application-consistent backups. DPM supports express full backups and parallel backups.

 Please note that when selecting clustered virtual machines, do not pick virtual machines from individual nodes; instead, point to the cluster to select virtual machines.

How it works...

With DPM, you have continued protection with VM live migration; live migration refers to the process in which a running VM moves to another physical machine, keeping memory, network connectivity, and storage intact, which implies the application continues to run as-is without any disruption. This can happen due to a host server crash or due to rebalancing the resources in a cluster. The DPM server continues to protect the VM even after live migration. If the VM moves to a different cluster, DPM integration with **System Center Virtual Machine Manager** (**SCVMM**) helps discover the VM on a node in the new cluster.

There's more...

Starting with Windows Server 2016, Microsoft introduced the cluster OS rolling upgrade feature, which is used to upgrade the cluster nodes' operating system, from Windows Server 2012 R2 to Windows Server 2016, and from Windows Server 2016 to Windows Server 2019 without stopping the Hyper-V or SOFS workloads. The cluster OS rolling upgrade ensures protection is not interrupted during OS upgrades. System Center 2016 Data Protection Manager or later continues to protect VMs during the upgrade, maintaining the backup **service level agreement** (**SLA**).

Now, consider the failure scenarios. What if the compute node goes down? There is no impact to the protected VMs on that node if the VM configuration version is 8.0 and later, because the tracking is done using RCT on the compute node. However, if the VM configuration version is still at 5.0 (Windows Server 2012 R2 support), the protected VM on that host will go into **Consistency-Check** (**CC**) mode since the filter tracking is on that node. Please check the *Protecting Hyper-V VMs with Resilient Change Tracking* recipe in this chapter.

See also

For more information on the cluster OS rolling upgrade process, please see the article here: `https://docs.microsoft.com/en-us/windows-server/failover-clustering/cluster-operating-system-rolling-upgrade#cluster-os-rolling-upgrade-process`.

Protecting Hyper-V shielded VMs

This recipe covers how to protect Hyper-V shielded VMs with SCDPM.

Getting ready

To protect Hyper-V shielded virtual machines, you need to make sure that your servers support **Trusted Platform Modules** (**TPM**). A TPM is a chip in the motherboard of computers that helps integrate cryptographic keys. These keys are used by BitLocker to protect the computer even if it is stolen. **Virtual TPM** (**vTPM**) is a new feature introduced in Windows Server 2016 Hyper-V and enhanced in Windows Server 2019 Hyper-V. With vTPM, you can use BitLocker and a virtual TPM chip to encrypt an entire VM, thereby protecting the VM. These VMs, called shielded VMs, can only be run on healthy and approved guarded hosts by the host guardian service in the fabric.

How to do it...

DPM 2016 or later supports backup and recovery of Windows shielded VMs that have their virtual hard disks (VHDXs) protected with vTPM. As of this writing, ILR and **Alternate Location Recovery** (**ALR**) to a location outside of the guarded hosts fabric is not yet available for shielded VMs backup.

Starting with DPM 2019 and DPM 1901, you can also protect Linux shielded VMs running on top of Windows Server 2019 Hyper-V.

How it works...

Windows Server 2016 and Windows Server 2019 Hyper-V provides shielded VMs to protect VM data and state from compromised and malicious fabric administrators. A shielded VM is a Generation-2 VM (it supports Windows Server 2012 and later) that has a virtual TPM.

DPM backups retain the protections provided by shielded VMs to ensure they can be recovered seamlessly and securely.

See also

- For more information about guarded fabric and Hyper-V shielded VMs, please check the following article: https://goo.gl/LpDEJb.
- For more information about virtual TPMs in Windows Server 2016 Hyper-V, please check the following article: https://goo.gl/Kimm4V.

Enabling DPM for scale-out Hyper-V protection

This recipe covers how to set up protection for a large-scale Hyper-V environment.

Getting ready

Starting with DPM 2012 SP1 and later, the DPM team introduced a new feature called *Scale-Out Protection* that makes it possible to protect large Hyper-V cluster environments. This is especially useful if you have a large cluster with more than 800 virtual machines.

In this scenario, you need multiple DPM servers to protect a large number of VMs. Therefore, DPM scale-out capability removes the limit of a one-to-one relationship between a Hyper-V cluster and a DPM server; the DPM protection agent that runs on the Hyper-V host can attach itself to multiple DPM servers. Thus, you can add the virtual machine to a protection group on any of the recognized DPM servers.

How to do it...

When leveraging *Scale-Out Protection*, the DPM agent needs to be installed on the Hyper-V server, or on each server in the Hyper-V cluster. Then, you need to use `Setdpmserver` from the command line with the `-Add` switch to make multiple DPM servers visible to the protected virtual machine, as follows:

```
Setdpmserver -Add -Dpmservername <Name of Second DPM Server>
```

If you don't specify the `-Add` switch, the previous (first) DPM server is overwritten.

Ensure that all servers that are running Hyper-V, and virtual machines are discovered by DPM before you begin to create protection groups.

How it works...

To deploy *Scale-Out Protection*, you must have a minimum of two DPM servers, which are visible to all nodes in the Hyper-V clusters and/or a stand-alone Hyper-V host. When you create protection groups on any of the two DPM servers, you can add any of the virtual machines for protection to any of the two DPM servers, as shown in the following diagram:

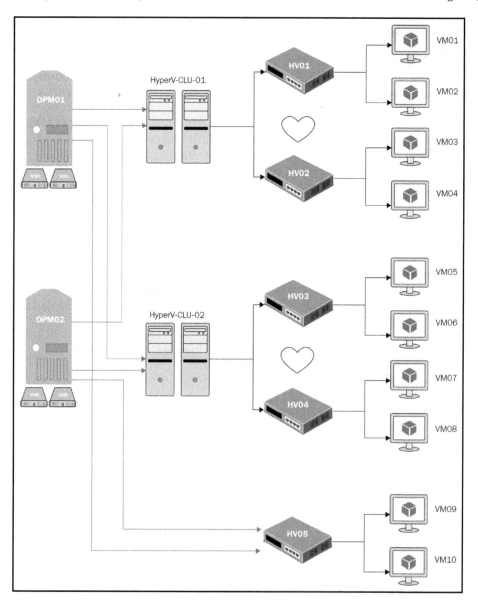

A virtual machine can only be protected by one DPM server that is a member of the *Scale-Out Protection* configuration. The VM will stay with the same DPM server unless you stop the protection of that VM. You cannot protect the same virtual machine with multiple DPM servers of the *Scale-Out Protection* configuration.

See also

For more information about protecting a large Hyper-V scale environment, please check the following article that is worth a read: `https://charbelnemnom.com/2017/03/deploying-system-center-data-protection-manager-2016-for-large-hyper-v-workloads-hyperv-dpm-scdpm-ws2016/`

Recovering a Hyper-V virtual machine

This recipe covers how to recover a Hyper-V protected virtual machine.

Getting ready

When you want to recover a virtual machine, you open the System Center Data Protection Manager Console and go to the **Recovery** task view.

How to do it...

1. Open the DPM Administrator Console, and go to the **Recovery** view. Browse or search for the data you want to recover:

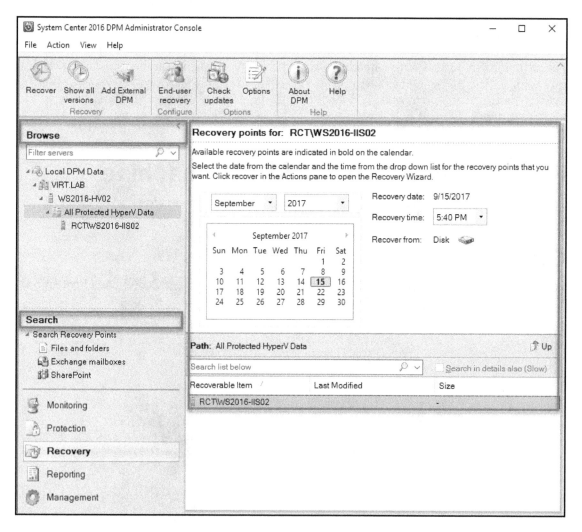

2. In the results pane, select the desired date in the calendar and desired time in the drop-down list next to **Recovery** time.
3. Under **Recoverable items**, right-click the server and choose **Recover...**; this will trigger the **Recovery Wizard**.
4. In the **Review Recovery Selection** step, click **Next >**.

5. In the **Select Recovery Type** step, specify the type of recovery you would like to perform. You can restore the virtual machine to the following:

- **Recover to the original location**.
- **Recover as virtual machine to any host**.
- **Copy to a network folder**.
- **Copy to tape**: If you are still using tapes, this option copies the volume that contains the selected data to a tape in a DPM library. When you select this option, click **Next** and, on the **Specify library** screen, select library details and tape options. You can compress or encrypt data on this screen.

6. Choose the **Recover as virtual machine to any host** option, and click on **Next >** to continue:

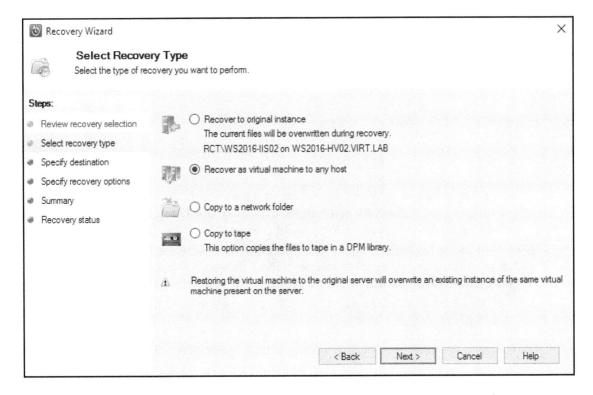

7. In the **Specify Destination** step, specify where you want to recover the virtual machine; you need to define the **Destination host** and the **Destination path** by clicking on the **Browse...** button. Point out to the destination Hyper-V host and desired volume.

8. Select **Destination host uses remote storage** if the destination host uses SMB share only. Click on **Next >** to continue:

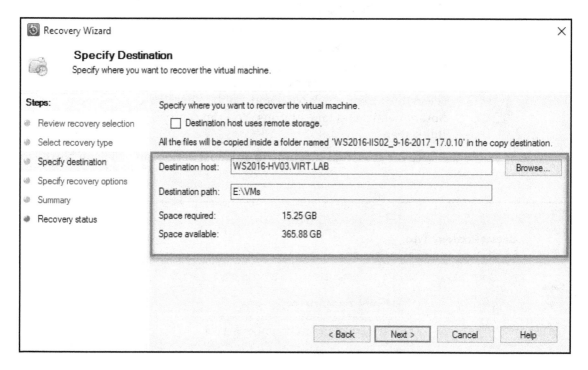

9. If the recovery will be restoring data over a poor WAN link, you can click the **Modify...** link in the **Network bandwidth usage throttling** part to define how much bandwidth the restore job should consume.

10. If you are using VSS hardware providers and a LUN presented for the SAN storage of the protected data source, select **Enable SAN based recovery using hardware snapshots** in the **SAN Recovery** part.

11. You can send an email to a specific user or users notifying them that the recovery has finished. You can enable this by checking the checkbox in the **Notification** part. However, this requires the DPM server to have an SMTP server configured in the DPM options. Please read the *Configuring email notifications* recipe in `Chapter 2`, *DPM Post-Installation and Management Tasks*. Click on **Next >** to continue.

12. In the **Summary** step, review the recovery settings and click on **Recover**.

13. In the **Recovery Status** step, you will be able to see the current state of recovery. The status could also be monitored in the **Monitoring task** view of the DPM console:

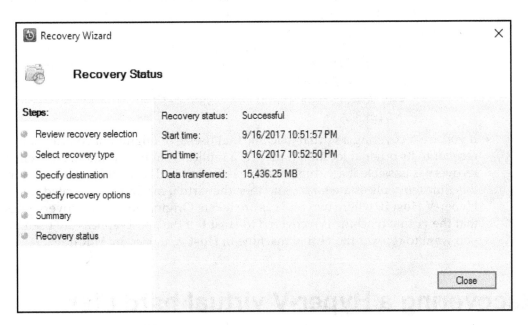

How it works...

When performing a virtual machine recovery that is protected by using RCT technology, Data Protection Manager will attach the virtual hard disks of the protected virtual machines on the DPM server as read-only. When DPM initializes the recovery job, it relies on the VSS architecture that is part of the Hyper-V host's operating system. When the recovery operation is completed, DPM will detach the VHDX.

There's more...

There are certain scenarios that you want to be aware of when you recover a virtual machine in your environment, such as the following:

- If you are recovering a virtual machine to an alternative stand-alone Hyper-V host, and if the recovered virtual machine was backed up in an online state, and it's in a saved state after recovery, then you need to delete the saved state of that virtual machine from the Hyper-V Manager console and start it.

- Always verify that the virtual machine's network configuration is correct after the alternative Hyper-V host recovery option.
- DPM saves the recovery virtual machine in a custom directory structure in the following format, `VMName_<backup-time>_<RecoveryTime>\`, with two subfolders:
    - `C-Vol\Program Files\Microsoft Data Protection Manager\DPM\RctVMBackupConfig\<Backup-Config-ID>\Virtual Machines`
    - `D-Vol\VirtualMachines\WS2016-RTM01\Virtual Hard Disks`
- If you are recovering a virtual machine that uses live migration, you can only recover to its original location if there is a replica from that location. For example, recovery is possible if a virtual machine is hosted on Hyper-V **Host A** and during this time ten replicas are taken, and then the virtual machine is migrated to Hyper-V **Host B**, where two replicas are taken. Original location recovery means that the virtual machine is recovered to **Host B** if the latest replicas are used. If you want to recover the virtual machine to **Host A**, it uses an ALR flow.

Recovering a Hyper-V virtual hard disk

This recipe covers the recovery process of a virtual hard disk (VHDX) file.

Getting ready

System Center Data Protection Manager can help you to recover a single virtual hard disk (VHDX) file in the the scenario where a virtual machine has lost its volume or the data has been corrupted.

How to do it...

1. Open the DPM Administrator Console, and go to the **Recovery task** view. **Browse** or **Search** for the data you want to recover.
2. In the **Recovery points** section, select the data. Available recovery points are indicated in bold on the calendar in the recovery points section. Select the bold date for the recovery point you want to recover.

3. In the **Recoverable Item** pane, double-click on the recoverable item you want to recover, and then right-click the VHD or VHDX file and choose **Recover...**; this will trigger the **Recovery Wizard**:

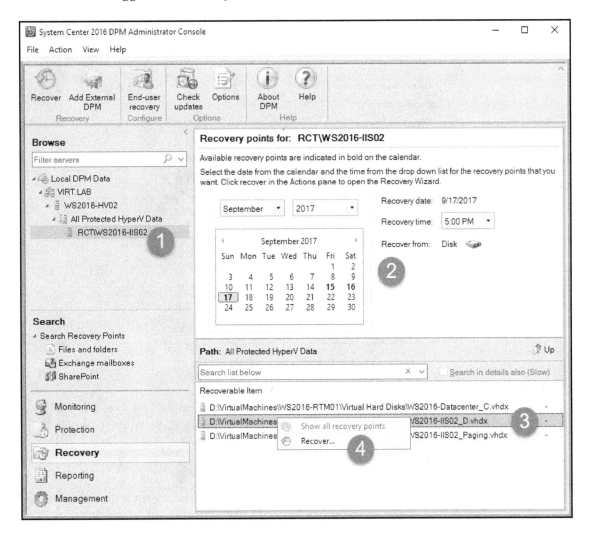

4. In the **Review Recovery Section** step, review the selection, and then click **Next >**. Note that the selected recovery element is a VHD and not the virtual machine:

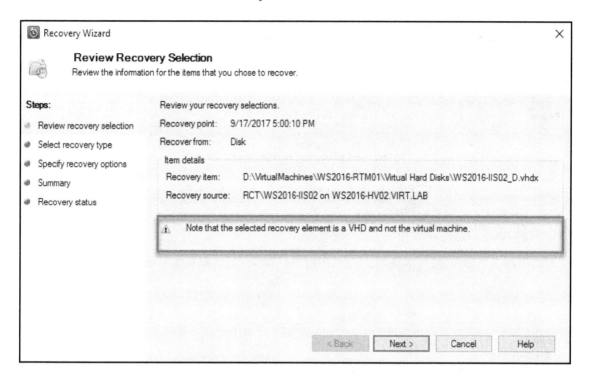

5. The next step is **Select recovery type**, where the only option you have is to **Copy to a network folder**; click on **Next >** to continue.

6. In the **Specify Destination** step, define the **Destination** and the **Destination path**. Click on the **Browse...** button to point out the location; click on **Next >** to continue.

7. In the **Specify Recovery Options** step, configure the specific options for recovery.

8. In the **Restore security** part, define how the restored data source should apply to the security setting in the targeted location. The restored data can either keep the security settings that are present in the recovery point version or apply the security settings of the targeted location.

9. If the recovery will be restoring data over a poor WAN link, click the **Modify...** link in the **Network bandwidth usage throttling** part to define how much bandwidth the restore job should consume.

10. If you are using VSS hardware providers and a LUN presented for the SAN storage of the protected data source, select **Enable SAN based recovery using hardware snapshots** in the **SAN Recovery** part.

11. You can send an email to a specific user or users notifying them that the recovery has finished. You can enable this by checking the checkbox in the **Notification** part. However, this requires the DPM server to have an SMTP server configured in the DPM options. Please read the *Configuring email notifications* recipe in `Chapter 2`, *DPM Post-Installation and Management Tasks*. Click on **Next >** to continue.

12. In the **Summary** step, verify the recovery configuration and click on **Recover** to start recovery:

13. In the **Recovery Status** step, you will be able to see the current state of recovery. The status could also be monitored in the **Monitoring task** view of the DPM console.

How it works...

When performing a virtual hard disk recovery, Data Protection Manager will attach the virtual hard disks (VHDX) of the protected virtual machines to provide the backup administrator with the ability to restore a single VHDX file; the restore process consists of several steps using temporary areas. When the operation is completed, DPM will detach the virtual hard disks.

There's more...

DPM saves the recovery item in a custom directory structure in the following format:

```
DPM_<BackupTime>\Recovered_At_<BackupTime>_<RecoveryTime>\D-
Vol\VirtualMachines\<VMName>\Virtual Hard Disks\<VHDX-Name>
```

If the recovery job fails, verify the alert under the **Monitoring task** view that DPM server will raise to inform you about what has happened. It also gives you a guide to rectify the issue for a possible scenario for the recovery to succeed.

Recovering a single file using Item-Level Recovery

This recipe covers how to restore a single file from a protected virtual machine using ILR.

Getting ready

As mentioned previously, DPM supports ILR, which allows you to perform a specific recovery of files, folders, and virtual hard disks from a host-level backup of Hyper-V virtual machines to a network share or a volume on a DPM protected server. The DPM agent doesn't have to be installed on the guest operating system of the virtual machine to perform Item-Level Recovery.

How to do it...

1. Open the DPM Administrator Console, and go to the **Recovery** task view.
   Browse or **Search** for the data you want to recover:

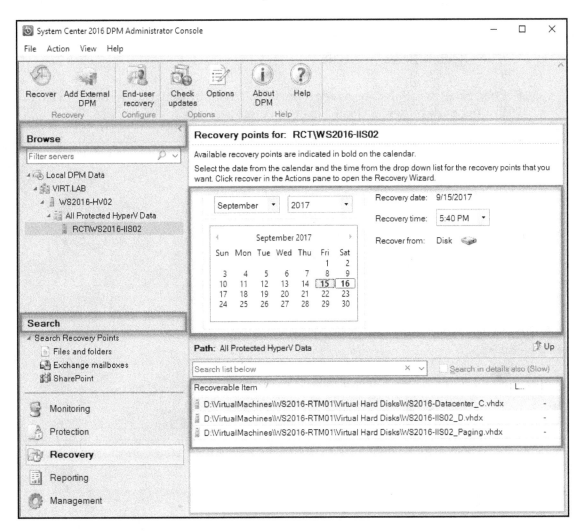

2. In the **Recovery points** section, select the data. Available recovery points are indicated in bold on the calendar in the recovery points section. Select the bold date for the recovery point you want to recover.

3. In the **Recoverable Item** pane, double-click on the recoverable item you want to recover, and then keep double-clicking the VHD or VHDX file till you find your desired file; right-click the flat file that you would like to recover. Choose **Recover...** and this will trigger the **Recovery Wizard**.

4. In the **Review Recovery Section** step, review the selection, and then click **Next >**.

5. The next step is **Select recovery type**, where the only option you have is to **Copy to a network folder**; click on **Next >** to continue:

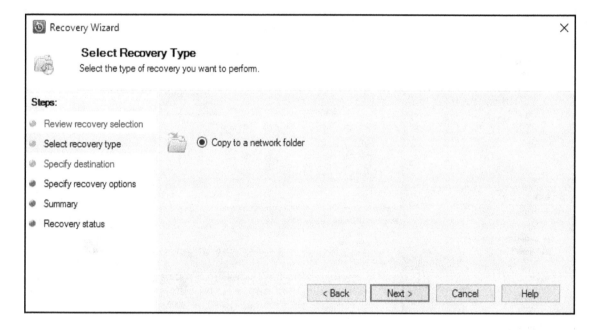

6. In the **Specify Destination** step, define the **Destination** and the **Destination** path. Click on the **Browse...** button to point out the location; click on **Next >** to continue:

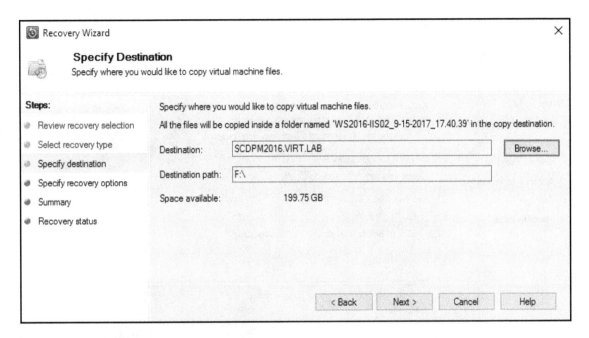

7. In the **Specify Recovery Options** step, configure the specific options for recovery.

8. In the **Restore security** part, define how the restored data source should apply to the security setting in the targeted location. The restored data can either keep the security settings that are present in the recovery point version or apply the security settings of the targeted location.

9. If the recovery will be restoring data over a poor WAN link, click the **Modify...** link in the **Network bandwidth usage throttling** part to define how much bandwidth the restore job should consume:

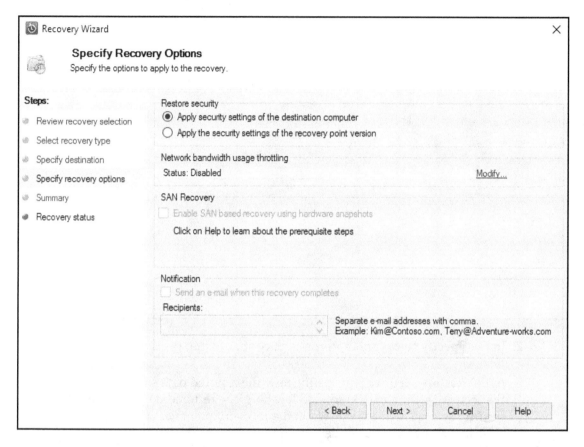

10. If you are using VSS hardware providers and a LUN presented for the SAN storage of the protected data source, select **Enable SAN based recovery using hardware snapshots** in the **SAN Recovery** part.

11. You can send an email to a specific user or users notifying them that the recovery has finished. You can enable this by checking the checkbox in the **Notification** part. However, this requires the DPM server to have an SMTP server configured in the DPM options. Please read the *Configuring email notifications* recipe in `Chapter 2`, *DPM Post-Installation and Management Tasks*. Click on **Next >** to continue.

12. In the **Summary** step, verify the recovery configuration and click on **Recover** to start recovery:

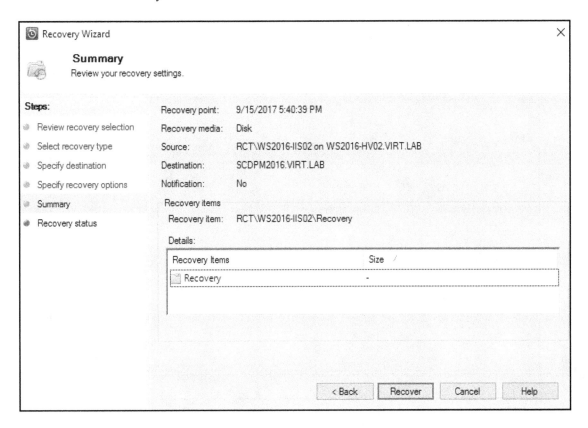

13. In the **Recovery Status** step, you will be able to see the current state of recovery. The status could also be monitored in the **Monitoring task** view of the DPM console:

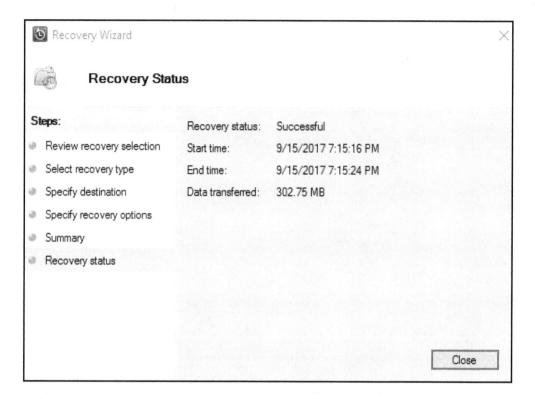

How it works...

When you double-click on the virtual hard disk file to perform ILR, Data Protection Manager will attach the VHDX of the protected virtual machines to provide the backup administrator with the ability to restore a single file; the restore process consists of several steps using temporary areas. When ILR operation is completed, DPM will detach the virtual hard disk.

There's more...

There are certain scenarios that you want to be aware of when using ILR in your environment, such as the following:

- You cannot select and recover multiple virtual hard disks at the same time.
- When you recover a virtual hard disk of a virtual machine that has Hyper-V checkpoints (formerly known as snapshots), the `.avhdx` files are not displayed in the **Recoverable Items** pane, but DPM recovers the parent virtual hard disk and all the associated `.avhdx` files.
- DPM saves the recovery item in a custom directory structure in the `VMName_<BackupTime>\<Path of the recovery item on the protected computer>` format, with the exact file system hierarchy that is used on a protected computer with the DPM protection agent installed.
- You must have the Hyper-V role enabled on the DPM server to perform item-level recoveries. Item-Level Recovery does not support recovery of an item to its original location. Item-Level Recovery is not supported if the differencing virtual hard disk and base (parent) virtual hard disk are on different volumes.
- You cannot browse the mount points when you explore a virtual hard disk for Item-Level Recovery.

4
Monitoring DPM and Configuring Role-Based Access

In this chapter, we will cover the following recipes:

- Monitoring DPM
- Publishing the DPM logs
- Monitoring DPM with SCOM
- Monitoring DPM without SCOM
- Installing the DPM Central Console
- Using the DPM Scoped Console
- Configuring remote administration
- Configuring and using role-based access
- Central reporting

Introduction

This chapter is designed to provide you with the skills and techniques for dealing with the post-deployment monitoring and management tasks of your Microsoft System Center **Data Protection Manager** (**DPM**) server. After reading this chapter, you will have the knowledge to carry out common DPM monitoring and management activities, such as monitoring DPM with **Microsoft System Center Operations Manager** (**SCOM**), monitoring DPM using native tooling, using the DPM Central Console, configuring and using role-based access control, and many more tasks.

To follow the recipes in this chapter, you need to have successfully installed Microsoft SCOM within your environment. For more information on how to deploy SCOM, please refer to the following article: `https://docs.microsoft.com/en-us/system-center/scom/deploy-overview`.

Monitoring DPM

An element of basic monitoring can be achieved by simply using the Microsoft System Center DPM Administrator Console. The DPM Administrator Console doesn't replace the need for a more comprehensive monitoring solution, but it does provide basic reactive capabilities. When combined with alert notifications, you can include email notifications for a slightly more comprehensive approach to monitoring your DPM environment.

Getting ready

To set up and configure email notifications with Microsoft System Center DPM, you will need to set up an SMTP relay server in advance, and then you can subscribe to alert notifications. For more details on setting up an SMTP relay server, take a look at the following article: `https://docs.microsoft.com/en-us/exchange/mail-flow-best-practices/how-to-set-up-a-multifunction-device-or-application-to-send-email-using-office-3`.

How to do it...

The following steps will guide you through monitoring alerts and setting up alert notifications in Microsoft System Center DPM server:

1. From the **Start** screen, select **Microsoft System Center Data Protection Manager**. The DPM Administrator Console will load and the **Monitoring** task area will be highlighted.
2. In the **Action** pane, click on **All Alerts**. Make sure that there are no critical errors reported in the DPM Administrator Console.
3. If you notice any critical or warning errors that disclose a problem, double-click the error to see more detailed information about the error.
4. Review the **Recommended Actions**, and research and determine any errors or inconsistencies as soon as is practical. Use the provided hyperlink associated with the error to determine the best course of action.

5. In the DPM Administrator Console, click the Subscribe icon on the ribbon bar and click the **SMTP Server** tab. Specify your **SMTP server name**, **SMTP server port**, and **"From" address** (here, the **From** email address must be a valid email address on the SMTP server):

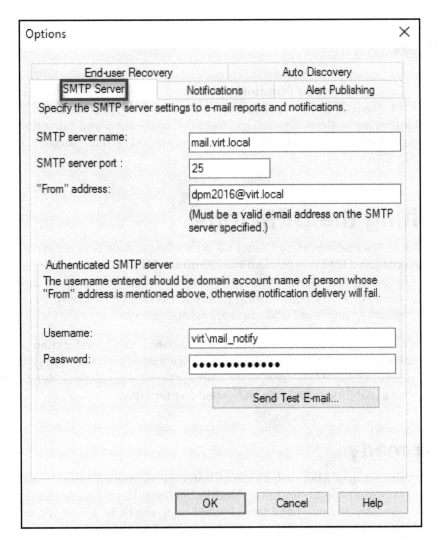

6. If you are using authentication, in **Authenticated SMTP Server**, type a valid username and password. Make sure to specify the name in the format of domain\username. Then, click **Send Test E-mail...** and specify where to send the test email. This will ensure that email notification is working correctly.

7. Click the **Notifications** tab. Select the types of alerts that you want to be notified about, for example, **Critical Alerts**, and then add recipients using the email address format. Use commas to separate multiple addresses. Click **Send Test Notification** to send a test message and then click **OK**.

How it works...

Microsoft System Center DPM out of the box publishes alerts only to the DPM Administrator Console. From the **Monitoring** task area's **Action** pane, you can see all of the published alerts for that DPM server. The alerts themselves are broken down into critical, warning, and information alerts. By configuring alert notification and subscribing to the type of alerts you want to be notified about, a configured SMTP relay server will forward alerts via email.

Publishing the DPM logs

The monitoring of Microsoft System Center Data DPM server alerts is not enabled by default. When enabled, DPM will publish alerts into the **DPM alerts** event log on the local DPM server. These alerts can then be seen in Windows Event Viewer. Once these alerts are published, you can use external monitoring tools such as SCOM or a third-party management product to monitor DPM and collect those events.

 SCOM has a number of capabilities that are much broader than just monitoring DPM, and so I would advise that you go to `https://docs.` `microsoft.com/en-us/system-center/scom/welcome` to understand the full capabilities of Microsoft System Center DPM.

Getting ready

To set up the monitoring of Microsoft System Center DPM, you will need to access the DPM Administrator Console to configure Alert Publishing. To be able to use the DPM Administrator Console, you will need to be logged on to the DPM server with a domain-based account that has membership of the DPM server's local administrators group.

How to do it...

The following steps will guide you through publishing alerts into Windows Event Viewer in a Microsoft System Center DPM server:

1. From the **Start** screen, select **Microsoft System Center Data Protection Manager**. The DPM Administrator Console will load and the **Monitoring** task area will be highlighted.

2. Click the **Options** icon on the ribbon bar and select the **Alert Publishing** tab. Click the **Publish Active Alerts** button and click **OK** to acknowledge that DPM alerts have been published to the DPM alerts event log:

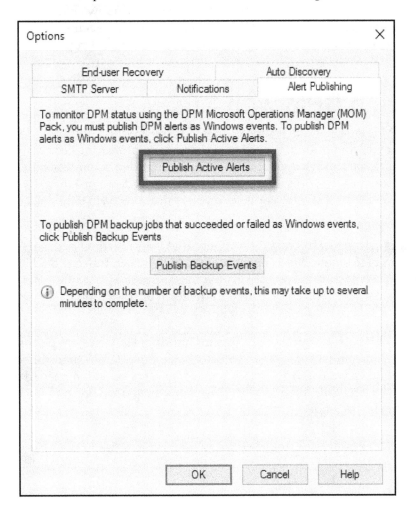

If you want backup events to be monitored by Microsoft SCOM, then you need to enable the publishing of these events as well. You can do this by clicking on the **Publish Backup Events** button.

How it works...

When Microsoft System Center DPM is initially installed, Alert Publishing is not enabled by default. You will only enable Alert Publishing if you decide to leverage an external monitoring product. When enabled, events are published into a dedicated event log named **DPM alerts**, and these alerts can be manually viewed by Windows Event Viewer. External monitoring tools such as Microsoft SCOM or a third-party management product can then be used to collect those alerts and store them centrally for processing.

Monitoring DPM with SCOM

Microsoft SCOM is a part of the System Center suite of products and provides cross-platform data center monitoring, as well as deep insight into various components within your environment, such as hardware; networking equipment or servers; core services, such as Active Directory or DNS; operating systems, either Windows or Linux; hypervisors, such as Microsoft Hyper-V or VMware vSphere; and applications from either Microsoft or third parties.

SCOM monitors systems of interest via an agent that is installed on each server. The agent monitors system performance and collects data, which is then transmitted back to a central management server. Agents are supplemented by service or application-specific management packs, which provide insight in the form of rules for data collection and reporting specific to a particular service or application.

SCOM also supports agentless monitoring. Here, system performance can still be monitored by using a proxy agent that has been installed on another system. Agentless managed systems are still managed as if there is an agent installed locally. However, not all management packs work in agentless mode.

Getting ready

The following recipe assumes that you have successfully installed SCOM within your environment and that a SCOM agent has been deployed to your DPM server. The SCOM infrastructure itself should include, as a minimum, the following management roles:

- **The management server**: This is used to administer the management environment and communicates with the operational database.
- **The operational database**: This is a SQL Server database that maintains all the configuration data for the management environment and stores the monitoring data that is collected from the systems that are being monitored.
- **The data warehouse database**: This is a SQL Server database that stores historical monitoring and alerting data. Here, data is written to the operational database and the data warehouse database sequentially, so reports always contain the most up-to-date data.

You can download the required SCOM Management Packs for Microsoft System Center DPM from the following location: `https://www.microsoft.com/en-us/download/details.aspx?id=56560`.

How to do it...

The following steps will guide you through downloading and importing Microsoft System Center DPM Server Management Packs into SCOM:

1. From the **Start** screen, select **Microsoft System Center** and then select **Operations Console**. The SCOM Operations Console will load and the **Monitoring** task area will be highlighted.
2. Select the **Administration** task area, right-click the **Management Packs** node, and then click **Import Management Packs**.

3. The **Import Management Packs** wizard will open; click the **Add** symbol, then choose **Add from disk**. On the **Open Catalog Connection** pop-up window, click **Yes** and import the following management packs: `Microsoft.SystemCenter.DataProtectionManager.Discovery.mp` and `.Library.mp`. Then, click **OK**:

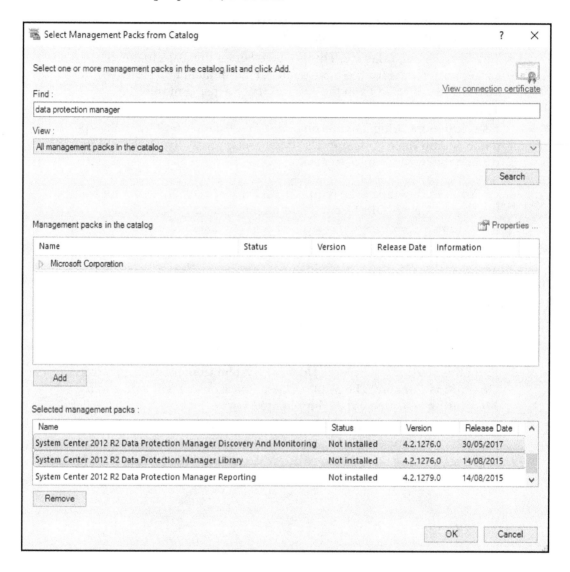

How it works...

Monitoring Microsoft System Center DPM Server Management Packs with SCOM provides the capability to centralize the monitoring and health status of your DPM server. You simply import the required management packs on the SCOM management server and your DPM server will be discovered and can be directly monitored via SCOM.

Monitoring DPM without SCOM

System Center is sold as a complete suite of products. The suite includes SCOM, so if you have purchased Microsoft System Center DPM, you automatically have a license for SCOM. So, it makes perfect sense to implement SCOM to monitor your DPM environment. However, DPM can be monitored without using SCOM, and this recipe will walk you through the various tools you can use to manually monitor DPM.

Getting ready

The approach to monitoring Microsoft System Center DPM without the use of SCOM takes a more manual approach. Here, you can do the following:

- Manually check the Windows Event Viewer to determine the overall state of not just DPM but the wider system state
- Use the DPM Administrator Console to view the state of DPM's overall health
- Use DPM reports to view the usage and health trends
- Use Performance Monitor to monitor the standard built-in operating system performance counters

To be able to use the DPM Administrator Console, you will need to be logged on to the DPM server with a domain-based account that has membership of the DPM server's local administrators group.

How to do it...

The following steps will guide you through monitoring Microsoft System Center DPM server without using SCOM, by using the DPM Administrator Console or native Windows troubleshooting tools.

Monitoring DPM operations through Windows Event Viewer

1. From the Windows Desktop, click the **Start** button, then type `Event Viewer`. Windows Event Viewer will load and the local node will be highlighted.
2. In Windows Event Viewer, in the console tree, expand **Windows Logs** and select the **System log**. Make sure that there no errors have been reported in the System event log that indicate a problem.
3. If you notice any error or warning events that disclose a problem, double-click the event to open the **Event Properties** window, and then read the information about the event.
4. Review, research, and determine any errors or inconsistencies as soon as is practical. Use Microsoft's Knowledge Base to help you: `https://support.microsoft.com/en-gb`.

Monitoring DPM operations through the DPM Administrator Console

1. From the **Start** screen, select **Microsoft System Center Data Protection Manager**. The DPM Administrator Console will load and the **Monitoring** task area will be highlighted.
2. Select **Alerts** and check the alerts on a daily basis to identify any potential data protection issues. Here, you will find errors, warnings, and informational messages that are currently active with your Microsoft System Center DPM system.
3. Select **Jobs** and check the jobs on a daily basis to verify that the jobs have run as expected. You can also view jobs that are scheduled to run or jobs that have run during your troubleshooting process.
4. From the DPM Administrator Console, select the **Monitoring** task area, select usage, and check the status of the volumes and shares within each protection group. Ensure the configuration of each protection group; for example, check that the recovery goals, disk allocation, and protection schedule are all configured correctly.
5. From the DPM Administrator Console, select the **Management** task area, select **Disk Storage**, and check regularly to verify the status of the storage pool volumes. Verify the status of the disks and check for the capacity of the disks in the storage pool, paying attention to used and free space.

6. Select **Agents**, check regularly to verify the status of the deployed DPM agents, and validate which versions of the agent you have running.

7. Select **Online** and check regularly to verify the connection status of the online subscription to Azure Backup.

8. Select **Libraries** and check regularly to verify the status of the attached tape libraries and drive on the DPM server.

Using DPM reports to view usage and health trends

1. From the DPM Administrator Console, select the **Reporting** task area, and generate and view reports on DPM operations that have occurred.

2. Ensure reporting is scheduled to occur automatically and subscribe to reports over email. Note that reporting is not used to monitor real-time events and was used more historically to help determine trends and usage patterns.

3. Consider running the **Status report**. The **Status report** provides an overview of the status of all recovery points for a specified time period. It lists recovery jobs and shows the total number of successes and failures for recovery points and disk-based and tape-based recovery point creations. This report can be used to show trends in the frequency of errors that occur and lists the number of alerts.

Using Performance Monitor to monitor the standard built-in operating system performance counters

1. From the Windows Desktop, click the **Start** button and type `Performance Monitor` (or `Perfmon` for short). Performance Monitor will load and the local node will be highlighted showing a summary of the current performance.

2. Click **Performance Monitor** under the **Monitoring Tools** node. Click the **Add** symbol (or *Ctrl + N*) and add the following performance counters:
   - **Memory**: Available MBytes
   - **Processor**: % Processor Time (for all instances)
   - **Physical Disk**: Current Disk Queue Length (for all instances)

The preceding performance counters can be used to measure the amount of memory that is available to processes running on your DPM server, the percentage of time the processor was busy, the number of disk requests that are currently queued, plus the disk requests currently being serviced during the sampling interval in Performance Monitor.

How it works...

It is certainly possible to monitor Microsoft System Center DPM server without leveraging SCOM. You can use Windows Event Viewer to determine whether there are any errors being reported in the System event log that might indicate a problem with your DPM server. You can also use DPM Administrator Console to view the operational status of your DPM server. By further enabling reporting and configuring email notifications, you can view usage and determine any health trends that might be occurring. Finally, you can use Performance Monitor and use standard performance counters to gain insight into the overall performance of your DPM server.

Installing the DPM Central Console

When you start to scale your Microsoft System Center DPM environment to multiple DPM servers, you will find that it becomes difficult to monitor and manage all your DPM servers individually. This is where the DPM Central Console comes in. The DPM Central Console allows you to manage individual DPM servers from one centralized location.

Getting ready

You can install Microsoft System Center DPM Central Console on a server operating system running Windows Server 2008 R2 or above, or a Windows client operating system running Windows 7 or above. However, you cannot install the Central Console on the DPM server itself. Before you can install the DPM Central Console, you need to have completed the following:

- You need to have installed the SCOM agent on your DPM server.
- You need to have imported the required two SCOM Management Packs. We completed this step in the previous *Monitoring DPM with SCOM* recipe.

How to do it...

The following steps will guide you through the process of installing the Microsoft System Center DPM Central Console on your SCOM management server:

1. Copy or make available the Microsoft System Center Data Protection Manager media to your System Center Operations Manager Management Server and click **Setup**.

2. In the setup screen for Microsoft System Center Operations Manager, select **Install Central Console**. Accept the license terms and conditions agreement and click **OK**.

3. In the Welcome to the Central Console Setup Wizard page, click on **Next**. Accept the default option, **Install Central Console server-side and client-side Components**, and click **Next**:

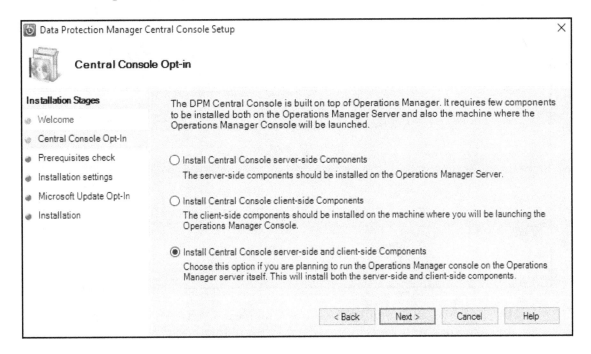

4. On the **Prerequisites Check** page, ensure that your system meets the software requirements for the DPM Central Console and click **Next**:

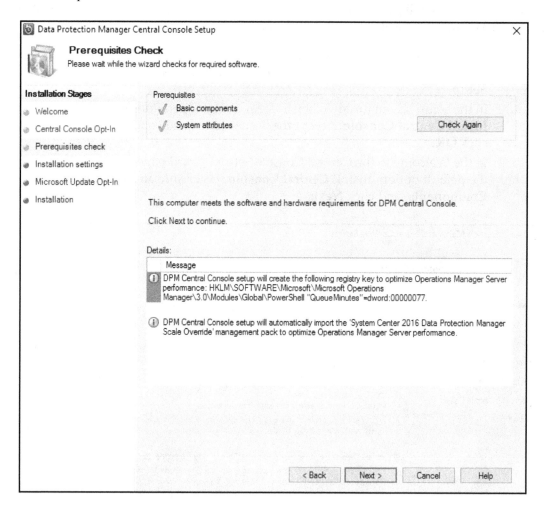

5. On the **Installation Settings** page, click on **Next**. On the **Microsoft Update Opt-In** page, click your preferred option for system updates, click **Install**, and then click **Close** when the Central Console has been successfully installed.

6. The DPM Central Console is integrated into the Operations Manager console. From the **Start** screen, select **Microsoft System Center** and then select **Operations Console**. The SCOM Operations Console will load and the **Monitoring** task area will be highlighted.

How it works...

To use the Microsoft System Center DPM Central Console to manage multiple DPM servers, you start off by installing the SCOM agent on the DPM server that you want to manage. After you install the SCOM agent, you then import the following SCOM Management Packs:

- `Microsoft.SystemCenter.DataProtectionManager.Discovery.mp`
- `Microsoft.SystemCenter.DataProtectionManager.Library.mp`

After you have imported the required Management Packs, you can progress to installing the DPM Central Console. As mentioned previously, the DPM Central Console can be installed in one of three ways:

- **Server and client components**: This option allows you to monitor the DPM server on which the SCOM agent is present and use the scoped DPM Administrator Console
- **Server components**: This option allows you to monitor DPM servers on which the SCOM agent is present but you cannot use the scoped DPM Administrator Console
- **Client components**: This option allows you to use the scoped DPM Administrator Console but you cannot monitor your DPM servers

Using the DPM Scoped Console

By installing the DPM Central Console, you enable a new feature of DPM, and this feature is called the DPM Scoped Console. The DPM Scoped Console can be used to help with troubleshooting. With the DPM Scoped Console, if alerts are raised in SCOM, you can click the **Troubleshoot** button and you will be directly taken to the DPM Administration Console, which you can then use to troubleshoot your DPM environment.

Getting ready

You must have the Microsoft System Center DPM Central Console installed. The DPM Central Console can be installed on a server operating system running Windows Server 2008 R2 or above, or a Windows client operating system running Windows 7 or above. In the previous recipe, we installed the DPM Central Console on the SCOM Server.

How to do it...

The following steps will guide you through using the DPM Scoped Console in SCOM:

1. From the **Start** screen, select **Microsoft System Center** and then select **Operations Console**. The SCOM Operations Console will load and the **Monitoring** task area will be highlighted.

2. Expand the **System Center Data Protection Manager** node, expand **Alert Views**, and select **All**. Select the alert – that is, critical event – and then in the **Alert Tas**k area, click **DPM: Troubleshoot Alert**. The DPM Scoped Console will load:

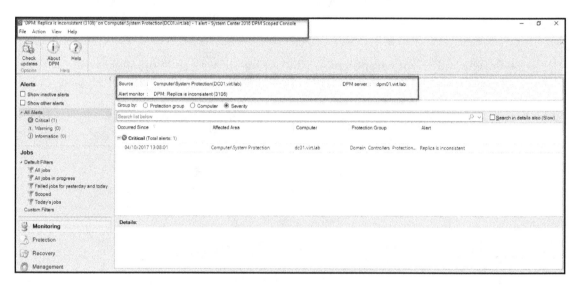

How it works...

The Microsoft System Center DPM Scoped Console is based on the DPM Administrator Console, but there are a few differences:

- The title bar provides you with some basic alert information, such as the alert monitor, and you are notified of the fact that you are using the Scoped Console.

- The context bar provides you with more details about the alert and where the alert was generated.

- The console itself only shows you the objects relating to the alert that is generated. It will also display some tasks that aren't associated with any specific protection group or server, as these jobs are common across all objects.

Configuring remote administration

With Microsoft System Center DPM, you have the ability to install the DPM Administration Console on a remote system, either on servers or workstations, so that you can manage a single DPM server instance without having to log on to the DPM server directly.

Getting ready

The DPM Administrator Console and the Management Shell can be installed on systems running Windows Server 2008 R2, Windows Server 2012, Windows Server 2012 R2, Windows Server 2016, Windows Server 2019, Windows 7, Windows 8, Windows 8.1, and Windows 10. The server or workstation must be running, at a minimum, .NET Framework 4.0.

How to do it...

The following steps will guide you through the process of installing the Microsoft System Center DPM Remote Console on a Windows 10 management workstation so that you can administer DPM remotely:

1. Copy or make available the Microsoft System Center Data Protection Manager media to your Windows 10 management workstation and click **Setup**.
2. In the setup screen for Microsoft System Center Operations Manager, select **DPM Remote Administration**. Accept the license terms and conditions agreement and click **OK**. The **Data Protection Manager Remote Administration Console Setup** wizard will appear.
3. Click **Next** to continue. On the **Prerequisites Check** page, ensure that all prerequisites are met and click **Next**. On the **Installation Settings** page, click **Next**.
4. On the **Microsoft Update Opt-In** page click your preferred option – **Use Microsoft update when I check for updates (recommended)** – and click **Install**. Finally, on the **Installation** page, click **Close**.

How it works...

The Microsoft System Center DPM Remote Console and the Management Shell can be installed remotely on a system, whether it be a server or management workstation. You have to make sure that the DPM installation media is available during installation and that the prerequisites are met. Once this has been achieved, you can install the DPM Remote Console by running SETUP and selecting DPM Remote Administration.

Configuring and using role-based access

Typically, most enterprise customers have a dedicated team that, among other duties and responsibilities, handles the day-to-day running of the backup service for their organization. Maintaining control over your DPM environment while effectively delegating tasks to a specific support team can be challenging, and this is where **role-based access control** (**RBAC**) in Microsoft System Center DPM comes in.

Getting ready

Microsoft System Center DPM provides eight default RBAC roles out of the box. These include the following:

- **DPM Read-Only Operator**: This can view everything, but can't modify or run anything
- **DPM Recovery Operator**: This can only perform recoveries
- **DPM Reporting Operator**: This can only run and manage reports
- **DPM Tier-1 Support**: This can resume backups, take automated recommended actions, and open a DPM Scoped Console to troubleshoot issues
- **DPM Tier-2 Support**: This can run backups on demand and perform corrective actions, such as enabling and disabling agents
- **DPM Tape Operator**: This can rerun backups or perform tape drive tasks
- **DPM Tape Admin**: This can perform all tape related actions
- **DPM Admin**: This can perform all actions on the DPM server

Before you can use RBAC with DPM, you need to have done the following:

- Imported the required SCOM Management Packs, which was previously carried out in a prior recipe in this chapter
- Installed the DPM Central Console, which was also previously carried out in a prior recipe in this chapter

How to do it...

The following steps will guide you through the process of installing the RBAC roles on the SCOM server:

1. From the **Start** screen, type CMD, right-click the **Command Prompt** option, and select **Run as Administrator**. Navigate to the following folder: %INSTALLDRIVE%\Program Files\Microsoft DPM\bin\.

2. Run the following executable: DefaultRoleConfigurator.exe. Then, press *Enter* to exit the utility:

```
Administrator: Command Prompt - DefaultRoleConfigurator.exe

C:\Program Files\Microsoft DPM\bin>DefaultRoleConfigurator.exe
----DPM Centralized Management Default Role Configurator ----

Skip list:
Skipping create role:   DPM Reporting Operator
Skipping create role:   DPM Read-Only Operator
Skipping create role:   DPM Tier-1 Support
Skipping create role:   DPM Tape Admin
Skipping create role:   DPM Tier-2 Support
Skipping create role:   DPM Admin
Skipping create role:   DPM Recovery Operator
Skipping create role:   DPM Tape Operator


Updating default roles in SCOM:
Updated role:DPM Reporting Operator
Updated role:DPM Read-Only Operator
Updated role:DPM Tier-1 Support
Updated role:DPM Tape Admin
Updated role:DPM Tier-2 Support
Updated role:DPM Admin
Updated role:DPM Recovery Operator
Updated role:DPM Tape Operator

---- END ----
If you want this tool to create the default roles again, delete the role from SCOM first

Hit Return to Exit!!
```

3. To view the role, from the **Start** screen, select **Microsoft System Center** and then select **Operations Console**. The SCOM Operations Console will load and the **Monitoring** task area will be highlighted.

4. Click the **Administration** task area, under the **Security** node, select **User Roles**. To delegate a role to somebody in your organization, you need to add that user to the relevant DPM RBAC role.

5. Right-click on the role you want to modify, select **Properties**, click the **Add** button, and search for the user in the Active Directory. Click **OK** in the **Select User & Groups** directory picker window and then click **OK** on the **User Role Properties** page.

How it works...

With Microsoft System Center DPM, you can create a centralized management model by using the DPM Central Console. The `DefaultRoleConfigurator.exe` executable extends the RBAC roles and provisions eight default roles. You can then add an Active Directory user or group to one of those roles by modifying the properties of that role.

Central reporting

Microsoft System Center DPM provides six standard reports that can be used for auditing and monitoring your production environment out of the box. With the integration of SCOM, the reporting infrastructure can be enhanced with the ability to create custom reports. The reporting framework integrates with SCOM via the DPM Central Console, so you can now even generate aggregated reports from numerous DPM Servers that are being managed by DPM Central Console.

Getting ready

To get Microsoft System Center DPM central reporting to work, you need to have done the following:

- You must have imported the required SCOM Management Pack, which was also carried out in a prior recipe in this chapter.

- You must have installed the DPM Central Console, which was also carried out in a prior recipe in this chapter.
- You must have ensured that the SCOM Data Warehouse is up and running. To verify this, ensure that all the SQL Server services with a service name containing the SCOM DB Instance name are started and running.

 If you want **service level agreement** (**SLA**) data in DPM reports, set SLA requirements on the DPM Server using the PowerShell commandlet Set-DPMProtectionGroupSLA –SLAInHours.

How to do it...

The following steps will guide you through importing the Microsoft System Center DPM Server Reporting Management Pack into SCOM:

1. From the **Start** screen, select **Microsoft System Center** and then select **Operations Console**. The SCOM Operations Console will load and the **Monitoring** task area will be highlighted.
2. Select the **Administration** task area, right-click the **Management Packs** node, and then click **Import Management Packs**.
3. The **Import Management Packs** wizard will open. Click the Add symbol, then choose **Add from disk**. On the **Open Catalog Connection** pop-up window, click **Yes** and import the `Microsoft.SystemCenter.DataProtectionManager.Reporting.mp` following management packs, and click **OK**.
4. A sample report can be viewed on the SCOM Operations Console by clicking the **Reporting** task area, navigating to the **System Center Data Protection Manager Reporting** node, and then double-clicking **DPM Executive Summary Report**.

How it works...

This additional Management Pack supports collecting reporting data from all of the Microsoft System Center DPM servers that have been deployed in your infrastructure. By importing the Management Pack, reporting data can be collected centrally and reported on.

Protecting Microsoft Workloads with DPM **5**

In this chapter, we will cover the following topics:

- Enabling file server protection with DPM
- Enabling SQL Server protection with DPM
- Enabling Windows bare metal protection with DPM

Introduction

Most organizations rely on Microsoft server workloads to run their businesses. Ensuring the protection of Microsoft workloads is a critical part of the business continuity strategy, and organizations need a backup solution to ensure their workload data is protected from being attacked by Ransomware and other malicious corruptions and deletions. With Microsoft **System Center Data Protection Manager** (**SCDPM**) and **Microsoft Azure Backup Server** (**MABS**), you can protect workloads such as Microsoft SQL Server, Microsoft SharePoint Server, Microsoft Exchange Server, and Hyper-V **virtual machines** (**VMs**) not only to disk or tape media, but also to Microsoft Azure. Please read Chapter 10, *Integrating DPM with Azure Backup*, to learn more about hybrid cloud backup solutions for your organization.

This chapter describes how DPM orchestrates backup and recovery of different Microsoft workloads.

Enabling file server protection with DPM

SCDPM provides a flexible data source protection solution for file server workloads, combining fast backup and restore scenarios, and is fully optimized. This recipe will cover how to configure file server protection by protecting shares that reside on NTFS, ReFS, or deduplicated volumes.

Getting ready

Before you enable file server protection, you need to make sure that the following prerequisites are satisfied:

- **Modern Backup Storage** (**MBS**) is configured as target disk storage to store all the backup data
- The file server you would like to protect is a supported version for DPM protection
- Install DPM agents on each of the file servers that need to be protected
- The agent status should report **OK** in the DPM management console

How to do it...

With the agents installed on the file servers that need to be protected, you can enable protection for the workloads. Complete the following steps to configure protection groups:

1. Open your DPM Administrator Console, click on **Protection** workspace, and then click on the **New** button in the top-left corner, as shown in the following screenshot:

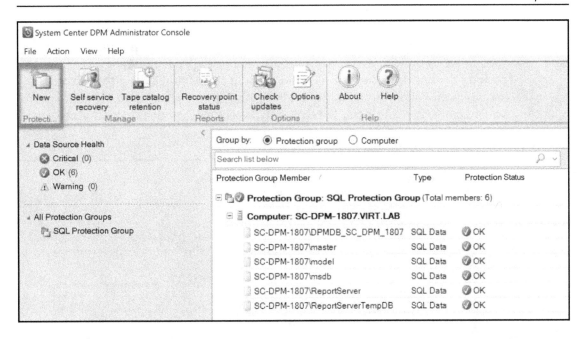

2. In the **Welcome to the New Protection Group Wizard** screen, select **Servers** and then click on **Next >** to continue.

3. In the **Select Group Members** window, select and expand the server(s) that you intend to protect, then select the file share, volume, or mount point that you would like to protect. If you would like to exclude specific file types, you can click on the **Exclude Files...** link at the bottom right-hand side of the wizard, as shown in the following screenshot. Please note that when you protect a file share, you cannot exclude folders. This can only be done by protecting the volume or a mount point containing sub-folders:

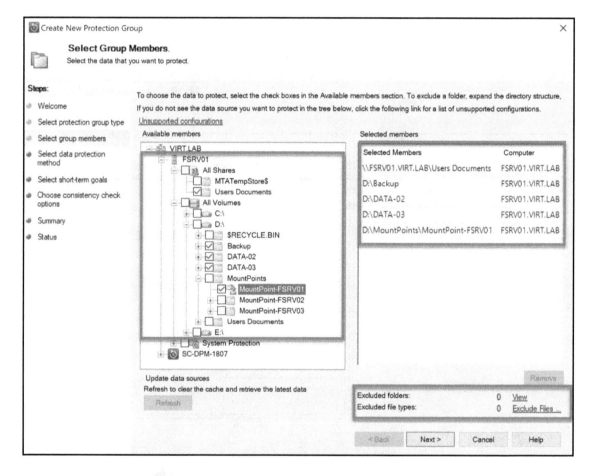

4. Once you have finished your selection, click on **Next >** to continue:

5. In the **Select Data Protection Method** page, select what method of protection you want to employ in order to protect your data and then type a value in the **Protection group name** field, as shown in the following screenshot. If Azure Backup is configured, you can select Azure as an online protection target. Please read `Chapter 10`, *Integrating DPM with Azure Backup*, to learn how Azure Backup can be configured and used as a long-term retention target. Click on **Next >** to continue:

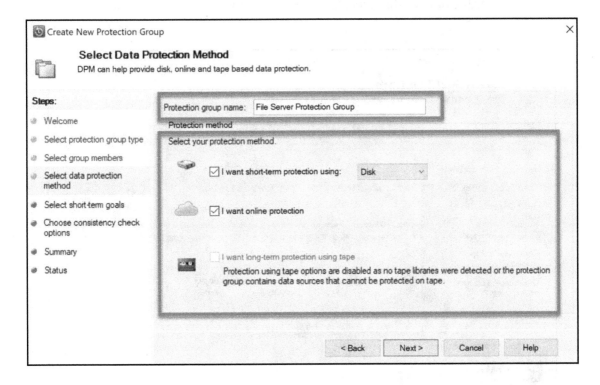

6. In the **Specify Short-Term Goals** page, select the **Retention range**, which is the number of days you want to keep the protected data in the backup storage. Next, specify the **Synchronization frequency**. The value specified here will set how often the DPM agent will replicate the block level changes from the protected data source. This can be as short as 15 minutes, up to 24 hours. You can also select to synchronize **Just before a recovery point**. In the **File recovery points** section, you can specify when to create a recovery point. If you click on **Modify...**, a new window will open, where you can choose the time of day as well as the days of the week. Click **OK** to confirm, and then click on **Next >** to continue:

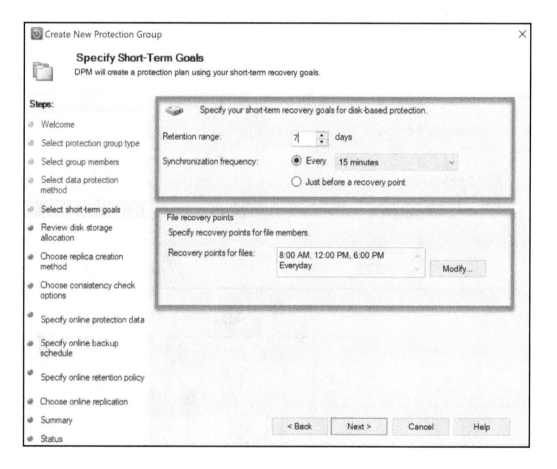

7. In the **Review Disk Storage Allocation** page, you can see the **Total data size**, and the **Disk storage to be provisioned on DPM**. You can also configure the **Average disk space allocated for change journal on protected volumes**. This isn't on the DPM server; this is on the source server, so you could click the **Modify...** link and change that 300 megabyte default value if you chose. You can also specify a **Target Storage** for each data source in case you have multiple volumes configured as target disk storage, or if you have configured **workload-aware storage** (**WAS**), so the volumes can be selected to preferentially store specific workloads. Click on **Next >** to continue:

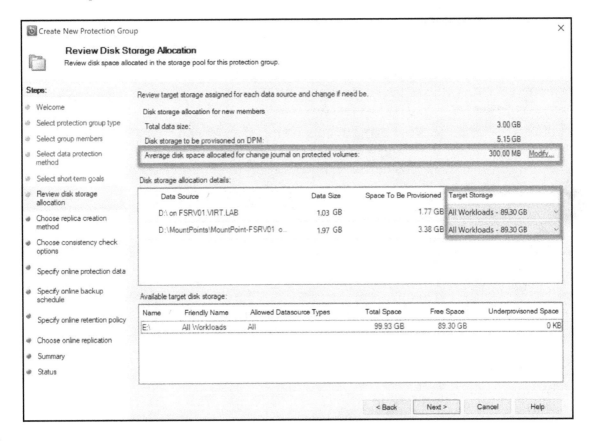

8. In the **Choose Replica Creation Method** page, you can define how the DPM sever should create the replica of the protected data source. You can create the replica **Now** over the network, or you can schedule the creation of the replica **Later**, maybe after working hours, because if you're bringing over a large dataset to the DPM server from the source, it could affect bandwidth. You could also create the replica manually using removable media if it's an enormous amount data and you don't have a quick network link. Click on **Next >** to continue:

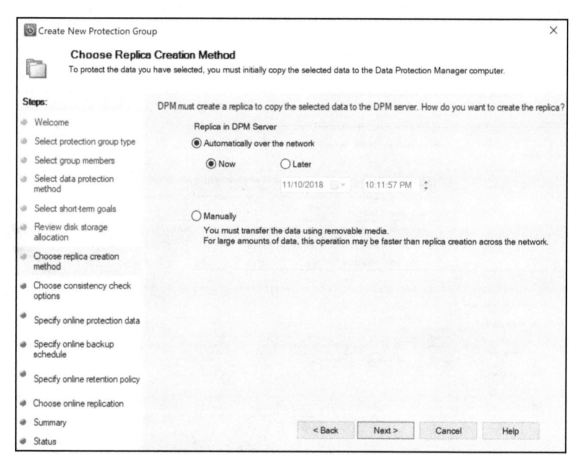

9. In the **Consistency check options** page, you can select the consistency check frequency. The default of running a consistency check if a replica becomes inconsistent is turned on, which is good if there's some kind of corruption. In this example, we will be proactive and turn on **Run a daily consistency check according to the following schedule**, which is going to be midnight for a maximum of **8** hours. Click on **Next >** to continue:

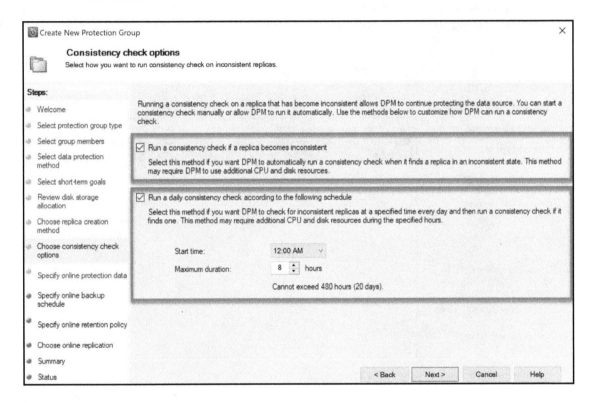

10. In the **Specify Online Protection Data** page, you can select the protected data source that you will include for Azure Backup (off-site protection). Click on **Next >** to continue:

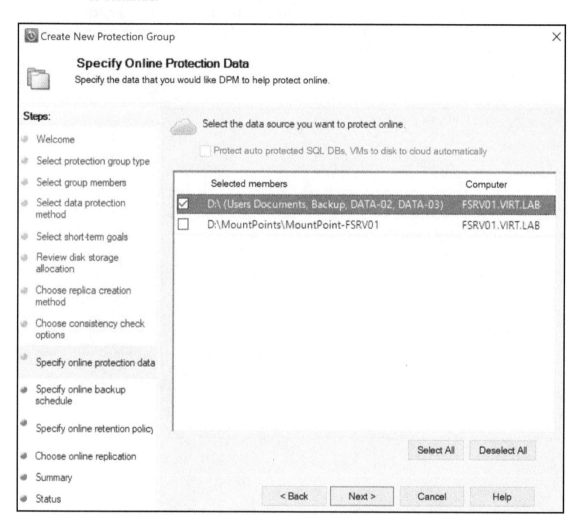

11. If you selected online protection in the previous step, then you have to utilize the **Specify Online Backup Schedule** option: when do you want to create backups? The maximum is twice per day. The default is **9:00 PM**. But you could also do it weekly, monthly, or yearly. In this example, we will leave it on daily with the default schedule. Click on **Next >** to continue:

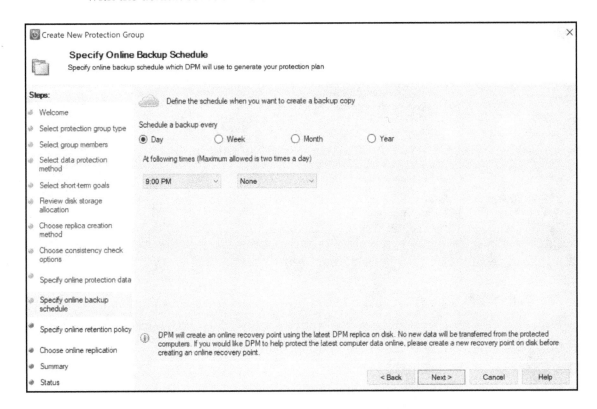

12. Now you need to utilize the **Specify Online Retention Policy** option. The default is **Daily** at **9:00 PM** for **180 Days**, but you've also got weekly, monthly, and yearly. You also have a **Modify** button for these if you want to make any changes. We are going to accept the defaults for the long-term retention policy in the cloud. Click on **Next >** to continue:

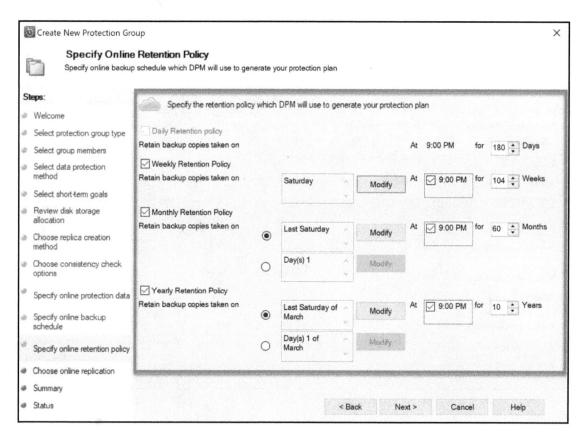

13. Last, but by no means least, you have to select the **Choose Online Replication** option: how should you create this initial backup from your protected file server in the Azure cloud? The default is **Automatically over the network**, but you could choose **Offline Backup** and specify the appropriate folders and other Azure information. We are going to do it over the network since it's not a large dataset. Click on **Next >** to continue:

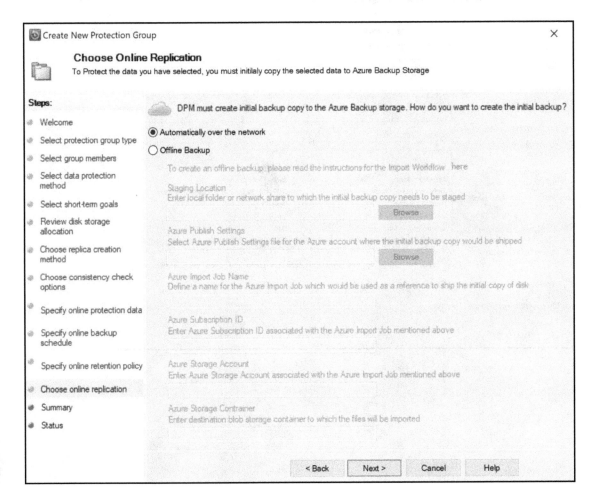

14. In the **Summary** page, you can see the results of your selections. Now click on **Create Group**:

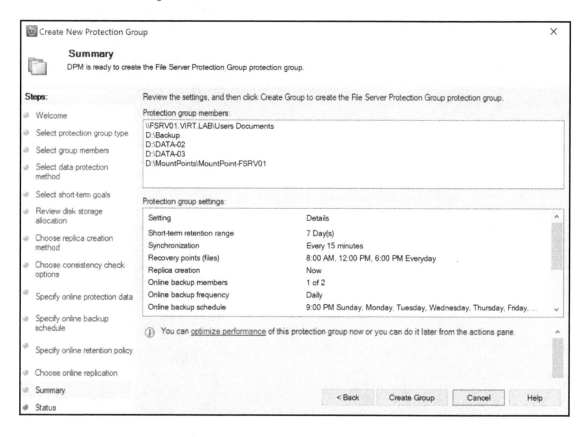

15. In the **Status** window, you can see that it's creating a protection group, allocating a replica for drive D:\ on our source machine, and updating the online backup policy. So, after a moment, you'll see that they've all succeeded. Click **Close**:

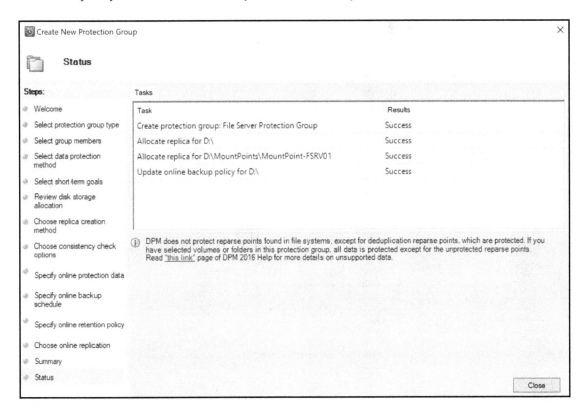

16. In the **Protection** workspace, you can now see that we have a new protection group called **File Server Protection Group**; it's got one server as a member. The replica creation process will take some time, depending on the amount of data you are protecting. You can also see the progress in the **Monitoring** workspace under **Informational**. And, after a moment, you can see that the protection status is now labeled as being **OK**. If you select any protected member, underneath you can see the details. There's a link you can click on for the replica path where that's stored on the DPM server. Also, you can see whether any recovery points have been taken. In this instance, because it's just nearly established, there is currently only one recovery point. You can also see the amount of storage space consumed, as demonstrated in the following screenshot:

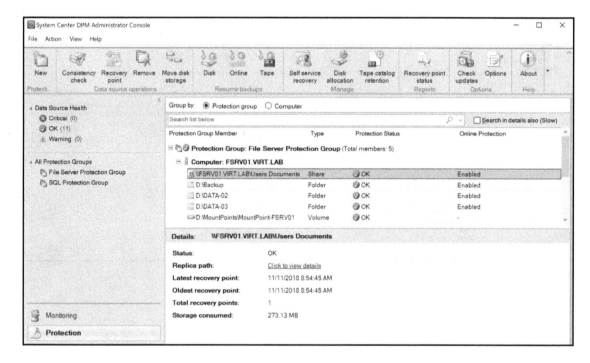

17. Now, interestingly also, if you wanted to, you could right-click on any protected member and select **Stop Protection of member**. This will remove a single protected member from the protection group. You could also right-click on the protection group and select **Stop Protection of group**. Now, when you do that, you get options to determine what it is that you want to remove. Do you want to retain any protected data or delete it? And do you want to delete the data source replicas from the DPM server disk and also online? This is important as regards data availability:

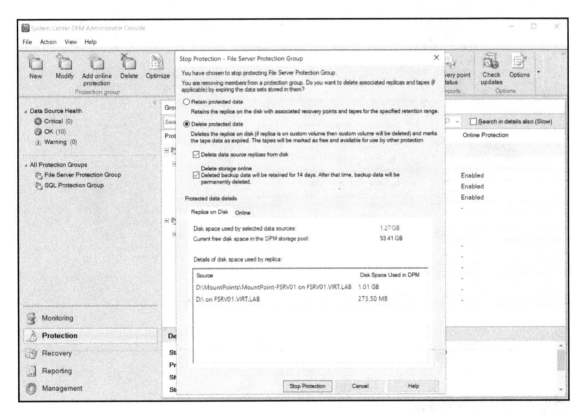

18. Now, at the same time, notice that when you right-click on a specific protected data, you can also choose the following options: **Perform consistency check...**, **Create recovery point...**, **Move disk storage...**, and so on. Please read `Chapter 2`, *DPM Post-Installation and Management Tasks*, to learn more about backup storage migration on DPM MBS:

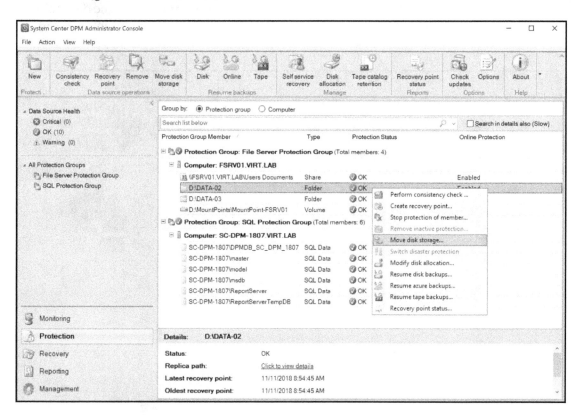

How it works...

SCDPM uses **Volume Shadow Copy Services** (**VSS**) and filter bitmaps to make the backup process more efficient. DPM leverages filesystem filter drivers to maintain a bitmap of changes between two synchronization jobs. With VSS volume snapshots, the set of changed blocks are tracked by the bitmap, and then transferred from the file server to DPM replica disk storage.

When you go to the **Recovery** workspace, you can see that on today's date, the day appears as a bold listed day, as opposed to the others on the calendar, and that's because there is data that was backed up on that day and you can recover from that point in time. This can be seen in the following screenshot:

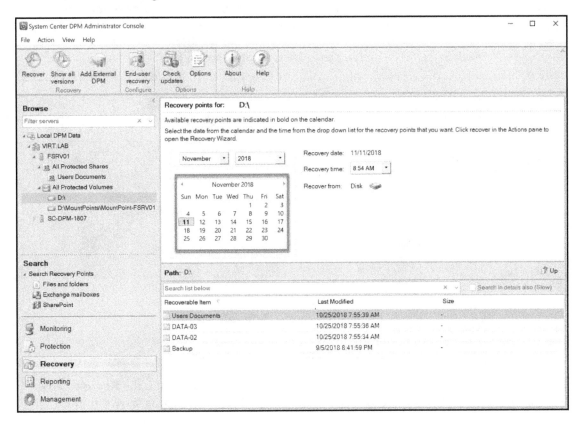

There's more...

When you create a protection group as demonstrated in this recipe, you can select multiple types of data sources and put them in a single protection group, but it's recommended that you segregate data sources based on their type and protection workloads; for example, file servers' workloads are in a dedicated protection group, and SQL databases in another group, since a protection group is a means to logically group data sources that have the same protection intent.

Once you configure DPM for protection, it calculates the size of the data being backed up. If many files and folders are being backed up together, as in the case of a file server, size calculation may take a long time. Starting with DPM 2016 and MABS version 3 onward, you can configure to accept the storage volume size as default, instead of calculating the size of each file and folder that's being backed up. To enable **Custom Size Allocation**, open **Registry Editor** and browse to the following path:
`HKEY_LOCAL_MACHINE\SOFTWARE\Microsoft\Microsoft Data Protection Manager\Configuration\DiskStorage`. Then create a string key named `EnableCustomAllocationOnReFSStorage` and set its value to 1, as demonstrated in the following screenshot:

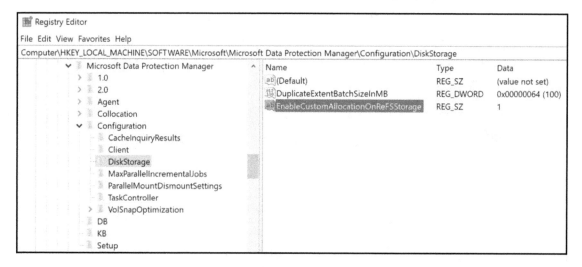

Once you enable **Custom Size Allocation**, you can set the **Data Size** in the **Review Disk Storage Allocation** step during the creation of the protection group, as shown in the following screenshot:

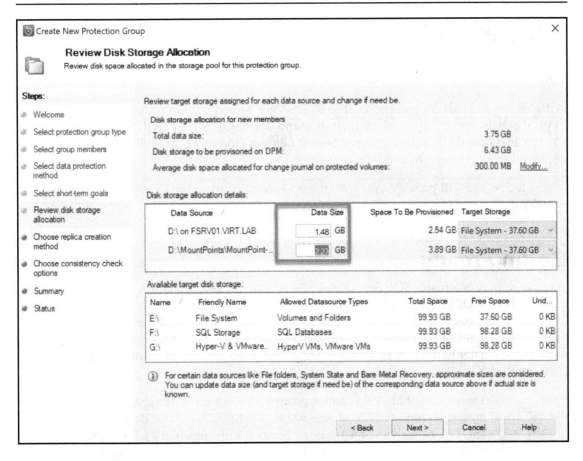

If you want to have the default size allocation with DPM, then set the `EnableCustomAllocationOnReFSStorage` key value to `0`.

Enabling SQL Server protection with DPM

One of the most important Microsoft workloads present in any modern data center is the SQL Server, on account of the majority of enterprise applications that use its functionality.

With Microsoft SCDPM, you can enable SQL Server protection in various configurations. Typical SQL Server configurations include standalone SQL Server, SQL Server **Failover Cluster Instance** (**FCI**) with Windows Server failover clustering, as well as SQL Server deployed as an AlwaysOn availability group.

In this recipe, we will provide you with the necessary information to protect SQL Server workloads.

Getting ready

You can deploy Microsoft SQL Server in a VM or in a physical machine. In either case, you must install the DPM agent on the SQL Server machine. If SQL Server is deployed in a clustered mode or as a SQL AlwaysOn, then the DPM agent must be installed on all the nodes that are part of the failover cluster for the SQL Server instance. And if you add any node to the cluster in the future, then the DPM agent must be installed on the newly added cluster node(s) as well.

 Please note that DPM cannot protect SQL Server when it has database files stored on remote SMB shares or on Windows **Server Scale-out File Server** (**SOFS**), as well as on **Clustered Shared Volumes** (**CSV**). DPM also cannot protect SQL Servers whose databases are stored on Microsoft Azure Blob storage.

Before you enable SQL Server protection, you must explicitly add the system account NTAuthority\System to the Sysadmin group on the SQL Server, as shown in the following screenshot:

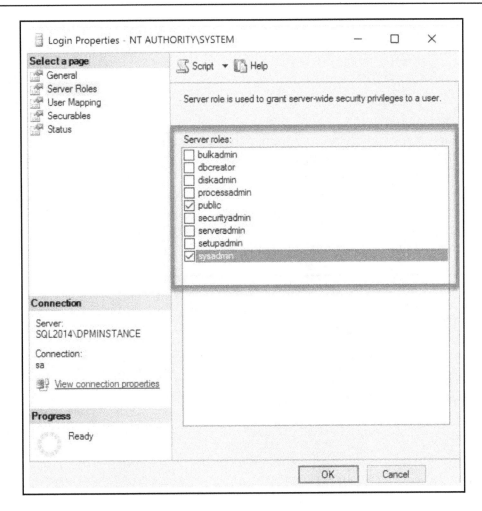

If you forget to add the system account NTAuthority\System to the Sysadmin group on SQL Server, then the DPM server will generate a critical alert stating **Unable to configure protection**, as shown in the following screenshot:

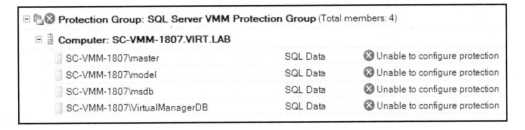

How to do it...

Before you enable protection, you should always verify that the targeted SQL Server is accessible and that the DPM agent is reporting **OK** in the DPM console. Now take the following steps:

1. Open your DPM Administrator Console, click on the **Protection** workspace, and then click on the **New** button up in the ribbon bar.
2. In the **Welcome to the New Protection Group Wizard**, select **Servers**, and then click on **Next >** to continue.
3. Next, you need to expand the appropriate server and then choose, for example, under the SQL items, where it says **All SQL Servers**, the appropriate server instance and, in that, the appropriate databases, as shown in the following screenshot. Click on **Next >** to continue:

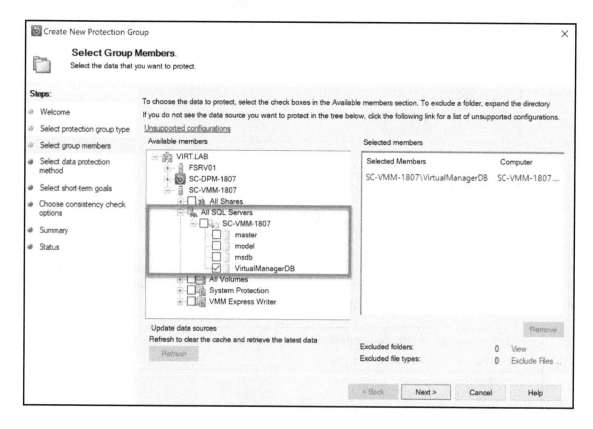

4. Now, what you could also do is enable auto protection mode of all databases within the SQL Server instance. This is useful in a dynamic environment where databases are added or deleted from a SQL Server instance; in this case, auto protection is enabled automatically without requiring backup administrator intervention. Please note that in auto protection mode, there is no mechanism to turn off backup of a subset of databases, so all databases within the selected SQL Server instance will be protected. You can enable auto protection by selecting the SQL instance name, as shown in the following screenshot. Click on **Next >** to continue:

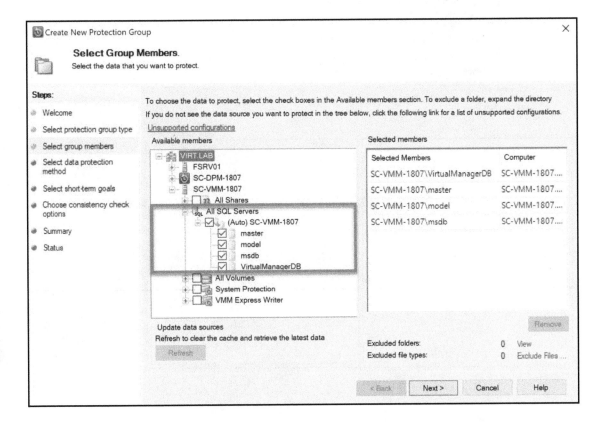

5. In the **Select Data Protection Method** page, select what method of protection you want to protect your data and then type a value in the **Protection group name** field, as shown in the following screenshot. In this example, we won't enable online protection; we will keep it on-premises, with local DPM disk storage. Click on **Next >** to continue:

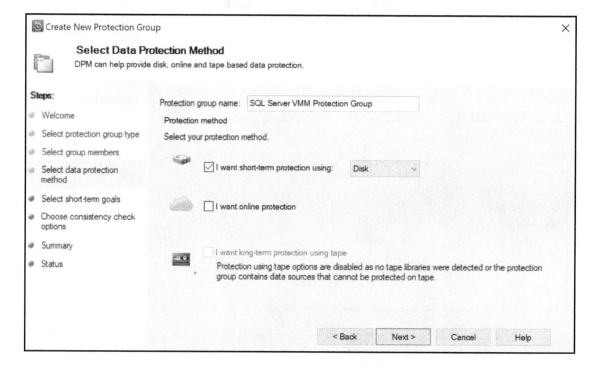

6. In the **Specify Short-Term Goals** page, select the **Retention range**, which is the number of days you want to keep the protected data in the backup storage for. Next, specify the **Synchronization frequency**; the specified value here will set how often the DPM agent will replicate the delta changes from the protected SQL Server; this can be as short as 15 minutes up to 24 hours. Now, this option will only be visible if you are protecting the entire SQL Server instance (auto protection mode) as discussed in the previous step, or if you select a database where it's **Recovery model** is set to **Full** and not **Simple**, in this case, DPM will be able to back up the transaction logs. You can also select to synchronize **Just before a recovery point**. In the **Application recovery points** section, you can specify when to create a recovery point. If you click on **Modify...**, a new window will open, where you can choose the time of day as well as the days of the week. Click **OK** to confirm, and then click on **Next >** to continue:

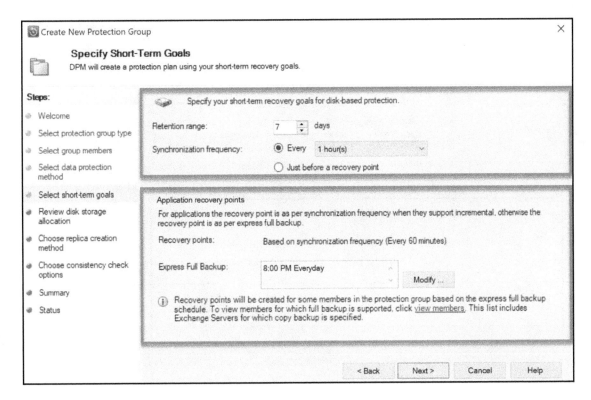

7. In the **Review Disk Storage Allocation** page, you can see **Total data size**, and the **Disk storage to be provisioned on DPM**. You can specify a **Target Storage** for each data source in case you have multiple volumes configured as target disk storage, or if you have configured **workload-aware storage** (**WAS**), so the volumes can be selected to preferentially store specific workloads or based on backup disk performance. Click on **Next >** to continue:

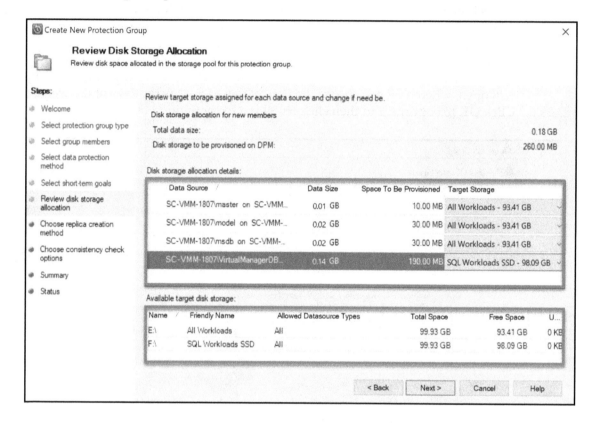

8. In the **Choose Replica Creation Method** page, you can define how the DPM sever should create the replica of the protected data source. You can create the replica **Now** over the network, or you can schedule the creation of the replica **Later**, maybe after working hours, because if you're bringing over a large dataset to the DPM server from the source, it could affect bandwidth. You could also create the replica manually using removable media if it's an enormous amount data and you don't have a quick network link. In this example, we will create the initial replica automatically over the network **Now**. Click on **Next >** to continue:

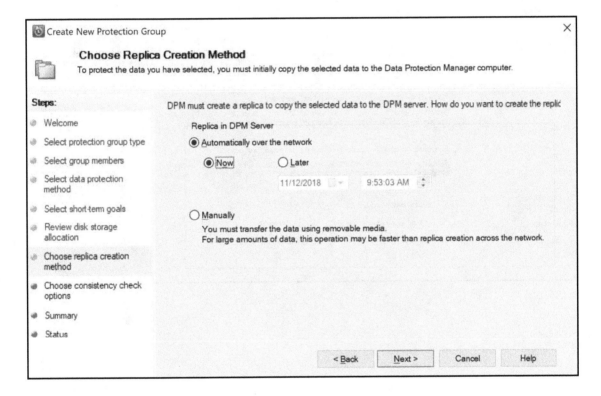

9. In the **Consistency check options** page, you can select the consistency check frequency. The default of running a consistency check if a replica becomes inconsistent is turned on, which is good if there's some kind of corruption. In this example, we will be proactive and turn on **Run a daily consistency check** according to the following schedule, which is going to be midnight for a maximum of **8** hours. Click on **Next >** to continue:

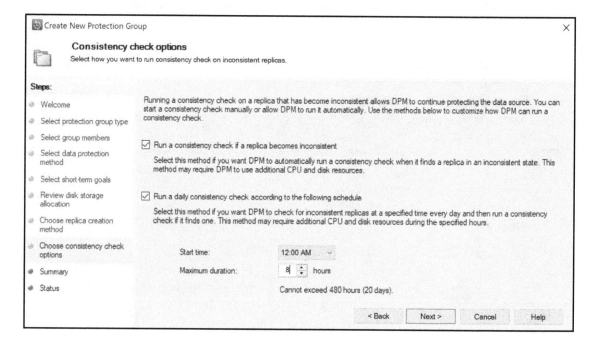

10. In the **Summary** page, you can see the results of your selections. Click on **Create Group**:

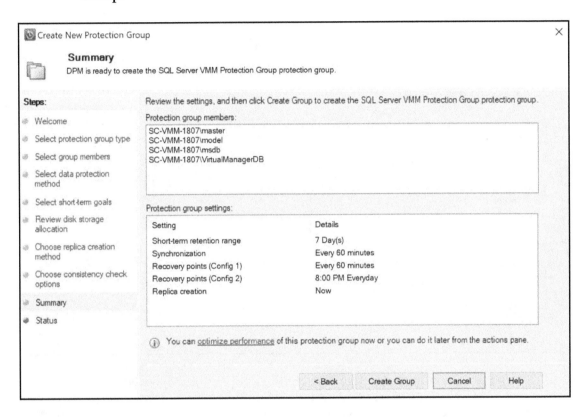

11. In the **Status** window, you can see that it's creating a protection group, allocating the replica for each database. So, after a moment, you'll see that they've all succeeded. Click **Close**:

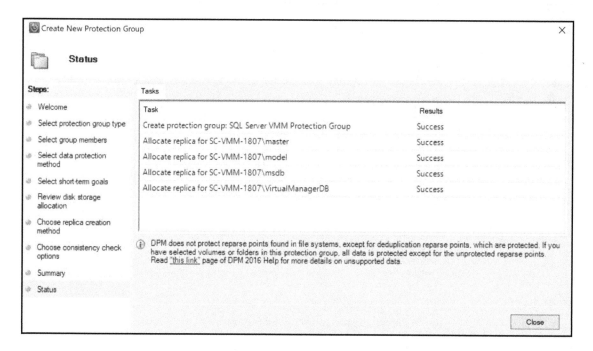

12. In the **Protection** workspace, you can see now that we have a new protection group called **SQL Server VMM Protection Group**; it's got one server as a member. The replica creation process will take some time, depending on the amount of data you are protecting. You can also see the progress in the **Monitoring** workspace under **Informational**. And, after a moment, you can see that the protection status is now labeled as being **OK**. If you select any protected member, underneath you can see the details. There's a link you can click on for the replica path where that's stored on the DPM server. Also, you can see whether any recovery points have been taken. In this instance, because it's just nearly established, there is currently only one recovery point. You can also see the amount of storage space consumed, as demonstrated in the following screenshot:

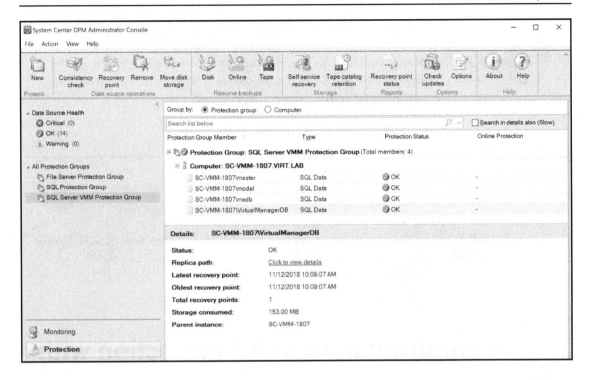

How it works...

Like file server backup, SCDPM uses VSS technology to take application-consistent snapshots of SQL Server. DPM tracks the blocks of SQL Server database files that are changed. For each synchronization job, SQL Server is quiesced to achieve a consistent state, a volume snapshot is taken, and a stable point in time of .mdf and .ldf files are copied to the DPM server. With DPM file system filters and the change bitmap, only the delta changes between synchronization jobs are copied to the DPM replica disk storage. With **Express full** backup, you can essentially do a full backup every day efficiently, both in terms of data transfer as well as storage on the DPM server.

In addition to **Express full** backup, DPM ships a transaction log to the DPM replica disk storage, thus minimizing data loss to up to 15 minutes. However, **Express full** backup is efficient in terms of data transfer on the DPM replica disk storage, but it requires high disk IOPS since storage snapshots are maintained on the production server while the backup data is being copied to the DPM. On the other hand, the **Transaction logs** backup is lightweight and enables up to a 15-minute **Recovery Point Objective** (**RPO**). However, this requires having the SQL database set its Recovery mode to **Full** and not **Simple**. In this case, DPM will be able to back up the **Transaction logs**.

Never use SCDPM and the SQL Server backup feature at the same time because the built-in SQL Server backup functionality will not update the SQL VSS information and, hence, it would interfere with DPM, the DPM agent will lose track of the changed blocks, and this could lead to a break in the transaction log chain.

See also

- Read this article to learn more about the supported SQL Server versions that could be protected with DPM: `https://docs.microsoft.com/en-us/system-center/dpm/dpm-protection-matrix?view=sc-dpm-1807`.
- Read this article to learn more about how to configure protection of SQL Server AlwaysOn configuration with DPM: `https://docs.microsoft.com/en-us/previous-versions/system-center/system-center-2012-R2/hh780998(v=sc.12)`.

Enable Windows bare metal protection with DPM

In this recipe, we'll enable **Windows bare metal** and **System state** protection. The **System state** backup enables you to recover when a machine starts but you've lost system files and registry. A **System state** backup includes the following:

- **Domain member**: Boot files, COM+ class registration database, registry
- **Domain controller**: Active Directory (NTDS), boot files, COM+ class registration database, registry, system volume (SYSVOL)
- **Machine running cluster services**: Additionally backs up cluster server metadata
- **Machine running certificate services**: Additionally backs up certificate data

On the other hand, **Bare Metal Recovery**, known as BMR, is useful. By definition, it includes a **System state** backup; for instance, it provides protection when a machine won't start and you have to recover everything.

Getting ready

Before you enable Windows bare metal protection, you need to make sure the following prerequisites are satisfied:

- The BMR feature only supports operating systems from Windows Server 2008 SP2 onward.
- Install DPM agents on each of the servers that need to be protected.
- The agent status should report **OK** in the DPM management console.

How to do it...

With the agents installed on the server that needs to be protected, you can enable bare metal protection. Complete the following steps to configure protection groups:

1. Open your DPM Administrator Console, click on the **Protection** workspace, and then click on the **New** button in the ribbon bar to start the wizard for creating a new protection group.
2. In the **Welcome to the New Protection Group Wizard** page, select **Servers**. Windows clients do not have an option for bare metal recovery, although you can protect them using system state only. Click on **Next >** to continue:

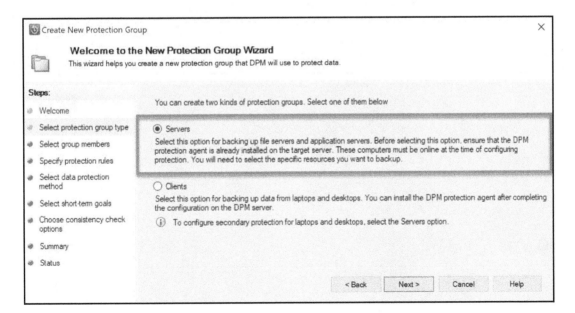

3. In the **Select Group Members** window, select and expand the server(s) that you intend to protect, and then expand **System Protection.** You could choose **System State**, which is essentially operating system files and also includes Active Directory if the server you are protecting is a domain controller. However, if you uncheck **System State** and instead check **Bare Metal Recovery**, notice that it will automatically turn on **System State**. Click on **Next >** to continue:

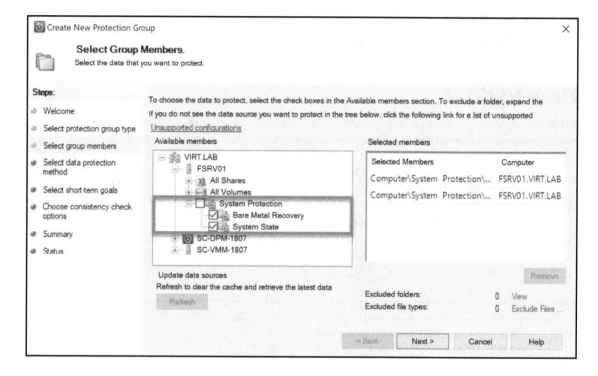

4. In the **Select Data Protection Method** page, select what method of protection you want to employ to protect your data and then type a value in the **Protection group name** field, as shown in the following screenshot. In this example, we won't enable online protection; we will keep it on-premises, with local DPM disk storage. Click on **Next >** to continue:

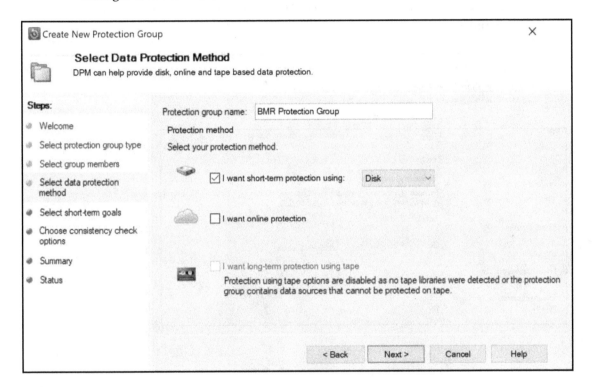

5. In the **Specify Short-Term Goals** page, select the **Retention range**, which is the number of days you want to keep the protected data in the backup storage. In this example, we'll set the retention range to 21 days. In the **Application recovery points** section, you can specify when to create a recovery point. If you click on **Modify...**, a new window will open, where you can choose the time of day as well as the days of the week. Click **OK** to confirm, and then click on **Next >** to continue:

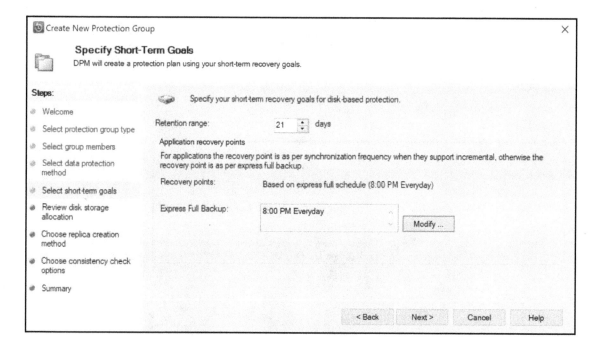

6. In the **Review Disk Storage Allocation** page, you can see **Total data size**, and the **Disk storage to be provisioned on DPM**. You can specify a **Target Storage** for each data source in case you have multiple volumes configured as target disk storage, or if you have configured **workload-aware storage** (**WAS**), so the volumes can be selected to preferentially store specific workloads or based on backup disk performance. In this example, we've got a total data size of **20.00 GB**, and disk storage to be provisioned on the DPM server is **34.24 GB**. Now, what's interesting is the fact that DPM is smart enough to filter out any storage that currently doesn't have enough space to accommodate what you're trying to protect. Click on **Next >** to continue:

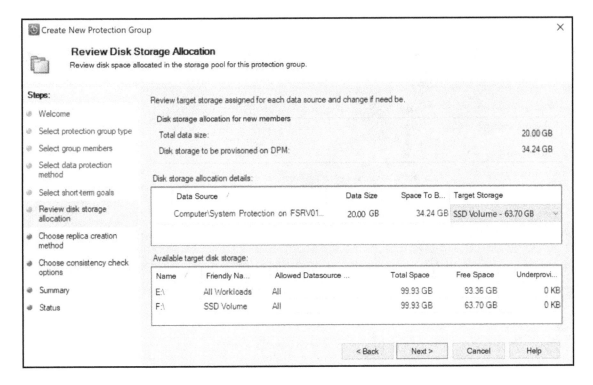

7. In the **Choose Replica Creation Method** page, you can define how the DPM sever should create the replica of the protected data source. You can create the replica **Now** over the network. Alternatively, because these are operating system files used for Bare Metal Recovery, you could choose **Later**, to defer this process until it's after work hours, for example. And there's always the manual option of using removable media. In this example, we will create the initial replica automatically over the network **Now**. Then click on **Next >** to continue:

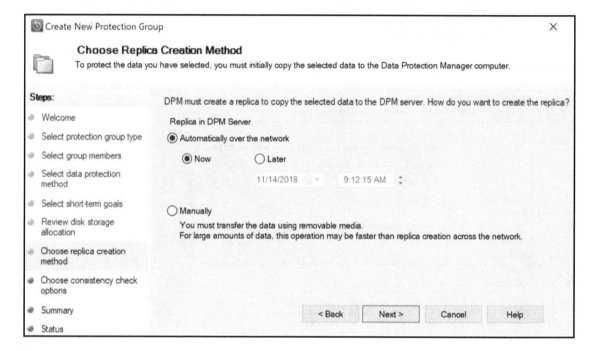

8. In the **Consistency check options** page, you can select the consistency check frequency. A consistency check can run only when the replicas become inconsistent, or on a daily schedule. In this example, we're going to turn on the daily consistency check, which will happen at midnight for a maximum of **8** hours. The purpose of this is to verify the integrity of the local backup replica on the DPM server. Click on **Next >** to continue:

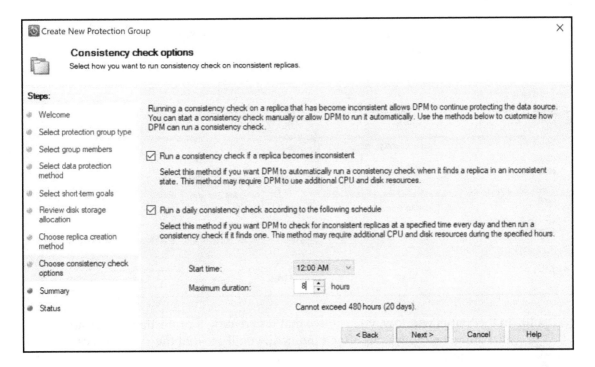

9. In the **Summary** page, you can see the results of your selections. Click on **Create Group**:

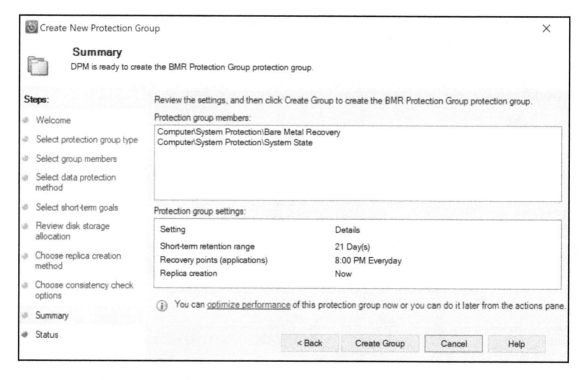

10. In the **Status** window, you can see that it's creating a protection group, and allocating the replica. So, after a moment, you'll see that they've all succeeded. Click **Close**.

11. Now that's because it could take a while. So, you could go to the **Monitoring** workspace in the bottom-left corner, and you can see under **Information**, that replica creation is currently in progress.

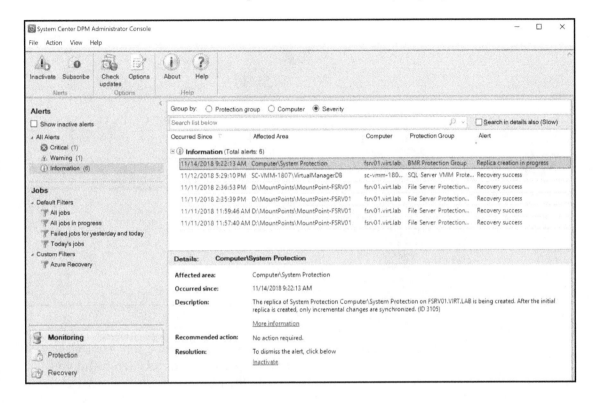

12. If you go back to the **Protection** workspace, the protection status for **Bare Metal Recovery** and **System State** is **OK**. And that's for the server in this example, FSRV01, as demonstrated in the following section:

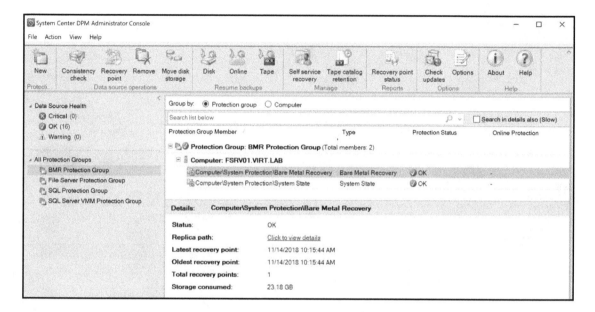

13. Now, as is the case with other protection groups, we have the option of right-clicking on something that's protected and then performing a consistency check, creating a recovery point, and even stopping protection of this item. And you have a lot of those same buttons available in the ribbon bar when you select the item that's being protected.

How it works...

When you choose a system state backup only, DPM communicates with **Windows Server Backup** (**WSB**) and requests a backup of the server's system state. By default DPM and WSB will use the drive with the most available free space, and the details pertaining to this drive are saved in the PSDataSourceConfig.XML file. This is the drive used by WSB to perform backups to.

On the other hand, when you choose the BMR option, which includes a system state backup, the backup job is performed directly to a share on the DPM server and not to a folder on the protected server. This share is created as follows:

1. The DPM server talks to WSB and shares out the replica volume for that BMR backup. In this step, it doesn't tell WSB to use the drive with the freest space, but instead it will create a specific share to use for the backup job.
2. When the backup finishes, the backup is transferred to the DPM server.
3. Finally, the logs are stored under `C:\Windows\Logs\WindowsServerBackup`.

There's more...

If you only perform system state backups, you can customize the drive that DPM uses for the system state backup. You can do this on the protected server, under `C:\Program Files\Microsoft Data Protection Manager\DPM\Datasources`. Open the `PSDataSourceConfig.XML` file for editing. Change the value of `<FilesToProtect>` to a different drive letter, as shown in the following screenshot. Save and close the file:

```
      <Size>1024</Size>
      <UseDRWithCC>true</UseDRWithCC>
    - <DatasourceCapabilities ExtendedCapabilityFlags="0" WaitForDatasourceServerTypeLock="false"
      DisplayTypeField="Disconnected Client" DisplayNameField="ComponentName"
      SupportedBackupType="Full">
          <DatasourceInfo xmlns="http://schemas.microsoft.com/2003/dls/DatasourceCapability.xsd"
              ValidateComponentFlags="15" Version="01.00.0000.00" WriterId="7b2e4c3d-876f-4535-b5c9-
              b344d4f05120"/>
          <OverlappedOperations
              xmlns="http://schemas.microsoft.com/2003/dls/DatasourceCapability.xsd"
              BackupRecovery="false" Recovery="false" Backup="0"/>
      </DatasourceCapabilities>
  </DatasourceConfig>
- <DatasourceConfig>
      <WriterId>8c3d00f9-3ce9-4563-b373-19837bc2835e</WriterId>
      <Version>01.00.0000.00</Version>
      <VssWriterInvolved>false</VssWriterInvolved>
      <LogicalPath>Computer</LogicalPath>
      <ComponentName>System Protection</ComponentName>
      <FilesToProtect>E:\WindowsImageBackup\*</FilesToProtect>
      <Size>51200</Size>
      <UseDRWithCC>true</UseDRWithCC>
    - <DatasourceCapabilities ExtendedCapabilityFlags="0" WaitForDatasourceServerTypeLock="false"
      DisplayTypeField="System Protection" DisplayNameField="ComponentName"
      SupportedBackupType="Full">
          <DatasourceInfo xmlns="http://schemas.microsoft.com/2003/dls/DatasourceCapability.xsd"
              ValidateComponentFlags="15" Version="01.00.0000.00" WriterId="8c3d00f9-3ce9-4563-b373-
              19837bc2835e"/>
          <OverlappedOperations
              xmlns="http://schemas.microsoft.com/2003/dls/DatasourceCapability.xsd"
              BackupRecovery="false" Recovery="false" Backup="0"/>
      </DatasourceCapabilities>
  </DatasourceConfig>
```

See also

- Read the following article to learn more about the support OS matrix for Windows bare metal in DPM **Long-Term Servicing Channel (LTSC)** and **Semi-Annual Channel (SAC)**: `https://docs.microsoft.com/en-us/system-center/` `dpm/dpm-protection-matrix?view=sc-dpm-1807`.
- Read the following article to learn more about the prerequisites and limitations for Windows bare metal and system state backup: `https://docs.microsoft.` `com/en-us/system-center/dpm/back-up-system-state-and-bare-metal?view=` `sc-dpm-1807#prerequisites-and-limitations`.

6
Securing Windows Client with DPM

In this chapter, we will cover the following recipes:

- Creating a plan for backing up end user data
- Plan for off-site end user backup
- Configuring DPM and Active Directory for end user protection
- Installing the agent automatically and manually on a client computer
- Performing image-level backups of client computers with DPM

 To follow the recipes in this chapter, you need to have successfully installed Microsoft System Center **Data Protection Manager** (**DPM**) and prepared your data storage repository for DPM.

Introduction

We all have user data, both personal and corporate data, and when it comes to corporate data, some of this data can often reside outside of our company's managed infrastructure. IT administrators often tend to struggle to protect corporate data that employees store and consume on their endpoint devices, be it a tablet, a laptop, or an all-in-one device.

When a company successfully implements a strategy to backup endpoint devices, the service often comes with restrictions on what is actually supported, the type of files that can be backed up, or the amount of data that can be backed up. Companies spend a lot of effort in the design and management of backing up servers and other critical IT systems that are permanently located inside the corporate network, and rightly so, but the greatest challenge can often be backing up endpoint devices that are recurrently disconnected from the corporate network.

You can deploy DPM to back up endpoint devices, along with client operating systems that are encapsulated inside a virtual machine when running on supported versions of Microsoft Hyper-V or VMware vSphere. Depending on the version of the client operating system, you can back up volumes, shares, folders, files, bare metal and system state, and even deduped volumes. DPM supports the following client operating systems (both 64-bit and 32-bit):

- Windows 10
- Windows 8 and 8.1
- Windows 7

Creating a plan for backing up end user data

Before you can start protecting Windows clients with Microsoft System Center DPM, you need to define a plan for backing up end user data and determine that all of the prerequisites for that plan are in place. The following recipe builds out this plan at a high level and shows you what things you need to check to ensure that you are in a position to support the backing up of end user data.

Getting ready

Before you can deploy Microsoft System Center DPM to protect Windows clients, you will need to verify that all of the deployment prerequisites have been met:

1. You will need to ensure that the version of the client operating system that you want to protect is actually supported by DPM. Supported client operating systems include the following:
   - Windows 10
   - Windows 8 and 8.1
   - Windows 7

2. A single DPM server can protect up to 3,000 client computers running either the 64-bit or 32-bit versions of the previously listed operating systems. If you have more than 3,000 client computers, then you will need to deploy more than one DPM server.

3. You will need to ensure that the endpoint devices you want to protect are in the same domain as your DPM server or in a domain that has a two-way trust relationship with the DPM domain.

DPM can actually protect computers that are in an untrusted domain or workgroup. You can authenticate these remote computers using local Windows Challenge/Response (NTLM) accounts or by using PKI certificates. However, this mechanism is not supported by client operating systems.

4. If the Windows client that you want to protect is behind a firewall, then you will need to set up firewall exceptions before you can install the DPM agent.

 If the Windows Firewall is configured on your client computer, the DPM agent during installation will set up the necessary exceptions. If you find yourself in the situation where you need to reset the Windows Firewall, then you can reconfigure it by running `SetDpmServer.exe`. If you are using a third-party firewall, then you will need to open the necessary ports manually.

5. You must have .NET Framework version 4.6 installed prior to installing the DPM agent.

6. DPM supports client computers that are wired or wirelessly connected to the **local area network** (**LAN**) and can back up client computers over a VPN. For VPN backup, including Direct Access, the ICMP protocol should be enabled on the client computer. The DPM agent can communicate via the following VPN protocols:

- Point-to-Point Tunneling Protocol (**PPTP**)
- Layer 2 Tunneling Protocol (**L2TP**)
- Secure Socket Tunneling Protocol (**SSTP**)
- Direct Access

 Direct Access is similar to a VPN connection but offers a transparent, always-on connection that is established at the machine level, rather than at the user level, like a VPN connection.

How to do it...

The following steps will guide you through creating a plan for backing up end user data:

1. From the **Start** screen, select **Microsoft System Center Data Protection Manager**. The DPM Administrator Console will load and the **Monitoring** task area will be highlighted.

2. Select the **Protection** task area. Click the **New** button on the ribbon bar and the **Welcome to the New Protection Group** wizard will appear.

3. In the **Welcome to the New Protection Group** wizard, click **Next**. On the **Select Protection Group Type** page, select **Client** and click **Next**.

4. On the **Select Group Members** page, either type the fully qualified domain name (FQDN) of the computer name you want to protect or add multiple computers in a single operation by using a text file and click **Next**.

   You can add multiple computers in a single operation via a text file. In the text file, you need to enter each computer on a new line. Microsoft recommends that you use the FQDN of the target computers. For example, would enter multiple computers in a `computers.txt` file as follows:
   `Win10a.virt.lab`
   `Win10b.virt.lab`
   `Win10c.virt.lab`

5. On the **Specify Inclusions and Exclusions** page, under **Folder Inclusions and Exclusions**, identify the folders to include or exclude from protection on the selected computers you are looking to back up. To select from a list of well-known folders, such as **Program Files**, **Desktop**, **Downloads**, or **My Videos**, click the drop-down list. Under **File type exclusions**, identify the file types to exclude by using their file extensions, separating multiple entries via a comma, and click **Next**:

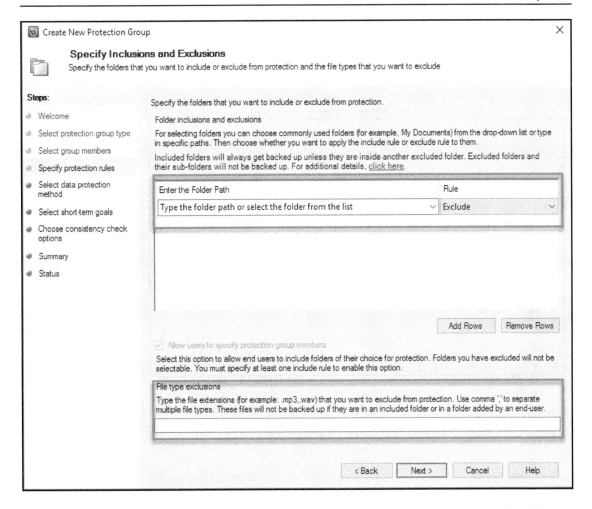

6. In the **Select Data Protection Method** page, identify how you want to handle short- and long-term backup and click **Next**.

Short-term backup always reverts to disk storage first, with the option of backing up from disk storage to public Azure with Azure Backup (for both short- or long-term backup). As an alternative to long-term backup to public Azure, you can also configure long-term backup to a supported standalone tape device or tape library that is connected to your DPM server.

7. In the **Select Short-Term Goals** page, identify your short-term recovery goals for disk-based protection. In **Retention Range**, identify how long you want to keep the data on disk; by default, this is five days. In **Synchronization Frequency**, identify how often you want to run an incremental backup to disk; by default, this is every 4 hours. In the **Alerting Option** field, identify the frequency of when you get alerted about a disconnected computer; by default, this is at 14 days. Click **Next**:

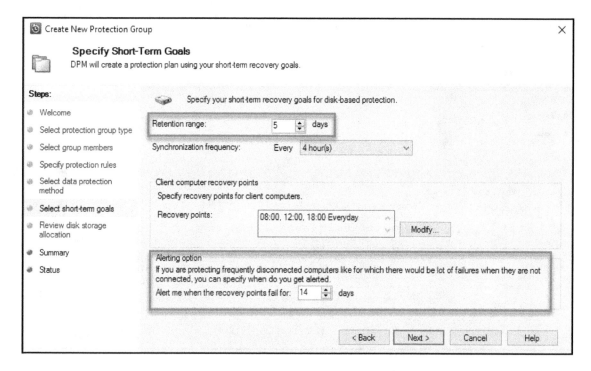

8. In the **Review Disk Storage Allocation page**, review the storage pool disk space that has been allocated to this protection group and click **Next**.

9. On the **Summary** page, review the settings that will be used to create the recovery group and click **Create Group**, and then click **Close**. After the initial replication of the data occurs, the newly created protection group status will show up as **OK** on the **Status** page. Backups then take place in line with the settings you have identified for the protection group.

How it works...

Before you can deploy Microsoft System Center DPM to protect Windows clients, there is an element of planning required. This ensures that you have met all of the prerequisites. Once those prerequisites have been verified, you can go ahead and start protecting Windows clients.

You start by creating a protection group. Here, you need to define that you are protecting clients (rather than servers). Next, you add members; this can be individually or you can bulk-add members by using a `.txt` file. Once members have been added to the protection group, you need to specify what you want to include and exclude from your backup.

Next, you configure your data protection method by specifying your short- and long-term backup requirements. Finally, you review the disk storage allocation requirements for your protection group and the first backup occurs.

See also

The following blog post shows you how to add or remove disk quotas for protected client computers that are protected by Microsoft System Center DPM: `https://blogs.technet.microsoft.com/dpm/2011/05/02/a-script-to-set-or-remove-disk-quotas-for-protected-client-computers-in-system-center-data-protection-manager/`.

Plan for off-site end user backup

In the previous recipe, we looked at the prerequisites that are required to set up Windows client protection and set up an initial protection group so that we could start an initial synchronization. Now, let's look a bit deeper into what is required when protecting clients off-site.

Getting ready

Microsoft System Center DPM can protect Windows clients when they are connected either via a VPN or DirectAccess connection. For Windows clients that are recurringly disconnected, it is recommended that the endpoint device has a minimum network bandwidth of 1 **megabit per second** (**Mbps**). For Windows clients that are permanently connected to the network, it is recommended that the endpoint device has a minimum network bandwidth of 256 **kilobits per second** (**Kbps**).

In DPM, when a backup or replica occurs, a complete copy of the protected data is transmitted from the DPM agent running on the protected machine to the DPM server. Creating a replica is one of the more resource intensive tasks in DPM, and greatly impacts network I/O. The performance of the replica creation will, for off-site users, be typically limited by the speed of the actual network connection between the DPM server and the protected machine. The following table shows the amount of time it would take, at varying network speeds, to transmit known amounts of data. Times are shown in hours, except where they are expressly shown in minutes:

Data size	Network speed 1 Gbps	Network speed 100 Mbps	Network speed 32 Mbps	Network speed 8 Mbps	Network speed 2 Mbps	Network speed 512 Kbps
1 GB	less than 1 minute	less than 1 hour	less than 1 hour	less than 1 hour	1.5	6
50 GB	less than 10 minutes	1.5 hour	5	18	71	284
200 GB	less than 36 minutes	6 hours	18	71	284	1137
500 GB	less than 1.5 hours	15	45	178	711	2844

The impact of replica creation on the overall network's performance can be reduced by using the on-the-wire compression capabilities in DPM.

How to do it...

The following steps will guide you through enabling on-the-wire compression for client protection:

1. From the **Start** screen, select **Microsoft System Center Data Protection Manager**. The DPM Administrator Console will load and the Monitoring task area will be highlighted.
2. Select the **Protection** task area. In the **Display** pane, select the client protection group that you previously created and click **Optimize** icon on the ribbon bar.
3. On the **Network** tab, check **Enable on-the-wire compression**. You can further optimize the performance of the protection group by offsetting the start time of synchronization jobs across this client protection group and other protection groups you have configured. Select the hours and minutes to offset the start of the synchronization job and click **OK**.

How it works...

When you create a protection group, you can optimize that protection group by enabling the following two properties of that protection group:

- By enabling compression on the protection group
- By offsetting the start time of synchronization jobs across your various protection groups

Launch the Microsoft System Center DPM Administration Console, go to the **Protection** task area, and select the client protection group that you want to optimize. Here, you can enable compression and offset the start time of your synchronization job for that particular protection group. Be aware that the maximum allowed value for the scheduled offset is the same as the synchronization frequency.

See also

The following blog post shows you how to configure client auto-deployment in Microsoft System Center DPM: https://docs.microsoft.com/en-us/previous-versions/system-center/system-center-2012-R2/hh758144(v=sc.12).

Configuring DPM and Active Directory for end user protection

Configuring Microsoft System Center DPM and **Active Directory** (**AD**) for end user protection allows you to empower your users to independently control their own backup, and it also provides the ability for the end-user to be able to recover their own data as well.

Getting ready

Before you can configure Microsoft System Center DPM and AD for end-user protection, you will need to verify that all of the deployment prerequisites have been met:

1. You will need to configure AD to support end user recovery by carrying out the following tasks:
   - By extending the AD schema
   - Creating an AD container object
   - Granting permissions to the DPM server to change the content of the previously mentioned container
   - Adding mappings between the source shares and the replica shares

2. You will need to enable the **Volume Shadow Copy** service on the protected Windows clients.

Where you already have both schema and domain administrator privileges in AD, the process to extend the schema, the creation of a container object, and granting permissions on the container object for the DPM server can be completed with a few simple steps within the DPM console. For non-schema and domain administrators, the DPMADSchemaExtension tool can be run manually to complete the configuration. The DPMADSchemaExtension tool can be located on the DPM server in the Microsoft System Center\DPM\DPM\BIN\1033 folder.

How to do it...

The following steps will guide you through enabling Active Directory for end user protection:

1. From the **Start** screen, select **Microsoft System Center Data Protection Manager**. The DPM Administrator Console will load and the **Monitoring** task area will be highlighted.

2. Select the **Management** task area. Click the **Options** icon on the ribbon bar. The **Options** dialog box will appear; on the **End-user Recovery** tab, click the **Configure Active Directory** button:

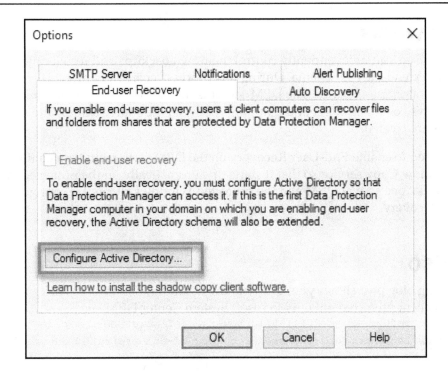

3. In the **Configure Active Directory** dialog box, select **Use current credentials** or specify the username and password of an account that has both the AD schema and domain administrator privileges, and then click **OK**.

4. In the **Active Directory Configuration for Data Protection Manager** dialog box, click **Yes**, and then click **OK**.

5. Next, select the **Recovery** task area. Click the **Options** icon on the ribbon bar. The **Options** dialog box appear. On the **End-user Recovery** tab, click the **Configure Active Directory** button.

6. Click the **End User Recovery** icon on the ribbon bar. On the **End-User Recovery** tab, enable the **End-User Recovery** checkbox and click **OK**.

7. Finally, before your users can begin to independently recover previous versions of their files and applications, the Volume Shadow Copy service must be configured to automatically start on the protected Windows client.

How it works...

Before your users can independently control their own backups and recover their own data, you need to extend the AD schema. During this process, a container object is created, called `MS-ShareMapConfiguration`. The DPM server is then granted permissions to change the contents of this container object and mappings between the source shares, and shares on the replicas are created.

Next, you need to enable **End-User Recovery** on the DPM server and then configure the Volume Shadow Copy service so that it starts up automatically on the protected Windows clients. This is done so that DPM and the protected Windows clients are configured for **End-User Recovery**.

See also

The following blog post shows you how to allow non-administrators to perform end-user recovery of client protected data in Microsoft System Center DPM: `https://blogs.technet.microsoft.com/dpm/2011/05/10/how-to-configure-the-dpm-client-to-allow-non-admin-users-to-perform-end-user-recovery-of-dpm-protected-data/`.

Installing the agent automatically and manually on a client computer

With Microsoft System Center DPM, there are two approaches to installing the DPM agent on client computers that you want to start protecting. The first approach is to push the agent installation automatically through the DPM Administrator Console, and the second approach is to install the agent manually. If you need to install the DPM agent on a number of client computers, then you can automate this process through scripting.

Getting ready

The Microsoft System Center DPM agent can be installed on computers that are in the same domain as the DPM server, in a workgroup, and in an untrusted domain. If you deploy the DPM agent manually, then you will need to attach the agent to the DPM server post deployment. For the DPM agent to be able to communicate with the DPM server through a firewall, specific firewall exceptions are required.

How to do it...

The following steps will guide you through installing the DPM agent automatically and then manually on client computers:

1. From the **Start** screen, select **Microsoft System Center Data Protection Manager**. The DPM Administrator Console will load and the **Monitoring** task area will be highlighted.
2. Select the **Management** task area. Click the **Install** icon on the ribbon bar. On the **Select Agent Deployment Method** page, click **Install Agents** radio button, and click **Next**.
3. On the **Select Computers** page, enter the computer name of the client you want to protect using the FQDN and click **Next**.
4. On the **Enter Credentials** page, type in the credentials for a domain account that is a member of the local administrators group on the selected client computer.
5. On the **Choose Restart Method** page, select the most appropriate method to use to restart the selected client computer, post the deployment of the DPM agent, and click **Next**. On the **Summary** page, click Install.

 The client computer must be restarted before you can start protecting data on this client. The restart is required to load the volume filter that DPM agent uses to track and transfer block-level changes between the DPM server itself and the protected client computer.

If you decide to deploy the DPM agent manually and the client computer is behind a firewall, you will need to ensure that the DPM agent can be pushed out through the firewall. With the Windows Firewall, you run the following command from an elevated Command Prompt:

```
netsh advfirewall firewall add rule name="Allow DPM Remote Agent Push"
dir=in action=allow service=any enable=yes profile=any remoteip=<IPAddress>
```

Here IPAddress is the actual IP address of the DPM server.

1. On the client computer that you want to protect, open an elevated Command Prompt window, and then type net use * \\DPMServerName\DriveWhereDPMIsLocated. Then, navigate to the \Microsoft System Center 2016\DPM\DPM\ProtectionAgents\RA5.0.322.0\amd64\1033 folder for 64-bit client computers or \i386\1033 for 32-bit client computers.

2. To manually install the protection agent, do the following:
    - For a 64-bit client computer, type `DpmAgentInstaller_x64.exe /q DPMServerName /IAcceptEULA`, where `DPMServerName` is the FQDN of the DPM server
    - For a 32-bit computer, type `DpmAgentInstaller_x86.exe /q DPMServerName /IAcceptEULA`, where `DPMServerName` is the FQDN of the DPM server

3. If you installed the DPM agent before you added the client computer to the DPM server, you must attach the client computer before the DPM server can begin to create backups.

4. From the **Start** screen, select **Microsoft System Center Data Protection Manager**. The DPM Administrator Console will loads and the **Monitoring** task area will be highlighted.

5. Select the **Management** task area. Click the **Install** icon on the ribbon bar. On the **Select Agent Deployment Method** page, click **Attach Agents** radio button. Ensure that the **Computer on Trusted Domain** radio button is also selected, and click **Next**.

6. On the **Select Computers** page, enter the computer name of the client you want to attach to the DPM server using the FQDN and click **Next**.

7. On the **Enter Credentials** page, type the credentials for a domain account that is a member of the local administrators group on the selected client computer and click **Next**. On the **Summary** page, click **Attach**, and then click **Close**.

How it works...

When you install the DPM agent automatically from the DPM administrator console, you first need to ensure that you have the required Windows Firewall exceptions in place on the Windows client to allow a push install to occur. Once you have specified the FQDN of the Windows client, provided your credentials to carry out the installation, and chosen a restart method for the DPM agent, the DPM agent will be deployed.

You can also manually deploy the DPM agent. You will find the required DPM agent software on the DPM server. Map a drive to this location (the volume where the DPM software is installed) and run `DpmAgentInstaller_x86.exe`. Once the DPM agent software has been successfully deployed, you will need to attach the client computer to the DPM server before backups can begin.

Performing image-level backups of client computers with DPM

Performing image-level backups of client computers with Microsoft System Center DPM is not a supported scenario. However, the ability to carry out an image-level backup of a client is a scenario that certain industry-vertical customers (such as those in manufacturing) ask for from time to time.

Getting ready

Microsoft System Center DPM and earlier versions of DPM are not natively able to perform image-level backups of any supported client operating systems that appear in the Microsoft support matrix. To protect a client's system state or perform an image-level backup, you will need to use the image backup feature in Windows 10 to first create an image-level backup. This backup option will include a full installation of the operating system itself, components of the operating system (such as settings, desktop, and Windows applications), and any personal data.

You can use the image backup feature in Windows 10 to carry out an image-level backup to a local drive and then let DPM back this data up. This is, however, a workaround, and not an ideal scenario.

How to do it...

The following steps will guide you through performing an image-level backup of a client computer:

1. In Windows 10, right-click on the **Start** button, click **Settings**, click **Update & Security**, and then click **Backup**.
2. In the **Settings | Backup** page, click the Plus sign next to the **Add Drive** option and select the local drive you are going to back up to. Ensure that **Automatically Backup my Files** is enabled. By default, **File History** runs hourly.
3. File History in Windows 10 will protect all of the folders in your `User` folder. To add other folders to **File History**, click the **More Options** link and scroll down to the Plus sign next to **Back up these Folders**.
4. You can also add a list of folders to specifically exclude from the backup. Scroll down to the Plus sign next to **Exclude these Folders** and select the folders you want to exclude.

How it works...

To be able to protect a client's system state or perform an image-level backup, you will need to use the image backup feature in Windows 10 and create an image-level backup. Here, your backup target is a local drive, or you can even use an external USB key. By default, the backup of a Windows 10 client computer occurs hourly, but this is configurable. You can identify both the folders that you want to include and exclude. Then, you simply use Microsoft System Center DPM to centrally back up this data.

7
Protecting Microsoft Azure Stack with DPM

In this chapter, we will cover the following recipes:

- Preparing to back up Azure Stack with SCDPM
- Backing up the Azure Stack infrastructure layer
- Backing up the Azure Stack tenant layer
- Overview of cloud recovery

Introduction

This chapter is designed to provide you with the insights, skills, and techniques for protecting Microsoft Azure Stack with a Microsoft **System Center Data Protection Manager** (**SCDPM**) server. After reading this chapter, you will have the knowledge to protect Azure Stack, by configuring data protection at both the infrastructure and tenant layers, but you will also be equipped with the ability to talk to your Azure Stack OEM provider about the basics of cloud recovery.

To follow the recipes in this chapter, you need to have installed Microsoft SCDPM successfully and also have either the **Azure Stack Development Kit** (**ASDK**) or a multinode Azure Stack appliance installed and configured.

Preparing to back up Azure Stack with DPM

Microsoft Azure Stack is not a traditional monolithic application, and so the topic of data protection with Microsoft Azure Stack is divided into two distinct and separate sets of tasks: infrastructure backup and tenant backup. The approach to each task is quite different. For instance, the infrastructure backup can't initially be backed up by an SCDPM server, so a component of Microsoft Azure Stack, the Backup Resource Provider, carries out this task. Subsequently, the backup repository created by the Backup Resource Provider requires data protection and this is where SCDPM comes in to support the infrastructure backup task.

The Microsoft Azure Stack infrastructure backup, Backup Resource Provider, requires a **Server Message Block** (**SMB**) 3.x file share to operate. This SMB 3.x file share must be external to the Microsoft Azure Stack appliance, so here you could leverage an existing SMB 3.x storage solution, such as a Windows file server or a third-party storage solution.

Placing the infrastructure backup on the **hardware lifecycle host** (**HLH**) may not be an operation that is supported by your **original equipment manufacturer** (**OEM**), so you should check with your OEM before thinking about using the HLH as a backup target. Your OEM will also provide instructions for manually backing up other components within the Azure Stack solution, such as the network switches and the HLH itself. You should also consider keeping these backup items in the same repository as the infrastructure backup. This will expedite any cloud recovery process.

Tenant data is less complex: Microsoft Azure Stack supports the backup of both Windows- and Linux-based virtual machines by deploying backup agents inside the virtual machine. Here, SCDPM can have access to the guest operating system and can easily protect operating system states, files, folders, and application data. If you so choose too, you can back up your data on-premises or to the cloud with public Azure.

Getting ready

Before you can start to protect your Microsoft Azure Stack appliance, there are a number of things that you need to consider and plan for. You need an SMB 3.x file share that is accessible from Microsoft Azure Stack, and this may mean that you need to modify your edge firewall to allow infrastructure backup. Typically, an outbound connection to either the IP address or the **fully qualified domain name** (**FQDN**) of the target file server is all that is required on port 445.

You also need to size your backup repository according to your needs. Microsoft recommends that you carry out an infrastructure backup at least twice a day (that is, every 12 hours), although this backup can be configured to occur every 4 hours minimum, and Microsoft further recommends that you keep no more than 7 days' worth of backups online. Again this is configurable, with the minimum retention period being 2 days and the maximum retention period being 14 days.

Each backup payload is projected to be around 10 GB in size and so the total space requirements, following those guidelines for every 12 hours with a retention period of 7 days, is around 140 GB.

How to do it...

To create a file share that can support Microsoft Azure Backup, follow these steps:

1. Create a local folder on your existing SMB 3.x storage solution. For example, create a folder called **AzSBackup** on the appropriate storage volume, so `V:\AzSBackup`.
2. Right-click the folder you have just created, and then click **Properties**.
3. Click the **Sharing** tab, and then click **Share**.
4. Enter the name of **Domain Computers**, and click **Add**.
5. In the **Permission level** column, select **Read/Write**, then click **Share**.

Make a note of the network path that is shown on the confirmation screen, as you will use this later when you are configuring infrastructure backup on your Microsoft Azure Stack appliance. The network path will be shown in the following format: `\\server-name\AzSBackup`.

Ensure that permissions on the folder, subfolders, and files are set to full control for the object, **Domain Computers**, you selected in the previous step. To do this, follow the steps:

1. Click the **Security** tab.
2. Select the object, **Domain Computers** that you added in the previous step.
3. Click **Advanced** and check that **Domain Computers** has full control and that this permission applies to the folder, subfolders, and files.
4. Click the **Effective Access** tab, then click **Select Domain Computers** and enter your user account credentials.
5. Click **View effective access** and check in the **Permission** column that the **Domain Computers** object has full control.

How it works...

Creating a file share is a necessary prerequisite before you can configure infrastructure backup in Microsoft Azure Stack. The file share is used to store all the infrastructure backup metadata and must be accessible to the Infrastructure Backup Resource Provider running on your Microsoft Azure Stack appliance. You can create a file share on your existing SMB storage solution, such as a Windows file server or on a third-party storage solution that supports SMB 3.x within your wider data center environment.

There's more...

To ensure your SMB 3.x file share is accessible from Microsoft Azure Stack, you can connect to the privileged endpoint via a remote PowerShell session. If you are completing this task from an **Azure Stack Development Kit** (**ASDK**), then these virtual machines have a prefixed name that is **AzS-ERCS01**. If you are using a Microsoft Azure Stack appliance, then there are three instances of this privileged endpoint that have a customer-defined prefix (Prefix-ERCS01, Prefix-ERCS02, and Prefix-ERCS03).

Before you begin, make sure you can access the privileged endpoint either via an IP address or through a DNS name. After the initial deployment of a Microsoft Azure Stack appliance, you can only access the privileged endpoint by IP address. This is because DNS integration may not have occurred yet. The first three octets of the IP address are customer-defined, but the fourth octet's starting address for Prefix-ERCS01 is x.y.z.224, and Prefix-ERCS03 is x.y.z.226.

On your **Privileged Access Workstation** (**PAW**), follow these steps:

1. From your PAW click **Start**, type `PowerShell`, right-click the **Windows PowerShell** application, and select **Run as administrator**.
2. Run the following command from within the elevated PowerShell session to add the IP address of the privileged endpoint as a trusted host:

```
winrm s winrm/config/client '@{TrustedHosts="x.y.z.224"}'
```

3. Run the following command to establish a remote session with the targeted privileged endpoint so that you can run a specific set of PowerShell commands:

```
$cred = Get-Credential

Enter-PSSession -ComputerName x.y.z.224 `
    -ConfigurationName PrivilegedEndpoint -Credential $cred
```

4. Run the following command to ensure that the SMB 3.x file share is accessible from Microsoft Azure Stack:

```
Test-Connection <IP_address_of_File_Server>\AzSBackup
```

See also

For further background information on the prerequisites, please check out https://docs.microsoft.com/en-us/azure/azure-stack/azure-stack-backup-reference.

Backing up the infrastructure layer

You can enable infrastructure backup either through the Microsoft Azure Stack Administration Portal or via a set of PowerShell cmdlets. You can then use these backups to restore your Microsoft Azure Stack appliance, by using cloud recovery in the event of a total failure of your appliance. Cloud recovery allows your cloud operators and tenants to log back in to either the Administration or Tenant Portal after a cloud recovery is complete.

Cloud recovery ensures that tenants have their subscriptions restored, including any roles and role-based access permissions, plans, offers, and any previously defined quotas for either compute, storage, or network. However, the Infrastructure Backup Service does not back up tenant **infrastructure as a service** (**IaaS**) virtual machines or network configurations, nor any storage resources, such as storage accounts, blobs, tables, and queues. So, when tenants log on after the cloud recovery process has completed, they will not see any of their previously existing resources or services. It is also worth noting that any **Platform as a Service** (**PaaS**) services and associated data are also not backed up. System administrators need to plan separately for backing up and restoring IaaS and PaaS resources.

Getting ready

Before you can configure the infrastructure backup service, there are a couple of things that you need to obtain first. You need to be able to log in to the Microsoft Azure Stack Administration Portal and/or connect to Microsoft Azure Stack using PowerShell. For this, you need a set of cloud admin credentials and, if you plan to connect via PowerShell, you will need PowerShell modules for Azure Stack loaded.

You also need to provide a preshared key when configuring infrastructure backup. The infrastructure backup is encrypted with AES 256 using this key. Take precautions to store this key securely. Once you have specified the preshared key for the first time, or have rotated this secret in the future, you can't view this key from the Administration Portal. To generate this key, run the following PowerShell commands (note this assumes you are running a Microsoft Azure Stack appliance in an internet-connected scenario):

```
# Install the AzureRM.Bootstrapper module. Select Yes when prompted to
install NuGet
 Install-Module -Name AzureRm.BootStrapper -Force

# Install and import the API Version Profile required by Azure Stack 1808
into the current PowerShell session.
 Use-AzureRmProfile -Profile 2018-03-01-hybrid -Force

 Install-Module -Name AzureStack -RequiredVersion 1.5.0

# Generate and view the encryption key for infrastructure backups

 $encryptionkey = New-AzsEncryptionKeyBase64
 $encryptionkey
```

If you are operating your Microsoft Azure Stack appliance in a disconnected scenario, you need to download the PowerShell modules to a machine that has internet connectivity and install the modules offline.

How to do it...

To enable infrastructure backup from the Administration Portal, follow these steps:

1. Log in to the Microsoft Azure Stack Administration Portal, select **All services**, and then under the **Administration** category select **Infrastructure backup**.
2. Enter the **Server Message Block (SMB)** 3.x file share path to the **Backup storage location,** for example, `\\server-name\AzSBackup`.
3. Type the **Username** and **Password** combination that has read and write access permissions to the SMB 3.x file share.

4. In the **Backup frequency in hours**, specify how often backups will occur. As a reminder, the default value is 12 and the Infrastructure Backup Scheduler supports a maximum of 12 hours and a minimum of 4 hours.

5. In the **Retention period in days**, specify how many days of backups will be preserved in the backup storage location. As a reminder, the default value is **7**. The scheduler supports a maximum of 14 and a minimum of 2 days. Backups that are older than the defined retention period will automatically be deleted from the backup storage location.

6. In the **Encryption key**, enter the previously generated encryption key and click **OK**.

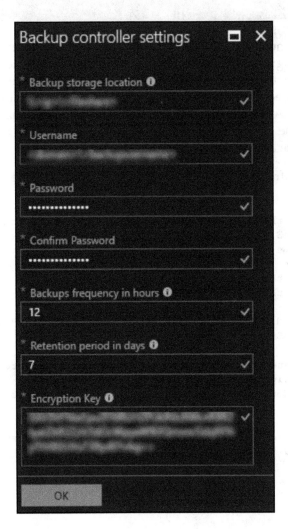

7. To initiate an on-demand backup, click on the **Backup now** button:

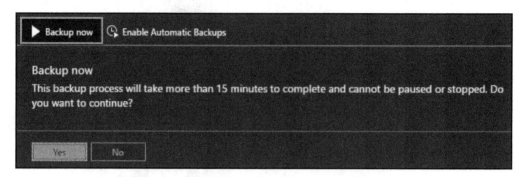

> There is no need to **Enable Automatic Backups** automatically when you are configuring the infrastructure backup service. When you enable the infrastructure backup service, **Automatic Backups** are scheduled for you. If you need to disable future scheduled backups, you can click on the **Disable Automatic Backups** button. Disabling automatic backups will retain the infrastructure backup service configuration and simply postpone any future scheduled backups.

8. To enable infrastructure backup from PowerShell, run the following PowerShell commands:

```
# Enter the Username that has read and write access permissions to
the SMB 3.x file share
$username = "domain\admin"

# Enter the SMB 3.x file share path
$sharepath = "\\serverIP\AzSBackupStore\"

$password = Read-Host -Prompt ("Password for: " + $username) -
AsSecureString

# Generate the encryption key for infrastructure backups
$Encryptionkey = New-AzsEncryptionKeyBase64
$key = ConvertTo-SecureString -String ($Encryptionkey) -AsPlainText
-Force

Set-AzsBackupShare -BackupShare $sharepath -Username $username -
Password $password -EncryptionKey $key
```

9. To confirm your infrastructure backup settings, run the following PowerShell commands:

```
Get-AzsBackupLocation | Select-Object -Property Path, UserName
```

10. To update your infrastructure backup settings, and specify the retention period and frequency of backups, run the following PowerShell commands:

```
# Set the infrastructure backup frequency and retention period
values.
$frequencyInHours = 12
$retentionPeriodInDays = 7

Set-AzsBackupShare -BackupFrequencyInHours $frequencyInHours -
BackupRetentionPeriodInDays $retentionPeriodInDays
Get-AzsBackupLocation | Select-Object -Property Path, UserName,
AvailableCapacity, BackupFrequencyInHours,
BackupRetentionPeriodInDays
```

How it works...

When you enable the Infrastructure Backup Service on your Microsoft Azure Stack appliance, with either the Administration Portal or via PowerShell, the infrastructure backup service takes periodic backups of the following items:

- Internal identity service and root certificate
- User plans, offers, and subscriptions
- Key vault secrets
- User RBAC roles and policies

You can access either the Microsoft Azure Stack Administration Portal or PowerShell to enable backups, start or pause backups, and get backup information.

There's more...

To execute an on-demand backup on Microsoft Azure Stack when the infrastructure backup service is configured, run the following PowerShell command:

```
Start-AzsBackup -Force
```

To confirm that the infrastructure backup has been completed from the Microsoft Azure Stack Administration Portal, follow these steps:

1. Log in to the **Microsoft Azure Stack Administration Portal**, select **All services**, and then under the **Administration** category, select **Infrastructure backup**.
2. Choose **Configuration** and find the **Name** and **Date Completed** of the backup in the **Available backups** list.
3. Verify the **State** is **Succeeded**.

To confirm that the infrastructure backup has been completed, run the following PowerShell command:

```
Get-AzsBackup
```

Backing up the Azure Stack tenant layer

You can use SCDPM to protect folders, files, and applications on Microsoft Azure Stack. To back up folders, files, and applications, install SCDPM as a virtual machine running on Microsoft Azure Stack. You can protect folders, files, and applications on any Microsoft Azure Stack virtual machine in the same virtual network.

Once you have installed SCDPM, you need to add additional Azure Stack storage to your SCDPM virtual machine to increase the local storage available for short-term backup data. If you operate your Microsoft Azure Stack in a connected scenario, then you can use public Azure for long-term retention.

If you are operating your Microsoft Azure Stack in a disconnected scenario, then you should consider leveraging an external disk array via iSCSI to support long-term retention.

Getting ready

SCDPM can perform both host- or guest-level backups. At the host level, an SCDPM protection agent is installed on the host server or cluster and protects the entire set of virtual machines and data files running on that host. However, Microsoft Azure Stack is a sealed appliance, where the infrastructure is secured, and so SCDPM protection agents running on the Microsoft Azure Stack nodes are not supported.

At the guest level, the SCDPM protection agent is installed on each supported **virtual machine** (**VM**) and protects folders, files, and the workload present in that VM. Here, you are basically treating the VM in the same way as you would treat a physical or bare-metal machine.

How to do it...

To enable backup of the Microsoft Azure Stack tenant layer, follow these steps:

1. In the SCDPM console, click **Protection** and in the toolbar, click **New** to open the **Create New Protection Group** wizard:

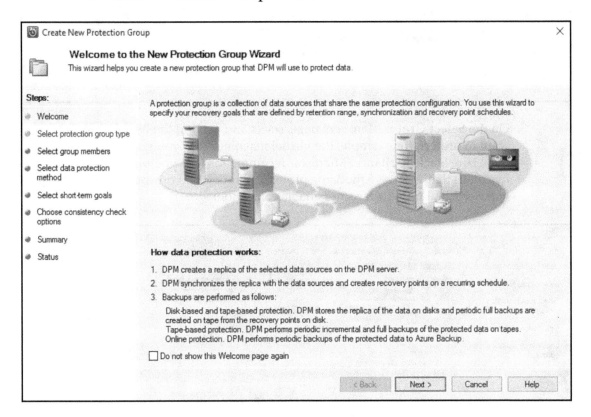

2. On the **Select Protection Group Type** page, choose **Servers** and click **Next**:

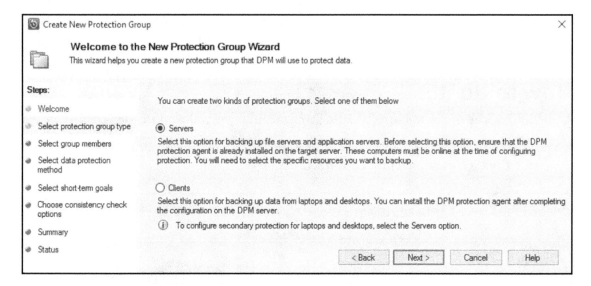

3. On the **Select Group Members** page, select and expand the list of items that you want to protect, for example, the virtual machines that you want to protect from the Azure Stack appliance. Microsoft recommends that you put all the virtual machines that will have the same protection policy into one protection group to make efficient use of space and enable colocation:

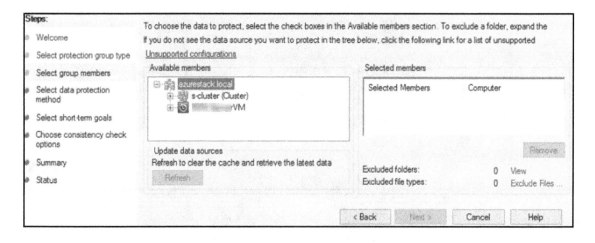

4. On the **Select Data Protection Method** page, type a name for your protection group, for example, **AzSBackup**. Select the checkbox for **I want short-term protection using disk** and optionally, if operating your Azure Stack in a connected scenario, select **I want online protection**. Then, click **Next**.

5. On the **Specify Short-Term Goals** page, choose how long to retain the recovery points saved to disk and when to save incremental backups. Then, click **Next**.

6. On the **Review disk allocation** page, review the storage pool disk space allocated for the protection group. Note, **Total data size** is the amount of data you want to protect, and **Disk space to be provisioned on DPM server**, is the space that SCDPM recommends allocating for your protection group. Then, click **Next**.

7. On the **Choose replica creation method** page, select how you want to handle the initial full data replication. If you decide to replicate over the network, Microsoft recommends that you choose an off-peak period. Then, click **Next**.

8. On the **Choose consistency check options** page, select how you want to automate consistency checks. Enable consistency checks to run only when data replication becomes inconsistent, or according to a schedule. Then, click **Next**.

9. If you opt to back up to public Azure, on the **Specify online protection data**, page make sure the workloads you want to back up to public Azure are selected. Then, click **Next**.

10. In the **Specify online backup schedule**, specify how frequently incremental backups to public Azure should occur. You can plan backups to run every day/week/month/year and the time/date at which they should run. Backups can happen up to two times per day.

11. On the **Specify online retention policy** page, you can specify how the recovery points created from the daily/weekly/monthly/yearly backups are retained.

12. On the **Choose online replication** page, specify how the initial full replication of data will occur. You can replicate over the network, or do an offline backup (offline prestaging).

13. On the **Summary** page, review your settings. After you click **Create Group**, the initial replication of your data will occur. When it is complete, the protection group status will appear as **OK** on the **Status** page. Backups will then happen according to the settings for the protection group you previously defined.

How it works...

System Center Data Protection Manager (SCDPM) supports guest-based backups. Microsoft Azure Stack virtual machines operate similarly to physical machines. This allows for a backup agent to be installed inside the virtual machine and allows for the backing up of that virtual machine as though it were physical.

Once you have installed and configured your SCDPM server, you can install the SCDPM protection agent inside the virtual machine. You will start by creating a new protection group and then select and expand the list of items that you want to protect. Next, you specify your short-term goals and review the disk allocation requirements. Finally, you specify the initial replication settings for your data and how you want to automate SCDPM consistency checks.

See also

Check out `Chapter 1`, *Installing and Upgrading DPM* and the *Installing DPM and Installing the DPM agents* recipes for more details on how to get Microsoft System Center Data Protection Manager up and running as a virtual machine on Microsoft Azure Stack, in the same virtual network as the tenant workloads that require protection.

Overview of cloud recovery

Today, Microsoft only supports a single Microsoft Azure Stack region and that Azure Stack region supports a single Microsoft Azure Stack scale unit. Currently, a scale unit is synonymous with a rack and consists of a minimum of four scale unit nodes and a maximum of 16 scale unit nodes, an HLH, two top-of-rack switches, one **baseboard management controller** (**BMC**) switch, power distribution units, and a rack. This exposes your Microsoft Azure Stack appliance to the risk of catastrophic events at your data center or failures due to hardware, operational, or product issues.

If such a disaster strikes, your Microsoft Azure Stack appliance goes offline. At that point, all of the data is potentially unrecoverable. Depending on the root cause analysis of your data loss, you may need to repair an infrastructure service with guidance from Microsoft Product Support, for example, Network Controller, or restore the entire Microsoft Azure Stack appliance.

Getting ready

If disaster strikes, you will be faced with a key decision to make: do you request your OEM to carry out a clean deployment of Microsoft Azure Stack or do you request that your Microsoft Azure Stack appliance is restored using cloud recovery mode? If you plan to recover your Microsoft Azure Stack appliance, then you will need to specify the following:

- Microsoft Azure Stack build version, for example, `1809`
- The storage location of the backup
- Encryption key used to protect the backup payload
- Credentials required to access the infrastructure backup file share
- The backup ID to restore (assume multiple infrastructure backups are available)
- The IP address of a reliable time server
- The password for the external certificates (ASDK recovery only)
- The public key infrastructure certificates and password (multinode recovery only)
- OEM-supplied deployment JSON files (multinode recovery only)

 Without access to the encryption key, the Microsoft Azure Stack infrastructure backup payload can't be decrypted. If this situation arises, your only option is to carry out a new deployment instead of a recovery, since you do not have access to the backup payload.

Recovery mode is limited to the following scope:

- Microsoft Azure Stack deployment inputs
- Internal identity
- Federated identity configuration used during a disconnected deployment
- Certificates used by the internal certificate authority
- **Azure Resource Manager** (**ARM**) configuration user data, such as subscriptions, plans, offers, and quotas for storage, network, and compute resources
- KeyVault secrets and vaults
- RBAC role assignments and policy assignments

None of the IaaS or PaaS services or resources are recovered during recovery mode. After cloud recovery completes, the Microsoft Azure Stack cloud operator can log back in to the Administrator Portal and install any add-on resource providers, virtual machines, and any associated data.

If you are restoring an ASDK, then you will need to prepare the host computer first. In the ASDK, download the Microsoft Azure Stack build (`cloudbuilder.vhdx`) that corresponds to the same version of Microsoft Azure Stack as executed the infrastructure backup. After the ASDK restarts from `cloudbuilder.vhdx`, your next step is to create a file share and copy your backup payload to it. The file share itself should be accessible to the account running the ASDK installation.

If you are restoring a Microsoft Azure Stack multinode appliance, you will need to coordinate your recovery tasks with your OEM. Your OEM will need to recreate the **deployment virtual machine** (**DVM**) on the **hardware lifecycle host** (**HLH**).

 By default within your environment, the DVM will not exist and this is why the DVM needs to be recreated when recovering a Microsoft Azure Stack multinode appliance. Please contact your OEM for further information on this topic.

How to do it...

To recover Microsoft Azure Stack when a disaster strikes, follow these steps:

1. Create an SMB 3x file share and copy your infrastructure backup payload to it. Run the following PowerShell commands, but modify them for your environment:

```
# Create the required SMB 3.x file share for cloud recovery

$shares = New-Item -Path "c:\AzSBackup" -Name "Shares" -ItemType
"directory"
$azsbackupshare = New-Item -Path $shares.FullName -Name
"AzSBackups" -ItemType "directory"
New-SmbShare -Path $azsbackupshare.FullName -FullAccess
($env:computername + "\Administrator")  -Name "AzSBackups"
```

2. Copy your latest Microsoft Azure Stack infrastructure backup files to the newly created share. The folder structure within the share should be
`\\<ComputerName>\AzSBackups\MASBackup\<BackupID>\`.

3. Start the deployment of your ASDK in recovery mode. Run the following PowerShell commands, but modify them for your environment:

```
# ASDK recovery mode deployment

cd C:\CloudDeployment\Setup
$adminPass = Get-Credential Administrator
```

```
$key = ConvertTo-SecureString "<Your backup encryption key>" -
AsPlainText -Force `
$certPass = Read-Host -AsSecureString

.\InstallAzureStackPOC.ps1 -AdminPassword $adminpass.Password -
BackupStorePath ("\\" + $env:COMPUTERNAME + "\AzSBackups") `
-BackupEncryptionKeyBase64 $key -BackupStoreCredential $adminPass -
BackupId "<Backup ID to restore>" `
-TimeServer "<Valid time server IP>" -ExternalCertPassword
$certPass
```

4. After you have completed a successful cloud recovery deployment, you will need to complete the restore process by using the `Restore-AzureStack` PowerShell command:

   ```
   Restore-AzsBackup -Name "<BackupID>"
   ```

5. To recover your multinode Azure Stack appliance, you are heavily dependent on your OEM. To initiate the recovery, your OEM will need to run the Microsoft Azure Stack deployment script on the HLH, similar to initiating a fresh deployment. However, this time they need to include additional syntax and include backup relate parameters.

How it works...

To initiate a recovery, you need to have a number of pieces of information available, some of which are more obvious than others. For example, you will not only need the storage location, credentials, and encryption key of the infrastructure backup, but also the version of the Microsoft Azure Stack build version used to carry out the infrastructure backup. Once you have collected all this information, you will potentially need to work with your OEM to carry out a recovery if you are recovering your multinode Azure Stack appliance.

Whether you are recovering an ASDK or a multinode appliance, the process is very similar to a fresh deployment. With an ASDK, the actual recovery is a two-step process, where you initiate a new deployment and provide details of the path to the infrastructure backup payload, and then, after completing a successful cloud recovery deployment, the actual restore process is initiated. With the recovery of a multinode Azure Stack appliance, the backup payload is pre-seeded into the deployment at installation time by your OEM.

8
Protecting Workgroups and Untrusted Domains

In this chapter, we will cover the following topics:

- Setting up DPM protection with NTLM authentication
- Setting up DPM protection with certificate authentication

Introduction

System Center Data Protection Manager (**SCDPM**) supports the protection of computers in workgroups and untrusted domains using local user accounts (NTLM authentication); however, local accounts increase security risks for attack and are not allowed in most organizations and, therefore, this solution does not work. As an alternative, starting with DPM 2012 and later versions, you can use certificates to authenticate computers in workgroups or untrusted domains.

This chapter describes how to set up DPM protection with NTLM authentication as well as certificate-based authentication to protect computers in workgroups or untrusted domains.

Setting up DPM protection with NTLM authentication

SCDPM can protect computers in workgroups and untrusted domains. You can handle authentication using NTLM or certificates. This recipe describes how to configure DPM protection using NTLM authentication.

For NTLM authentication, DPM supports the following workloads as standalone only and not clustered:

- SQL Server
- File Server
- System State
- Hyper-V

Getting ready

For NTLM authentication to work in workgroups and untrusted domains, first you'll need to install the DPM agent on the computer that you want to protect, then you'll need to configure the agent to recognize the DPM server, and, lastly, you'll need to attach the protected computer to the DPM server.

How to do it...

Use the following procedure to install the DPM agent on the computer you want to protect:

1. From the DPM server, copy the DPM agent file manually to the computer you want to protect under the `C:\DPMAgent` folder:
   - The agent files can be found on the DPM server at the following location. Please note that the agent number in bold, which follows, will be different in your case, based on the DPM version you are running. In this example, DPM server is installed under the `D:\` drive:
     - For x64-bit, run the following code:

```
D:\Program Files\Microsoft System
Center\DPM\DPM\agents\RA\5.1.375.0\amd64\1033
```

   - For x86-bit, run the following code:

```
D:\Program Files\Microsoft System
Center\DPM\DPM\agents\RA\5.1.375.0\i386\1033
```

2. To install the protection agent on the targeted computer, open an elevated Command Prompt window and navigate to one of the following paths: `C:\DPMAgent\agents\RA\`**`5.1.375.0`**`\am64\1033\` or `C:\DPMAgent\agents\RA\`**`5.1.375.0`**`\i386\1033\`.

     - For x64-bit, run the following command:

       `DPMAgentInstaller_KB4293623_AMD64.exe`

     - For x86-bit, run the following command:

       `DPMAgentInstaller_KB4293623.exe`

   On the **Microsoft Software License Terms** page, click **Accept**. After a moment, the DPM agent will be installed:

```
Administrator: Command Prompt

C:\DPMAgent\agents\RA\5.1.375.0\amd64\1033>DPMAgentInstaller_KB4293623_AMD64.exe

C:\DPMAgent\agents\RA\5.1.375.0\amd64\1033>_
```

3. In this step, we need to configure the agent by running the `SetDPMServer.exe` executable with `-isNonDomainServer` switch, as follows:

   1. Open an elevated Command Prompt window and navigate to the following path: `C:\Program Files\Microsoft Data Protection Manager\DPM\bin`.

   2. Type the following command:

      `SetDpmServer.exe –DpmServerName <DPMserverName> –isNonDomainServer –UserName <userName>`

      - `-DpmServerName`: Specifies the name of the DPM server. You can use either an FQDN, if the DPM server and the protected computer are accessible to each other using FQDNs, or a NETBIOS name.
      - `-IsNonDomainServer`: This is used to indicate that the server is in a workgroup or untrusted domain.
      - `-UserName`: Specifies the name of the account you want to use for NTLM authentication. A local user account will be created and the DPM agent will be configured to use this account for NTLM authentication.

3. You will be prompted to provide a password for the local user account. Enter the password and confirm it a second time.

4. The `SetDPMServer.exe` executable will configure the DPM server settings and firewall exceptions that are created for the required ports. Lastly, you will receive a confirmation message, **Configuration completed successfully!!!**, as shown in the following screenshot:

```
C:\Program Files\Microsoft Data Protection Manager\DPM\bin>SetDpmServer.exe -DPMServerName SC-DPM-18
07 -isNonDomainServer -Username dpmworkgroup
Make sure that this computer is not part of a perimeter network. DPM does not support protection of
computers on a perimeter network.
Enter the password for 'dpmworkgroup' to connect to 'SC-DPM-1807':
Retype the password to confirm:
Enter the password for 'dpmworkgroup' to connect to 'SC-DPM-1807':
Configuring dpm server settings and firewall settings for dpm server =[SC-DPM-1807]

The following firewall exceptions has been added:
        - Exception for DPMRA.exe in all profiles.
        - Exception for Windows Management Instrumentation service.
        - Exception for DCOM communication on port 135 (TCP and UDP) in all profiles.
Configuration completed successfully!!!
C:\Program Files\Microsoft Data Protection Manager\DPM\bin>
```

4. Switch to the DPM server, open the **DPM Administrator console**, and go to **Management**. Click on **Production Servers** and, at the top-left corner of the console, click on the **Add** button to start the **Production Server Addition Wizard**.

5. In the **Select Production Server type** page, select **Windows Servers**. Click on **Next** to continue.

6. Under the **Select Agent Deployment Method** page, click **Attach agents**, followed by **Computer in a Workgroup or untrusted domain**. Click the **Next >** button to continue:

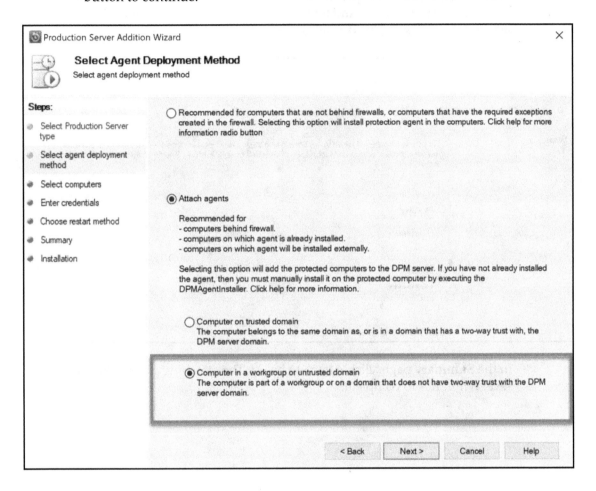

7. Enter the **Computer name**, **Username**, and **Password** for the computer that you want to attach to. These should be the credentials you specified when you installed the agent in the previous step; please note that you can only enter one server at a time. Click on **Add >** to add the computer to the **Selected computers** list, and then click the **Next >** button to continue:

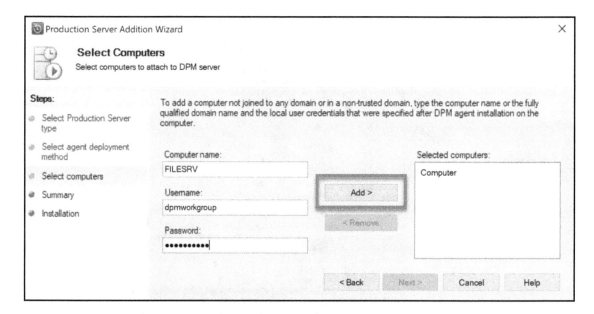

8. In the **Summary** page, click **Attach** to begin. The attaching process may take several minutes to complete:

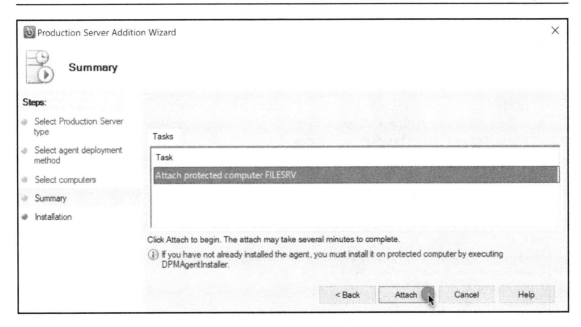

9. If the credentials are correct and the protected server is reachable by the DPM server, you will receive a **Success** message, as shown in the following screenshot. Click on **Close**:

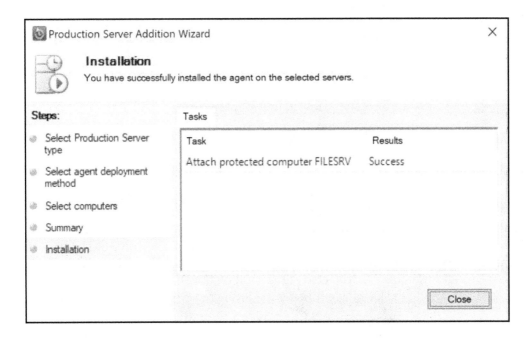

Optionally, you can run the Windows PowerShell `Attach-NonDomainServer.ps1` command instead of running the preceding wizard. To do this, take a look at the example in the *There's more...* section.

10. Lastly, when you want to create a Protection Group or include the workgroup server in an existing Protection Group, you will find the workgroup member server under the **Workgroup** node:

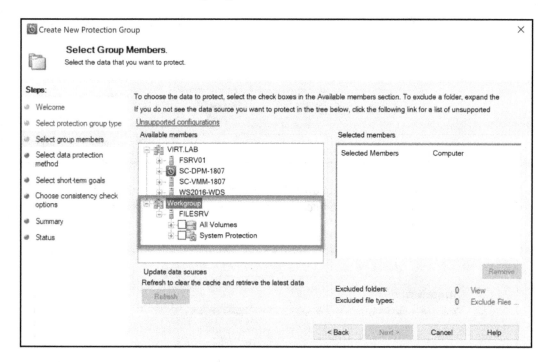

How it works...

The `setDpmServer.exe` executable command has the ability to configure the DPM agent to set which DPM server the DPM agent reports to. It also provides the configuration needed for the local Windows Firewall so that the DPM agent can start reporting to the DPM server. Additionally, a local user account will be created and the DPM agent will be configured to use this account for NTLM authentication. This account is provided both in the agent configuration on the protected server and on the DPM server side; the DPM server authenticates to the DPM agent using the local credentials of the dedicated user account:

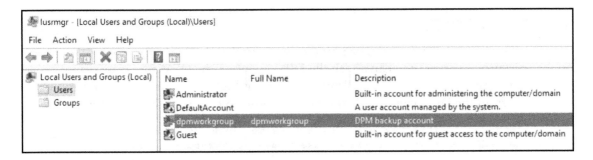

 Please make sure that you have a good naming convention for the local accounts that you use for workgroup and untrusted domain protection.

After you attach the protected server to the DPM server, you will see the **Domain** column in the DPM console reports as **Workgroup**:

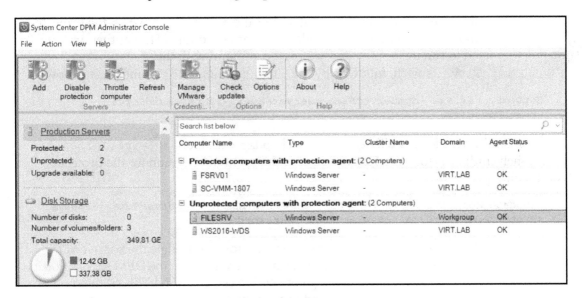

There's more...

After you run the `SetDPMServer.exe` executable with the `-isNonDomainServer` switch on the workgroup server, you can attach the DPM agent on the DPM server by using the `Attach-NonDomainServer.ps1` Windows PowerShell command instead of running the wizard from the DPM console. To do this, you need to run the following command:

```
.\Attach-NonDomainServer.ps1 -DpmServerName <DPMserverName> -PSName
<ProtectedServerName> -UserName <userName> -Password <Password>
```

Please note that you cannot remove a workgroup server from the DPM console—you can remove the server through the command line only. To do this, you need to run the `Remove-ProductionServer.ps1` PowerShell cmdlet as follows:

```
.\Remove-ProductionServer.ps1 -DpmServerName
<DPMserverName> -PSName <ProtectedServerName>.
```

You can also configure a workgroup computer after the agent is installed on the protected server, for example, in case you want to update the password for NTLM authentication. To do this, you need to run the `SetDPMServer.exe` command with the `-isNonDomainServer` switch, followed by the `-updatePassword` parameter, as follows:

```
SetDpmServer.exe -dpmServerName <serverName> -isNonDomainServer -
updatePassword
```

Then, on the DPM server, you'll need to run the `Update-NonDomainServerInfo.ps1` PowerShell cmdlet, as follows. This will refresh the agent information for the protected computer:

```
.\Update-NonDomainServerInfo.ps1 -DpmServerName <DPMserverName> -PSName
<ProtectedServerName> -NewPassword <Password>
```

When you want to configure, attach, remove, or update the password for the DPM agent on the protected server as well as on the DPM server, you want to use the same naming convention (FQDN or NETBIOS) that you did when you first configured protection. In other words, if you use FQDN for the DPM server name on the server that you want to protect, then you want to use FQDN for the protected server name on the DPM server side as well, otherwise the agent won't recognize and report to DPM server.

Finally, if the protected server is in a workgroup or untrusted domain, then make sure that the password for the local user account on the DPM server and the protected server is set to never expire (**Password never expires**), otherwise the **Agent Status** in the DPM console will report with **Error** status when the password expires:

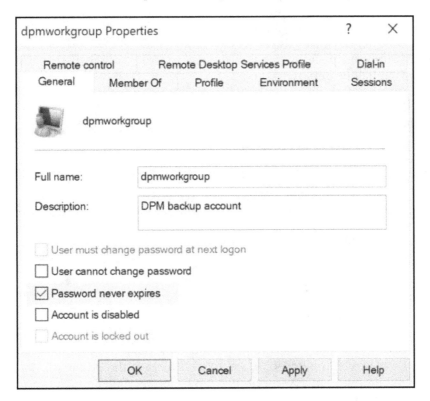

See also

Read the following article for more information about the DPM protection agent in a workgroup or untrusted domain: `https://charbelnemnom.com/2015/03/dpm-protection-agent-failed-because-the-service-did-not-respond-internal-error-code-0x8099090e-sysctr/`.

Setting up DPM protection with certificate authentication

SCDPM can protect computers in workgroups and untrusted domains. You can handle authentication using NTLM or certificates. Using certificates over NTLM authentication is the preferred and recommended approach to ensure a high level of security. This recipe describes how to set up DPM protection with **certificate-based authentication** (**CBA**).

For CBA, DPM supports the following workloads, regardless of whether they are deployed in clustered or standalone deployments:

- SQL Server
- File Server
- Hyper-V

The following workloads are not supported for CBA when they are NOT in trusted domains:

- Exchange server
- Windows clients
- SharePoint server
- Bare metal recovery
- System State
- End user recovery of a file and SQL

 Please note that if you are protecting a primary DPM server by another DPM server known as a secondary DPM, then the Primary DPM server and Secondary DPM server need to be in the same domain or mutually trusted domain. Certificate-based authentication between Primary and Secondary DPM servers is not supported.

Getting ready

Before you get started, you will want to validate the following prerequisites:

1. You need a **Certificate Authority** (**CA**) role installed with a **Clear Revocation List** (**CRL**). This recipe will not cover the installation and setup of a CA.

 Please read the following article for guidance: `https://docs.microsoft.` `com/en-us/windows-server/networking/core-network-guide/cncg/` `server-certs/install-the-certification-authority`.

2. Each computer you want to protect with CBA should have at least .NET Framework 3.5 with SP1 installed.
3. Each computer you want to protect with CBA (including virtual machines) must have its own certificate.
4. The certificate you use for CBA must comply with the following:
    *   X.509 V3 certificate
    *   **Enhanced Key Usage** (**EKU**) should have client authentication and server authentication
    *   Key length should be at least 1024 bits
    *   Key type should be **exchange**
    *   The subject name of the certificate and the root certificate should not be empty
    *   The revocation servers of the associated Certificate Authorities are online and accessible by both the protected server and DPM server
    *   The certificate should have an associated private key
    *   DPM doesn't support certificates with CNG Keys
    *   DPM does not support self-signed certificates

How to do it...

The overall steps to set up DPM protection with CBA are as follows:

1. Add HTTP CRL Distribution Point.
2. Create the DPM Certificate Template.
3. Configure the certificate on the DPM server.
4. Install the DPM agents on the protected systems.

5. Configure the certificate on the protected computer.

6. Attach the computer to DPM.

7. Test backing up the VMs.

For the remainder of this example, we are going to protect a Hyper-V host deployed in a different forest; there is no trust relationship between the two forests. Please note that the same concept will apply to SQL Server and File Server.

 The process of configuring DPM protection with certificate-based authentication is a bit long, so please make sure to follow each of the following steps carefully.

Adding a HTTP CRL Distribution Point

Before we start creating the certificate, we need to add HTTP to the CRL on the Enterprise CA server in the TRUSTED forest, because the CA server must be online and reachable by the protected computer.

On the CA server, make sure that the following is set:

1. Connect to the Enterprise CA with the appropriate credentials and open the **Certification Authority** console. To access the console, right-click on the **Start** button, type `certsrv.msc` in the Search field, and press the *Enter* key.

2. Right-click the CA name and select **Properties**.

3. On the **Extensions** tab, check the following CRL:

   - `http://<ServerDNSName>/CertEnroll/<CaName><CRLNameSuffix><DeltaCRLAllowed>.crl`
   - In the lower box, check the following and click **Apply**:
     - **Include in CRLs. Clients use this to find Delta CRL locations.**
     - **Include in CDP extensions of issued certificates.**

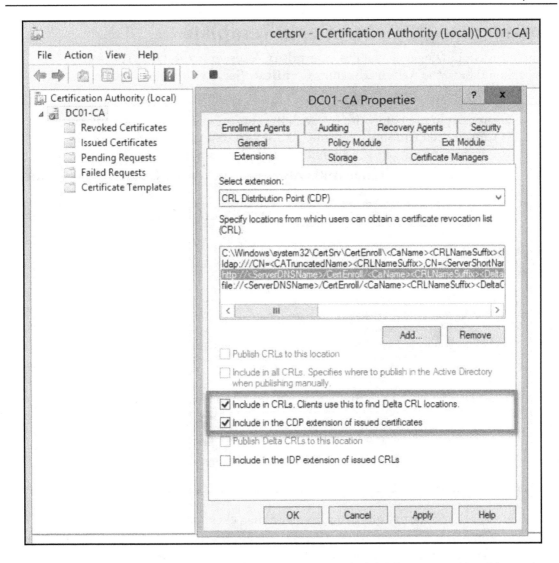

4. On the **Certification Authority** box message, click **YES** to restart the CA service and click **OK.**

Creating the DPM Certificate Template

Complete the following steps on the Enterprise CA server in the TRUSTED forest. The server should have the **Active Directory Certificate Services** installed and configured as your Enterprise CA:

1. Connect to the Enterprise CA with the appropriate credentials and open the Certification Authority console. To access the console, right-click on the **Start** button, type `certsrv.msc` in the Search field, and press the *Enter* key.

2. Expand the **Certification Authority** so that you can see **Certificate Templates**:

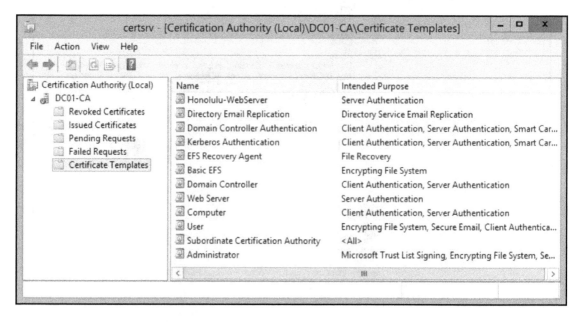

3. Right-click **Certificate Templates** and then click **Manage**.

4. In the details pane of the **Certificate Templates** console, right-click the **RAS and IAS Server** template and then click **Duplicate Template**:

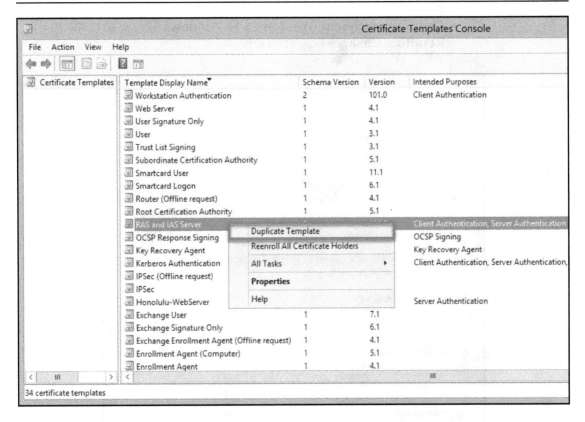

5. On the **Compatibility** tab, select the following:
    - **Certificate Authority**: **Windows Server 2003**: The certificate authority has to be set to Windows Server 2003 for the template to show up in the advanced **Certificate Request** page under **Certificate Template** on the **Web Enrollment** pages. If you set it to Windows Server 2012 or 2012 R2, it won't show up on the protected computer.

- **Certificate recipient: Windows 8.1 / Windows Server 2012 R2**: In the **Resulting Changes** box, click **OK**:

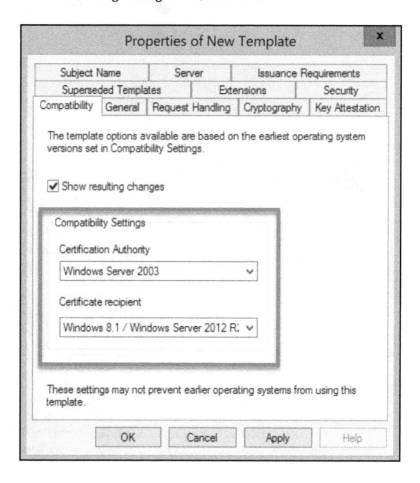

6. On the **General** tab, under **Template display name**, type the following:

- **DPMAUTH**: This name should NOT include spaces. Although the **Template name** is actually used when referencing the template, it is a best practice to set the **Template display name** to be the same as well.
- **Template name**: DPMAuth.
- **Validity period**: **5 Years.**
- **Renewal period**: **6 Weeks.**
- Select **Publish certificate in Active Directory**:

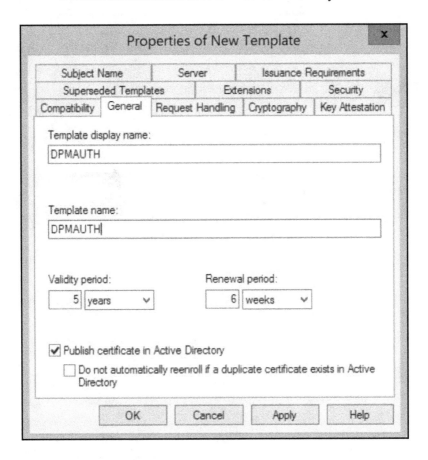

7. On the **Request Handling** tab, select the following:
   • **Allow private key to be exported**:

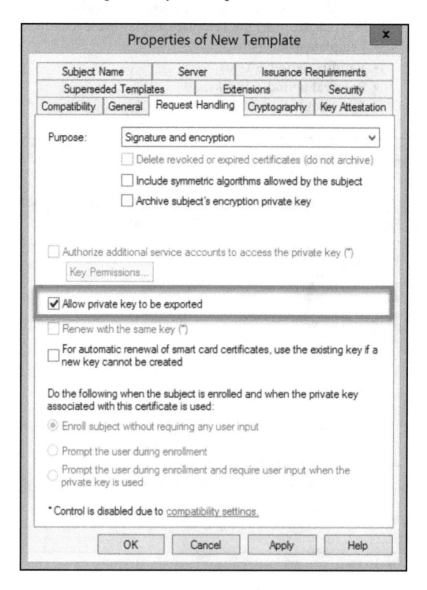

8. On the **Cryptography** tab, type/select the following:
   - **Minimum key size**: 2048

   - **Requests must use one of the following providers**:
     - **Microsoft RSA SChannel Cryptographic Provider**:

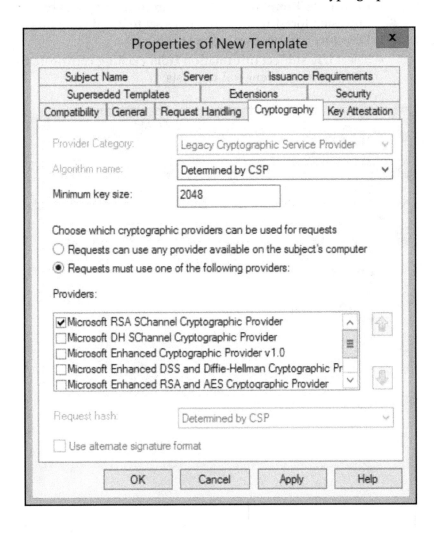

9. On the **Subject Name** tab, select the following:
   - **Supply in the request**: In the **Certificate Templates** box, click **OK**. The certificate authority has to be set to **Supply in the request** for the template to show up in the advanced **Certificate Request** page under **Certificate Template** on the **Web Enrollment** pages on a system in an untrusted forest/workgroup. If it's set to **Build from this Active Directory information**, it won't show up.
   - Select **Use subject information from existing certificate for autoenrollment renewal requests**:

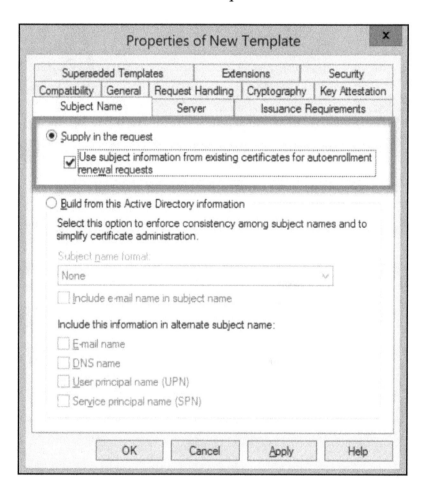

10. On the **Security** tab, you must ensure that the computer account that you want to protect has the ability to enroll for the template. To do so, set the following to enroll:

- For **Authenticated Users**:
  - Set the entry to at least enroll permissions and grant them. Choose **Enroll** and click **OK**.

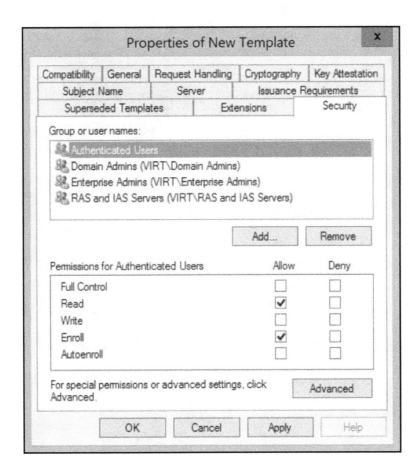

11. Close the **Certificate Templates** console and return to the **Certificate Authority** console.

12. In the **Certification Authority** window, right-click on **Certificate Templates** in the left navigation pane and then select **New** | **Certificate Template to Issue**:

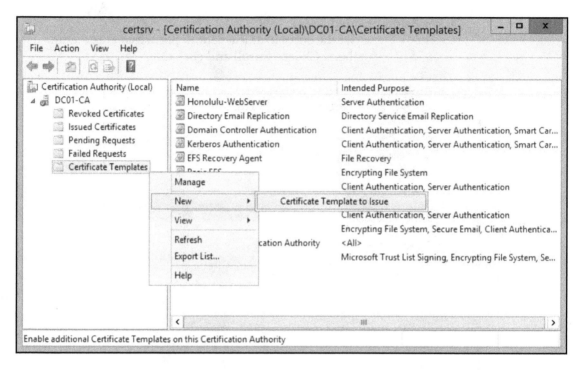

13. In the **Enable Certificate Templates** window, select **DPMAUTH** and click the **OK** button:

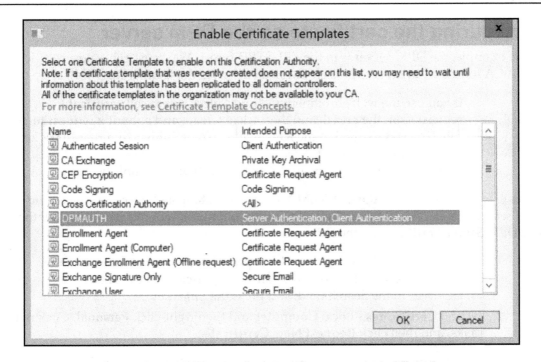

14. The template will now be available when you request a certificate:

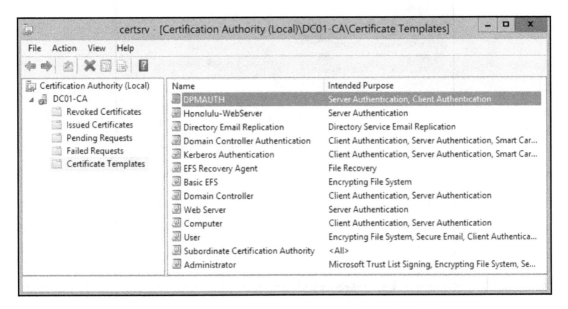

Configuring the certificate on the DPM server

In this example, the DPM server is in the TRUSTED forest. You must generate a certificate from a CA for the DPM server via **Web Enrollment** or via the **Certificates** MMC snap-in.

 If you use the web enrollment method, select **Advanced certificate request** from the portal, and then select **Create and submit a request to this CA**. Make sure that the **Key Size** is 1024 or higher, and that **Mark key as exportable** is selected. Note that this option allows you to select the desired Certificate Template (**DPMAUTH**) that was published earlier.

In this example, we will use the **CERTLM** MMC snap-in to install the certificate on the DPM server in a TRUSTED forest. In the following steps, you will request and enroll the new DPM Server Certificate on the DPM server:

1. Connect to the DPM server with the appropriate credentials and open the **Certificates** console. To access the console, right-click on the **Start** button, type `certlm.msc` in the Search field, and press the *Enter* key.

2. Expand **Certificates - Local Computer** and then right-click **Personal**. Click **All Tasks**, and then click **Request New Certificate...**

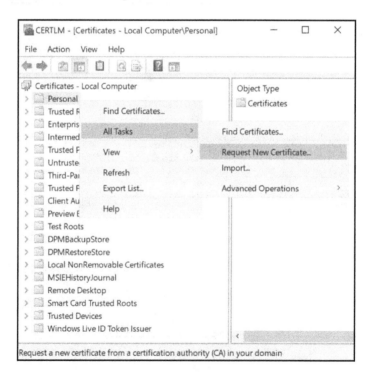

3. On the **Before You Begin** page, click **Next**. On the **Select Certificate Enrollment Policy** page, ensure that **Active Directory Enrollment Policy** is selected, and then click **Next**:

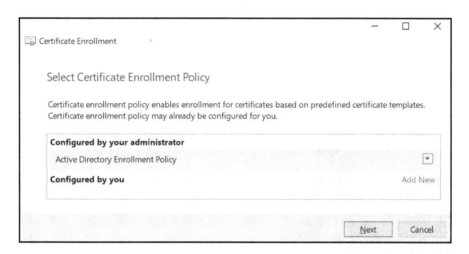

4. On the **Certificate Enrollment** page, select the new template; in this example, it's **DPMAUTH**.

   - Click on **More information is required to enroll for this certificate. Click here to configure settings**:

5. On the **Certificate Properties** page, select **Subject** tab, and type/select the following:
   - **Subject name:**
     - **Type: Common name**
     - **Value:** `<DPMServerFQDN>`
     - Click **Add >**
   - **Alternative name:**
     - **Type: DNS**
     - **Value:** `<DPMServerFQDN>`
     - Click **Add >**
   - Click **Apply.**

6. On the **Certificate Properties** page, select the **General** tab and type the following:

   - **Friendly name**: SRV-DPM-CERT

   - **Description**: DPM Server Certificate

   - Click **OK**:

7. On the **Certificate Enrollment** page, click **Enroll**, and then click **Finish**:

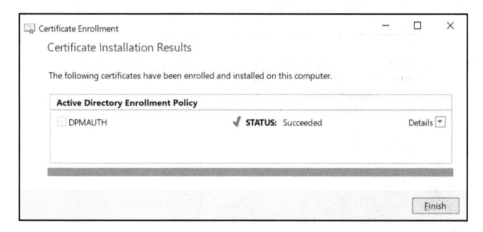

8. The new certificate should now show under the `Personal | Certificates` store:

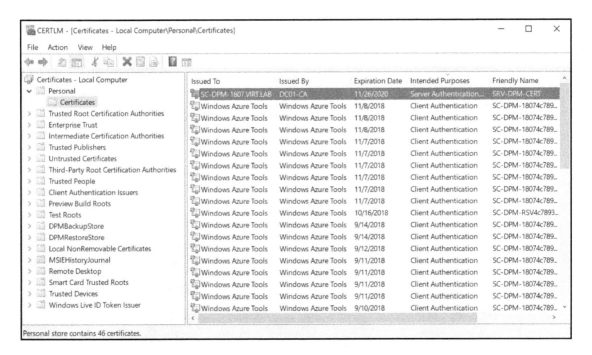

9. Next, we need to configure the DPM server to use this certificate. In the **Certificates** store, double-click on the certificate. Select the **Details** tab and scroll down to the **Thumbprint**. Click it, and then *highlight and copy it*. Paste the thumbprint into Notepad and *remove any spaces*:

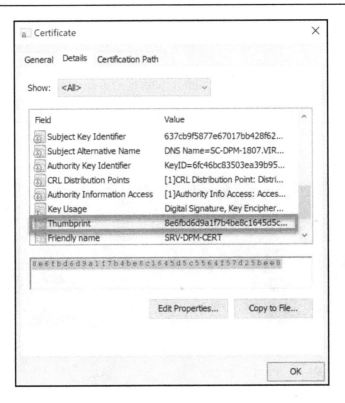

10. On the DPM server, create the following two folders: `C:\DPMCERT` and `C:\Temp`. Make sure that both folders exist before you move on to the next step.

11. Create a text file with the following details in it as a single line:

```
Set-DPMCredentials [-DPMServerName <String>] [-Type
<AuthenticationType>] [Action <Action>] [-OutputFilePath <String>]
[-Thumbprint <String>] [-AuthCAThumbprint <String>]
```

- `-Type`: Indicates the type of authentication. **Value: certificate**.
- `-Action`: Specifies whether you want to perform the command for the first time, or regenerate the credentials. Possible values include **regenerate** or **configure**.
- `-OutputFilePath`: Location of the output `.bin` file.
- `-Thumbprint`: Copies from the Notepad file (previous step).
- `-AuthCAThumbprint`: Thumbprint of the CA in the trust chain of the certificate. This parameter is optional. If not specified, root will be used.

12. Open an **Administrative PowerShell** window and change the directory to the `.bin` folder of the DPM installation path. In this example, it's `D:\Program Files\Microsoft System Center\DPM\DPM\bin`.

13. Run the command that you created before, as shown in the following screenshot. This command will generate a metadata file (`.bin`) that is required at the time that each DPM agent is installed in an untrusted domain. Note that if the `.bin` file is lost or deleted, you can recreate it by running the same script with the `-Action Regenerate` option:

```
Path
----
D:\Program Files\Microsoft System Center\DPM\DPM\bin


CharbelNemnom.com #> Set-DPMCredentials -DPMServerName SC-DPM-1807 -Type Certificate -Action Configure -Output
FilePath C:\DPMCERT\ -Thumbprint 8e6fbd6d9a1f7b4be8c1645d5c5564f57d25bee8 -Verbose
WARNING: Connecting to DPM server: SC-DPM-1807
VERBOSE: Configures DPM server SC-DPM-1807 for certificate-based authentication.
Configuration completed successfully.
Firewall exception for DPMCPWrapperService communication has been added on port 6076 (TCP and UDP) in all prof
iles.
CharbelNemnom.com #>
```

14. Copy the `xxx.BIN` file from the DPM server to the following folder on the target computer(s) you want to protect: `C:\DPMCERT\xxx.BIN`. In this example, we are protecting a Hyper-V host:

   - The `C:\DPMCERT\` folder on the protected computer is a temporary location because the DPM agent is not installed yet. Therefore, the `C:\Program Files\Microsoft Data Protection Manager\DPM\bin` folder does not exist yet (more on this in the next step).
   - The `xxx.BIN` file will be used later in the *Configure the Certificate on the protected computer* step.

Installing the DPM agents on the protected systems

In this step, we will install the DPM agent on the protected system. If protecting a VM on a standalone Hyper-V host, install the agent on the Hyper-V host. If protecting VMs in a Hyper-V cluster in the UNTRUSTED forest, then you need to install the agent on each of the nodes in the cluster.

In this example, we will install the protection agent on the Hyper-V host, and then attach it to the DPM server using a PowerShell script later. Use the following procedure to install the DPM agent on the computer you want to protect:

1. From the DPM server, copy the DPM agent file manually to the computer you want to protect under the `C:\DPMAgent` folder:

   - The agent files can be found on the DPM server at the following location; please note that the following agent number in bold will be different in your case, based on the DPM version you are running. In this example, DPM server is installed under the `D:\` drive.

   - For x64-bit, run the following command:

     ```
     D:\Program Files\Microsoft System
     Center\DPM\DPM\agents\RA\5.1.375.0\amd64\1033
     ```

   - For x86-bit, run the following command:

     ```
     D:\Program Files\Microsoft System
     Center\DPM\DPM\agents\RA\5.1.375.0\i386\1033
     ```

2. To install the protection agent on the targeted computer, open an elevated Command Prompt window, and navigate to one of the following paths: `C:\DPMAgent\agents\RA\5.1.375.0\am64\1033\` or `C:\DPMAgent\agents\RA\5.1.375.0\i386\1033\`.

   - For x64-bit, run the following command:

     DPMAgentInstaller_KB4293623_AMD64.exe

   - For x86-bit, run the following command:

     DPMAgentInstaller_KB4293623.exe

   - On the **Microsoft Software License Terms** page, click **Accept**. After a moment, the DPM agent will be installed.

```
Administrator: Command Prompt

C:\DPMAgent\agents\RA\5.1.375.0\amd64\1033>DPMAgentInstaller_KB4293623_AMD64.exe

C:\DPMAgent\agents\RA\5.1.375.0\amd64\1033>_
```

Configuring the certificate on the protected computer

In this step, we will configure the certificate on the Hyper-V host that we generated earlier.

TIP

Please note that in order to complete certificate installation via the web enrollment method, the website for the CA must be configured to use HTTPS authentication and not HTTP.

1. If you have not already done this step, retrieve the `xxx.BIN` file that was generated on the DPM server and copy it to the following location on the server that you want to protect in the untrusted forest/workgroup: `C:\Program Files\Microsoft Data Protection Manager\DPM\bin\xxx.BIN`.

2. Next, we need to generate a dedicated certificate from the Enterprise CA server for the protected computer, via the Web Enrollment method:

   1. Ensure that **Internet Enhanced Security** is turned off on the protected server during this process; you can turn it on once you complete this step.

   2. Launch the browser on the protected server and type in **FQDN** for your CA, followed by `/certsrv`.

   3. You will be prompted to enter your credentials for the TRUSTED forest.

   4. Select **Request a certificate**:

3. Click on **Advanced certificate request**, and then click **Create and submit a request to this CA**:
   - On the **Web Access Confirmation** box, click **YES**:

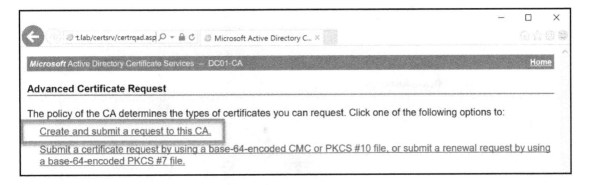

4. On the **Advanced Certificate Request** page, select the following:
   - **Certificate Template: DPMAUTH**
   - **Name:** <SERVER-NAME>
   - In the **Key Options** section, do the following:
      - Select **Create new key set**
      - **Key Usage: Exchange** (this is not configurable)
      - **Key Size:** 2048
      - Select **Mark keys as exportable**
   - In the **Additional Options** section, select the following:
      - **Friendly Name:** SRV-HYPER01-DPM

- Click **Submit >**
- On the **Web Access Confirmation** box, click **YES**:

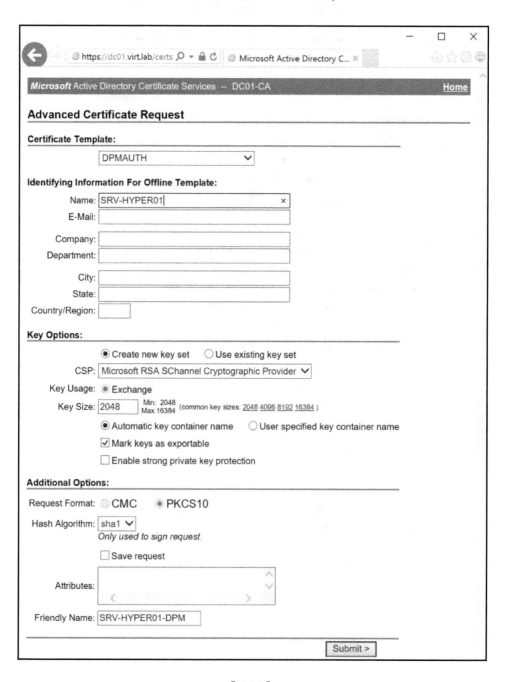

5. Click on **Install this Certificate**. Note that if this the first time you are installing the certificate on the system that you want to protect, you will see a message stating that this CA is not trusted. To trust certificates issued from this certification authority, click **Install this CA certificate** and then click **Open**. On the **Open File – Security Warning** window, click **Open**. Please do not close the browser yet:

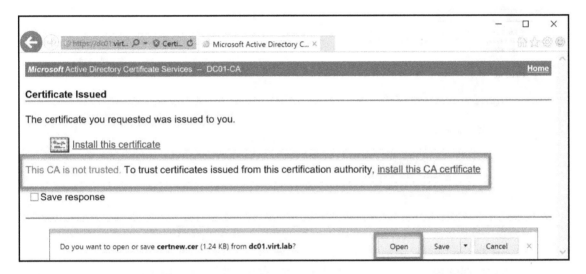

6. On the **Certificate** page, click **Install Certificate**. On the **Certificate Import Wizard** page, make sure that the **Store Location** is set to **Current User** and then click **Next**. Select **Place all certificates in the following store**. Click **Browse...** In the **Select Certificate Store** window, select **Trusted Root Certification Authorities** and click **OK**. Click **Next**, and then click **Finish**. On the **Security Warning** box, click **Yes**.

On the **Certificate Import Wizard** box click **OK**, and then click **OK** to close the **Certificate** window:

7. Switch to the browser again and refresh the page. On the **Web Access Confirmation** box, click **YES**. Click on **Install this Certificate** again, and the new certificate will be installed, as shown in the following screenshot:

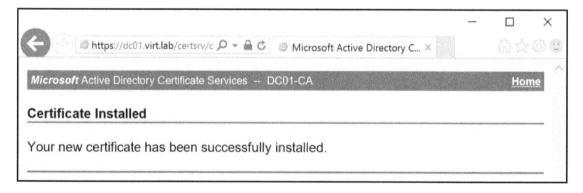

8. Once done, we need to open up an MMC and add the certificate snap-in for both the **Current User** and **Local Computer**. Remember that, by default, the certificate will be installed in the **Current User** store only.

9. On the protected system in the untrusted forest/workgroup, open an administrative Command Prompt, then type CERTMGR and press *Enter*:
   - Make sure **Certificates – Current User** is selected.
   - Expand **Personal** and then click on **Certificates**.
   - Right-click on the certificate (in this example, it's SRV-HYPER-01) and select **All Tasks-Export...**

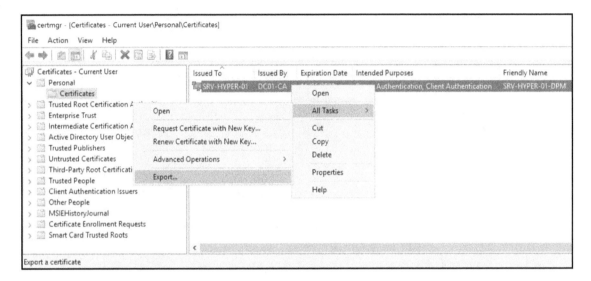

10. On the **Welcome to the Certificate Export Wizard** page, click **Next**.
11. On the **Export Private Key** page, select **Yes, export the private key**. Click **Next**:

12. On the **Export File Format** page, select the following and click **Next**:
    - **Personal Information Exchange – PKCS #12 (.PFX):**
        - **Include all certificates in the certification path if possible**
        - **Export all extended properties:**

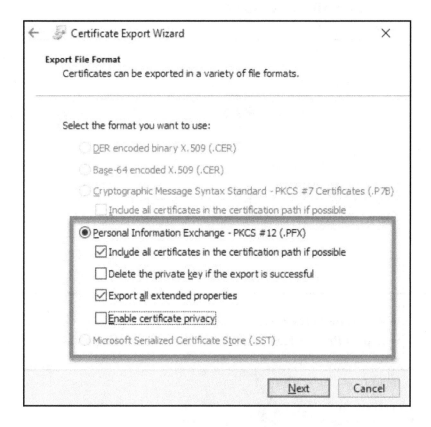

13. On the **Security** page, set a password for the file and confirm it. Click **Next**:

14. On the **File to export** page, type the path and the name for the file (that is, C:\DPMCERT\SRV-HYPER-01.pfx). Click **Save** and then click **Next**.

15. On the **Completing the Certificate Export wizard** page, click **Finish**. On the **Certificate Export Wizard** box, click **OK**.

16. Next, we need to select **Import PFX file** and install the certificate in the **Computer Store**.

17. On the protected system in the untrusted forest/workgroup, open an administrative Command Prompt, type CERTLM, and press *Enter*:

    - The **Certificates – Local Computer** console will open.
    - Right-click on **Personal** store and select **All Tasks – Import...**
    - On the **Welcome to the Certificate Import Wizard** page, click **Next**.
    - On the **File to Import** page, browse to the certificate (that is, C:\DPMCERT\SRV-HYPER-01.pfx). Click **Open**. Back on the **File to Import** page, click **Next**.

- On the **Private key protection** page, complete the following steps and then click **Next**.
  - Type the password
  - Select **Mark this key as exportable**
  - Select **Include all extended properties**:

18. On the **Certificate Store** page, keep the default and click **Next**.

19. On the **Completing the certificate Import Wizard** page, click **Finish**. On the **Certificate Import Wizard** box, click **OK**. You will now see the imported certificate (SRV-HYPER-01) under the **Personal** | **Certificates** store:

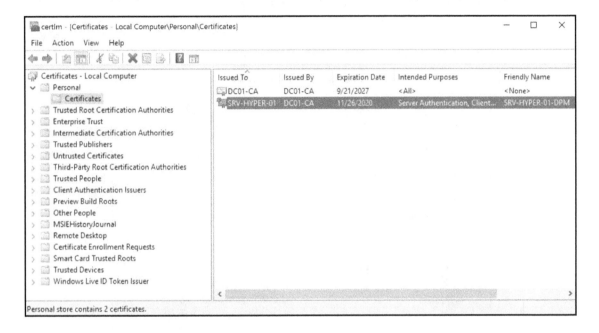

20. Now, we need to validate that the certificate has the URL of the CA server under CRL Distribution Points. In the **Certificates** store, double-click on the certificate. Select the **Details** tab and scroll down to the **CRL Distribution Points**. Then, in the box below, scroll to the bottom and you should see the full URL, as shown in the following screenshot. If you browse to that URL on the protected system, you will see that it will prompt you to download a small file with a `.crl` extension. This verifies that the revocation server of the associated Certification Authority is online and reachable by the protected system:

21. Next, we need to obtain the **thumbprint** for this certificate. In the **Details** tab, scroll down to the **Thumbprint**. Click it, then highlight and copy it. Paste the **thumbprint** into Notepad and **remove any spaces**.

22. Next, we need to configure the security accounts, permissions, and firewall exceptions that are necessary for the agent to communicate with the DPM server. On the protected system in the untrusted forest/workgroup, open an administrative Command Prompt and navigate to the `C:\Program files\Microsoft Data Protection Manager\DPM\bin` folder.

23. Run the `SetDpmServer.exe` executable command. Here, `-DPMCredential` is the full name of the `.bin` file that we copied from the DPM server, `-OutputFilePath` is the path of the `.bin` file that will be generated after running this command, and `-Thumbprint` is the thumbprint that we obtained previously. You will receive a confirmation message (**Configuration completed successfully!!!**), as shown in the following screenshot:

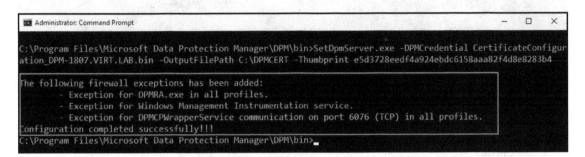

24. Copy the newly generated `.bin` file from the protected computer under `C:\DPMCERT\xxx.BIN` to the following location on the DPM server: `C:\Windows\System32`. In this example, it's `C:\DPMCERT\CertificateConfiguration_SRV-HYPER-01.bin`. When you attach the agent to the DPM server in the next step, by default, the attach process will check for the file under this location: `C:\Windows\System32`. This will make the attach process easy instead of specifying the full path for the `.bin` file.

Attaching the computer to the DPM server

In this step, we will attach the protected computer in the workgroup or untrusted forest to the DPM server using the `Attach-ProductionServerWithCertificate.ps1` PowerShell script:

1. On the DPM Server, open a PowerShell Command Prompt with **administrative privilege** and navigate to `C:\Program files\Microsoft Data Protection Manager\DPM\bin`. In this example, the DPM server is installed under the `D:\` drive.

2. Run the following command: `Attach-ProductionServerWithCertificate.ps1 [-DPMServerName <String>] [-PSCredential <String>] [<CommonParameters>]`.

   - `-DPMServerName`: Name of the DPM server.
   - `-PSCredential`: Name of the `.bin` file. If you placed it in the `Windows\System32` folder, you can only specify the file name. Be careful to specify the `.bin` file that you created on the protected server. If you specify the `.bin` file that was created on the DPM server, you'll remove all of the protected computers that are configured for certificate-based authentication:

3. After you attach the protected server in the workgroup or untrusted forest to the DPM server, you will see that the **Domain** column in the DPM console now reports as **(Untrusted - Certificates)**:

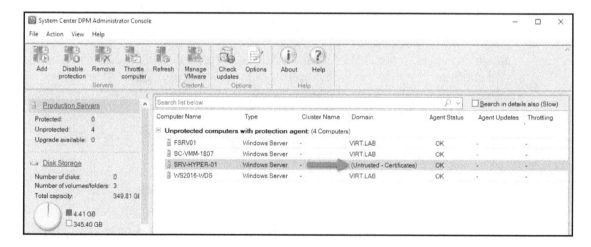

If you are protecting a Hyper-V cluster, or SQL Server cluster in the workgroup or untrusted forest, then you need to repeat the previous steps for the remaining nodes in the cluster as well.

Test backing up the VMs

The final test it to create a Protection Group and back up the virtual machines from the Hyper-V host running in the workgroup or untrusted forest:

1. Open your DPM Administrator Console, click on **Protection** workspace, and then click on the **New** button in the top-left hand corner.
2. In the **Welcome to the New Protection Group Wizard** screen, select **Servers**, and then click on **Next >** to continue.
3. You will find the untrusted protected server listed under the (**Untrusted - Certificates**) node, as shown in the following screenshot. Select the desired VM and click on **Next >** to continue:

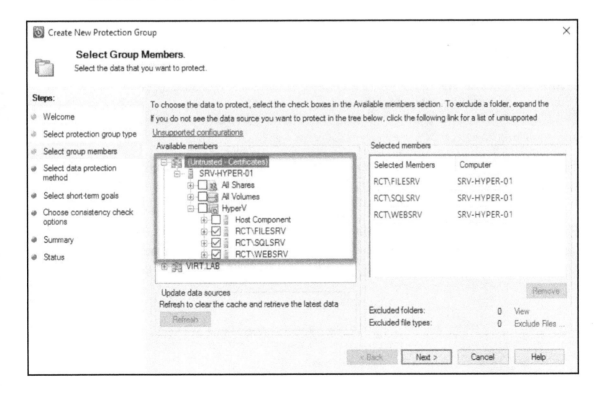

4. Complete the remaining wizard to start the VM backup.

5. Finally, confirm that the virtual machines are completely backed up, as shown in the following screenshot:

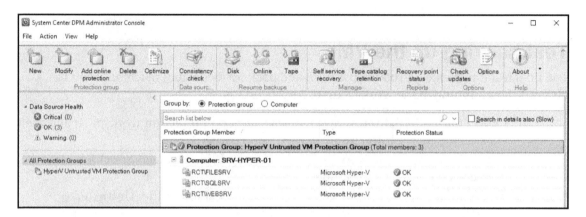

How it works...

The `setDpmServer.exe` executable command has the ability to configure the DPM agent on the protected server to authenticate to the DPM server using certificates, which is more secure than NTLM authentication. It also provides the configuration needed for the local Windows Firewall to create a new firewall rule named `CPWrapperServiceForDPMException` so that the DPM agent can start communicating and reporting to the DPM server over TCP port `6076`.

The `Set-DPMCredentials` PowerShell cmdlet on the DPM server has the same ability to configure the DPM service (`DpmCPWrapperService`) to authenticate and communicate with the protected server using certificates over the same TCP port, that is, `6076`.

Finally, certificate-based authentication uses both certificates and the `.bin` files that were generated by the DPM server and the protected server to authenticate and start protecting your workloads in the workgroup or untrusted forest over a secure channel.

There's more...

To back up VMs in a cluster (on a `Clustered Shared Volume` folder) in an untrusted forest, you must grant each computer node administrative privilege on all other nodes. You must add the machine accounts of all the nodes of the cluster to the **Local Administrators** group in all the nodes of the cluster. This step is only required if you're protecting virtual machines in a Hyper-V cluster in an untrusted forest.

On every member node of the Hyper-V cluster, you should do the following:

1. Log in to one of the Hyper-V nodes in the cluster (that is, `SRV-HYPER-01`) in the untrusted forest.
2. Add the computer account(s) of all the remaining nodes in the cluster to the local Administrator's group (that is, `SRV-HYPER-02$`, `SRV-HYPER-03$`, `SRV-HYPER-04$`).
3. Save these settings.
4. Repeat the same three steps on every node in the cluster.
5. Finish.

If you do not perform the preceding steps, the backup of the virtual machines in the cluster will fail. The Consistency Check on the DPM server will fail and you will receive the following error in the DPM job log: `An unexpected error occurred while the job was running. (ID 104 Details: Access is denied (0x80070005))`.

Recovering Data from Backup
9

In this chapter, we will cover the following recipes:

- Recovering file server data with PowerShell
- Recovering SQL data using the Self-Service Recovery Tool (SSRT)
- Recovering a failed server using bare-metal recovery
- Recovering data from Azure Backup
- Recovering data from an external DPM server
- Recovering data from a secondary DPM server

Introduction

Data recovery has been a natural component of the business continuity plan for many years. Restore is the key for all the backup story. The most important fact to realize is that backup without validating the restore does not guarantee that your backup plan is completed and the data is recoverable. The recovery can be presented in many shapes and can also be transformed over a period of time within companies and organizations.

In this chapter, we will cover how to restore data for different workloads to make sure that the backed-up data is recoverable and accessible when a disaster strikes.

Recovering file server data with PowerShell

In this recipe, we'll recover a file server data using DPM. You can recover items, as you can perform most administrative tasks in DPM, either using the DPM administrator console, or using PowerShell cmdlets. In this recipe, we will use DPM PowerShell cmdlets to restore file server data.

For more information on how to enable file server protection with DPM, please check `Chapter 5`, *Protecting Microsoft Workloads with DPM*.

Getting ready

Before you start the recovery, you should always verify that the targeted data source is accessible, and that the DPM agent is reporting **OK** in the DPM console.

How to do it...

Open the Windows PowerShell session on your DPM server and observe the following steps:

1. Open a connection to a DPM server by typing the following command:

   ```
   Connect-DPMServer -DPMServerName $env:COMPUTERNAME
   ```

2. Query all protection groups and store the results in a variable called $PGroup: $PGroup = Get-DPMProtectionGroup. You can see their name under the Name column, and, under ProtectionMethod, you can see whether they're using short-term storage using local DPM disks, or, in the case of our file server protection group, using Azure online protection:

   ```
   CharbelNemnom.com #> $PGroup = Get-DPMProtectionGroup
   CharbelNemnom.com #> $PGroup

   Name                         ProtectionMethod
   ----                         ----------------
   SQL Protection Group         Short-term using disk
   File Server Protection Group Short-term using disk | Online protection
   ```

3. This is an object collection. There were two objects in this collection based on what we're seeing. Bear in mind, in PowerShell syntax, what you could do is type in $PGroup, and if you were to incorporate square brackets, [1], that would refer to the second object in the collection, which, in this case, is the file server protection group object. Now, if you want to drill deeper into that protection group and look for recovery points, what you could do is take that further. For example, we will create a new variable named $PObjects, equal to the result of Get-DPMDatasource; so, we will use a different cmdlet here, followed by the parameter -ProtectionGroup. We are going to refer to our previous variable, $PGroup, and we are specifically interested in the file server protection group. You can make that reference in this case with square brackets: in this example, it's [1]. The full syntax will look like this: $PObjects = Get-DPMDatasource -ProtectionGroup $PGroup[1].

```
CharbelNemnom.com #> $PObjects = Get-DPMDatasource -ProtectionGroup $PGroup[1]
CharbelNemnom.com #> $PObjects

Computer  Name                                      ObjectType
--------  ----                                      ----------
FSRV01    D:\MountPoints\MountPoint-FSRV01 Volume
FSRV01    D:\                                       Volume
```

4. The next thing we are going to do is see what recovery points are available for that protection group, in other words, `Get-DPMRecoveryPoint`, space, and `-Datasource`, well, in this case, `$PObjects`, our previous variable. Again, this is an object collection. There were two objects in this collection based on what we're seeing. In this example, we are interested in recovering from `D:\MountPoints\MountPoint-FSRV01`, so we insert `[0]` in square brackets; this would refer to the first object in the collection. Then, we will sort by the property name, `RepresentedPointInTime`, to select the first recovery point, since we have multiple recovery points. Finally, we will store the result in a new variable. The full syntax will look like this:

   $RecoveryPoint = Get-DPMRecoveryPoint -Datasource $PObjects[0] | Sort -Property RepresentedPointInTime -Descending | Select-Object - First 1

```
CharbelNemnom.com #> Get-DPMRecoveryPoint -Datasource $PObjects[0] | Sort -Property RepresentedPoint
InTime -Descending

Name                                      BackupTime               Datasource
----                                      ----------               ----------
D:\MountPoints\MountPoint-FSRV01 11/11/2018 11:37:13 AM D:\MountPoints\MountPoint-FSRV01 on comp...
D:\MountPoints\MountPoint-FSRV01 11/11/2018 8:53:59 AM  D:\MountPoints\MountPoint-FSRV01 on comp...


CharbelNemnom.com #> $RecoveryPoint = Get-DPMRecoveryPoint -Datasource $PObjects[0] | Sort -Property
 RepresentedPointInTime -Descending | Select-Object -First 1
CharbelNemnom.com #> $RecoveryPoint

Name                                      BackupTime               Datasource
----                                      ----------               ----------
D:\MountPoints\MountPoint-FSRV01 11/11/2018 11:37:13 AM D:\MountPoints\MountPoint-FSRV01 on comp...
```

5. In this step, we will drill down further to restore a single item using the **Item-Level Recovery** (**ILR**) feature instead of restoring an entire recovery point. To do so, we will use a new `Get-DPMRecoverableItem` cmdlet, space, –`RecoverableItem`, space—well, in this case, $RecoveryPoint, our previous variable—then another space, –`BrowseType`, space, and finally `Child`. This will get all the recoverable items in the parent and child nodes of the recovery point. In this example, we are interested to restore the item that starts with the *BRK1026* name, and, finally, we will store the result in a new variable. The full syntax is as follows:

```
$RecoverItem = Get-DPMRecoverableItem -RecoverableItem
$RecoveryPoint -BrowseType Child
```

```
CharbelNemnom.com #> $RecoverItem = Get-DPMRecoverableItem -RecoverableItem $RecoveryPoint -BrowseType Child
CharbelNemnom.com #> $RecoverItem

Name                                                              BackupTime             Datasource
----                                                              ----------             ----------
$RECYCLE.BIN                                                      11/11/2018 11:37:13 AM D:\MountPoints\Moun...
BRK1000 - What's new in Microsoft Project.mp4                    11/11/2018 11:37:13 AM D:\MountPoints\Moun...
BRK1001 - Driving success with Project Online.mp4                11/11/2018 11:37:13 AM D:\MountPoints\Moun...
BRK1025 - Preparing for IoT in IT- Microsoft's IoT Vision and Roadmap.mp4 11/11/2018 11:37:13 AM D:\MountPoints\Moun...
BRK1026 - Getting started with Microsoft Azure and Azure Portal.mp4 11/11/2018 11:37:13 AM D:\MountPoints\Moun...
Sub-mountpoint                                                    11/11/2018 11:37:13 AM D:\MountPoints\Moun...

CharbelNemnom.com #> $RecoverItem = Get-DPMRecoverableItem -RecoverableItem $RecoveryPoint -BrowseType Child | Where-Obj
ect {$_.Name -like "*BRK1026*"}
CharbelNemnom.com #> _
```

6. Next, we need to create a recovery option by using a new cmdlet, `New-DPMRecoveryOption`, that restores the file to a server name, `SC-DPM-1807.virt.lab`, and the `RecoveryLocation` type is `CopyToFolder` to `AlternateLocation`. It will overwrite the file if it exits and restore the original security settings. Finally, we will store the result in a new variable as well. The full syntax is as follows:

```
$RecoveryOption = New-DPMRecoveryOption -TargetServer "SC-
DPM-1807.virt.lab" -RecoveryLocation CopyToFolder
-FileSystem -AlternateLocation "D:\Copytofolder" -OverwriteType
Overwrite -RestoreSecurity -RecoveryType Restore
```

```
CharbelNemnom.com #> $RecoveryOption = New-DPMRecoveryOption -TargetServer "SC-DPM-1807.virt.lab" -RecoveryLocation Copy
ToFolder
>> -FileSystem -AlternateLocation "D:\Copytofolder" -OverwriteType Overwrite -RestoreSecurity -RecoveryType Restore
CharbelNemnom.com #> $RecoveryOption


DsmProperties                   : Microsoft.Internal.EnterpriseStorage.Dls.XsdClasses.MTA.DsmPropertiesType
AlternateLocation               : D:\Copytofolder
LibraryId                       : 00000000-0000-0000-0000-000000000000
SourceServer                    :
TargetServer                    : SC-DPM-1807.VIRT.LAB
RecoverToReplicaFromTape        : False
IsSANRecovery                   : False
ReferencedRecoveryOptions       :
```

7. In the final step, we will trigger the restore process by using a new
cmdlet, `Restore-DPMRecoverableItem`, followed by `-RecoverableItem`, `$RecoverItem` in this case, which is our previous variable
from *Step 5*, then `-RecoveryOption`, and then `$RecoveryOption`, which is our
previous variable from *Step 6*. The full syntax is as follows:

```
CharbelNemnom.com #> # Item-Level Recovery (ILR) single item Restore
CharbelNemnom.com #> Restore-DPMRecoverableItem -RecoverableItem $RecoverItem -RecoveryOption $RecoveryOption

JobCategory         Status      ProtectionGroupName            DataSources
-----------         ------      -------------------            -----------
RestoreAsFilesFromSC InProgress File Server Protection Group D:\MountPoints\MountPoint-FSRV01
```

8. If you want to restore the entire recovery point instead of a single item, then you
need to replace the variable for the `-RecoverableItem` parameter—well, in this
case, `$RecoverItem`—with `$RecoveryPoint` instead. The full syntax is as
follows:

```
Restore-DPMRecoverableItem –RecoverableItem $RecoveryPoint –
RecoveryOption $RecoveryOption
```

9. If you open Windows Explorer under `D:\Copytofolder`, you will see that the
single file is restored, as demonstrated in the following screenshot:

How it works...

In all the restore processes involving either the DPM administrator console or PowerShell, DPM will rely on the VSS architecture present both in the operating system and on the application layer for a successful restore that is both optimal and fully supported.

See also

Please check this reference guide that provides cmdlet descriptions and syntax for the System Center DPM cmdlets: `https://docs.microsoft.com/en-us/powershell/module/dataprotectionmanager/?view=systemcenter-ps-2016`.

Recovering SQL data using the Self-Service Recovery Tool (SSRT)

In this recipe, we'll recover SQL data using DPM. You can recover SQL databases, as you can perform most administrative tasks in DPM, either using the DPM administrator console, via PowerShell, or using the SSRT. In this recipe, we will use the SSRT in DPM to restore SQL data.

For more information on how to enable SQL Server protection with DPM, please check `Chapter 6`, *Protecting Microsoft Workloads with DPM*.

Getting ready

You can enable self-service recovery for a group of users in SCDPM. The first step is to configure a DPM role using the **Self-Service Recovery** option in the **Protection** workspace in the DPM console. The second step is to install the SSRT on the SQL DBA's computer.

How to do it...

1. Open your **DPM Administrator Console**, click on the **Protection** workspace, and then click on the **Self service recovery** button at the top of the ribbon, as shown in the following screenshot:

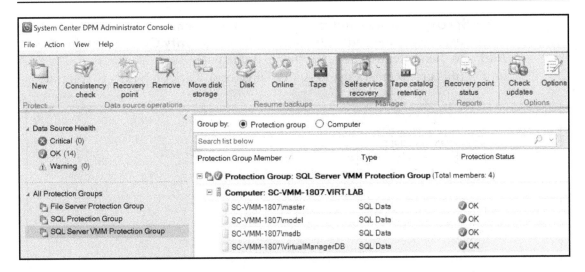

2. In the **DPM Self Service Recovery Configuration Tool for SQL Server** window, click **Create Role**.

3. In the **Welcome to the DPM Role Configuration Wizard** window, click on **Next >** to continue:

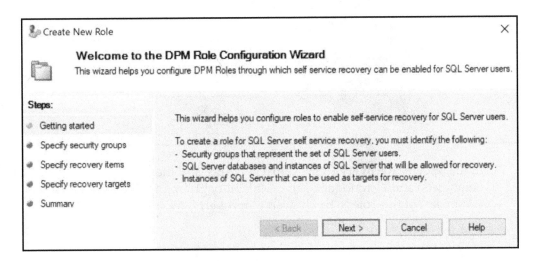

4. In the **Specify Security Groups** step, enter a **Role Name** and **Description** that will be used to uniquely identify this role. In the **Security Groups** section, click **Add**, and then enter a `Security Group` domain in `<domain\group>` format (this group must exist in Active Directory). Click on **Next >** to continue:

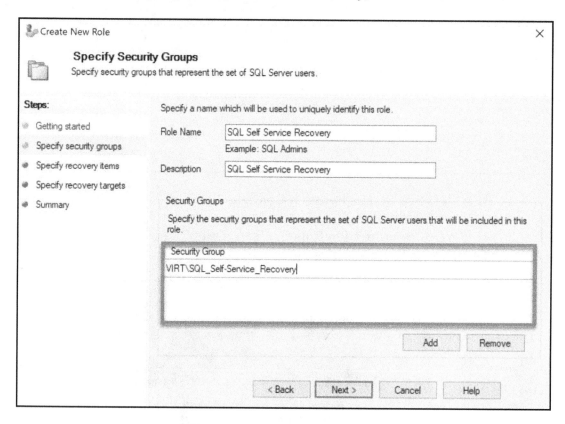

5. In the **Specify Recovery Items** step, click **Add**, and then specify the SQL Server database(s) and instance(s), or the availability group of SQL Servers that you want users of this role to be allowed to recover. Click on **Next >** to continue:

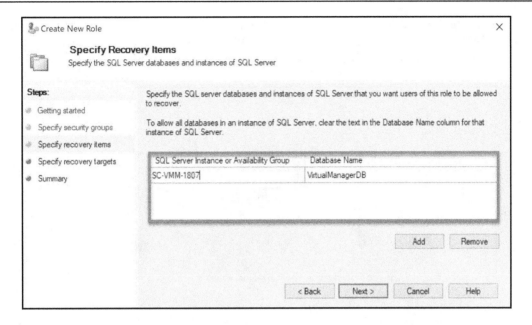

6. In the **Specify Recovery Target Locations** step, specify whether you want to **Allow users to recover the databases to another instance of SQL Server.** In all instances, users are not allowed to overwrite the original database. To allow users to recover the database as files only, you do not need to configure **Recovery Target Locations**. At the time of recovery, users can specify any location where they have permission to write. Click on **Next >** to continue:

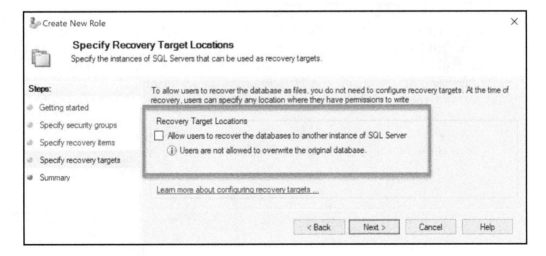

7. In the **Summary** page, you can see the results of your selections. Click on **Finish**. After a moment, you can see that the DPM role configuration has been successfully saved. Click **Close**:

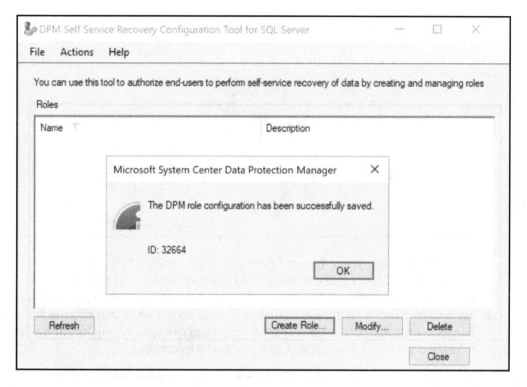

8. Now, switch to a Windows client machine, mount/extract System Center Data Protection Manager ISO media, and then launch `Setup.exe`. Before you start the installation, make sure that .NET Framework 3.5 SP1 is installed on the computer. You can enable the .NET Framework 3.5 through the Windows **Control Panel | Turn Windows features on or off**. This option requires an internet connection.

9. In the **Welcome** screen, click the **DPM Self Service Recovery** link, as demonstrated in the following screenshot:

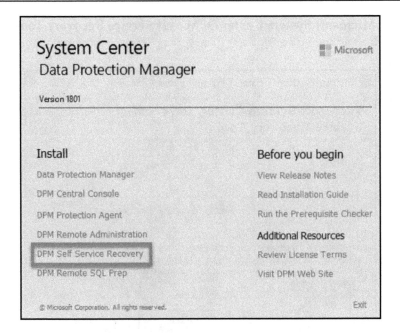

10. Read and agree to the **Microsoft Software License Terms**, and then click **Accept**:

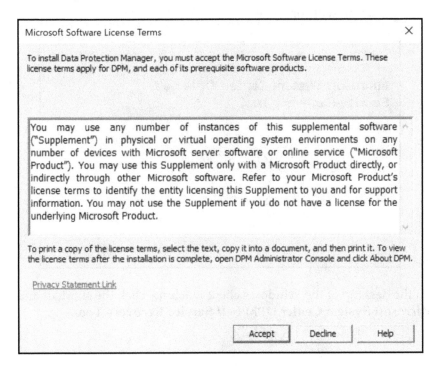

11. In the **Microsoft System Center DPM Self Service Recovery Tool** setup, click **Install**:

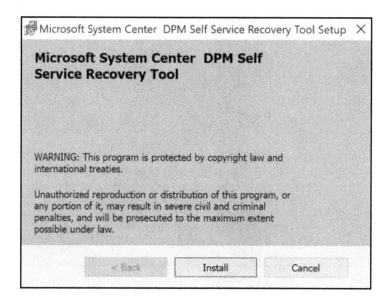

12. The installation will complete very quickly. Click **Finish**:

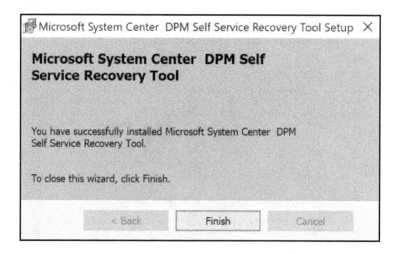

13. On the desktop of the Windows client machine, click the shortcut and launch **Microsoft System Center DPM Self Service Recovery Tool**.

14. In the **DPM Self Service Recovery Tool** window, click **Connect to Server...** and enter the name of your DPM Server as FQDN and click **Connect**, as demonstrated in the following screenshot:

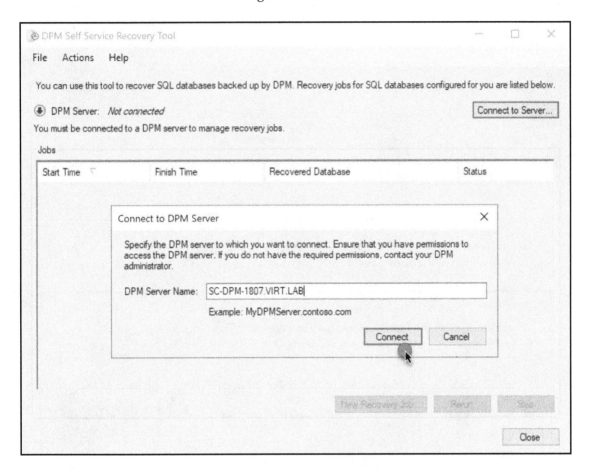

15. In the **DPM Self Service Recovery Tool** window, click **New Recovery Job...** in the bottom-right corner, as shown in the following screenshot:

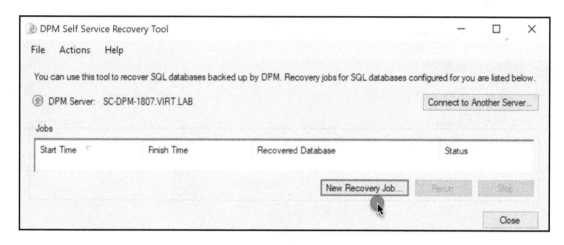

16. In the **Welcome to the Start New Recovery Job Wizard** window, click **Do not show this Welcome page again**, and then click on **Next >** to continue:

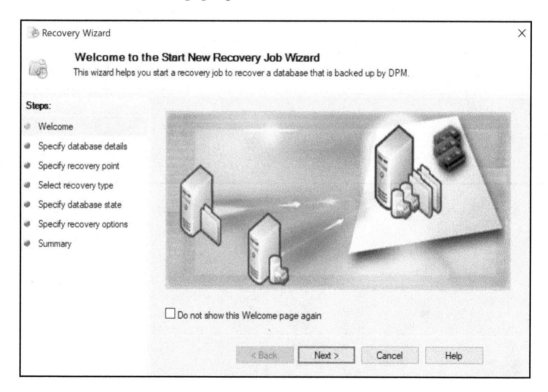

17. In the **Specify Database Details** page, specify the details of the database you want to recover and where it resides. Click on **Next >** to continue:

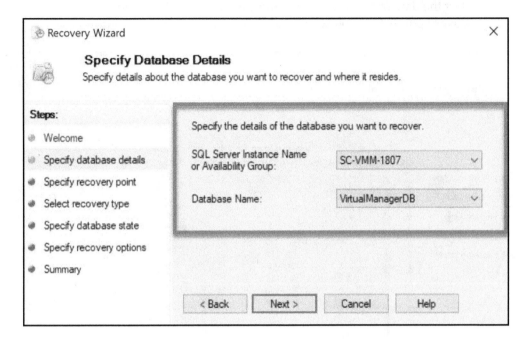

18. In the **Specify Recovery Point** page, please select which recovery point to use for recovery. The available recovery points are indicated in bold on the calendar. Select the date from the calendar and the time from the drop-down list for the recovery points that you want, and then click on **Next >** to continue:

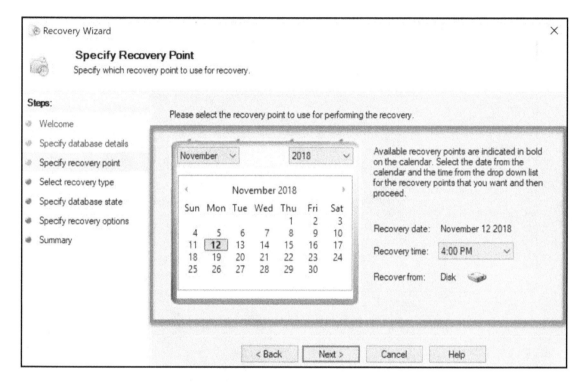

19. In the **Select Recovery Type** page, select the type of recovery you want to perform. Since we did not select **Specify Recovery Target Locations** to **Allow users to recover the databases to another instance of SQL Server** in the previous step, we can only recover to a network folder. Click on **Next >** to continue:

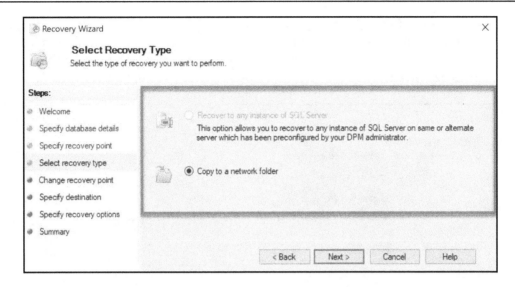

20. In the **Change Recovery Point** page, please specify a recovery point that has full backup, because users are not allowed to recover the databases to another instance of SQL Server. Hence, DPM can only copy files from a recovery point associated with an express full backup. Click on **Next >** to continue:

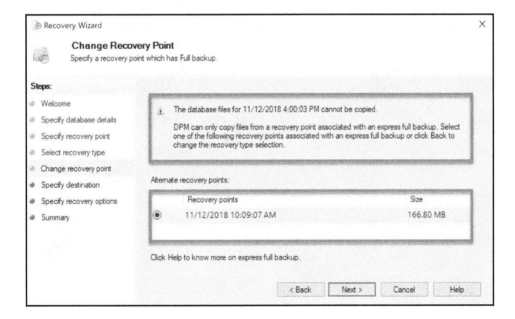

21. In the **Specify Destination** page, please specify where you would like to copy the database files. Enter the destination server as FQDN and a destination folder. Please note that the destination server specified here must have the DPM agent installed; otherwise, recovery will fail. Click on **Next >** to continue:

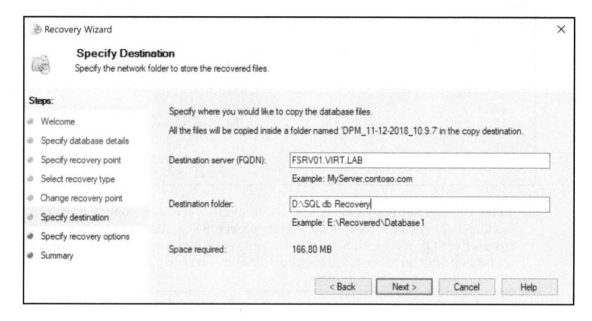

22. In the **Specify Recovery Options** page, please specify whether you want to restore the security of the destination computer or the recovery point version. Click on **Next >** to continue:

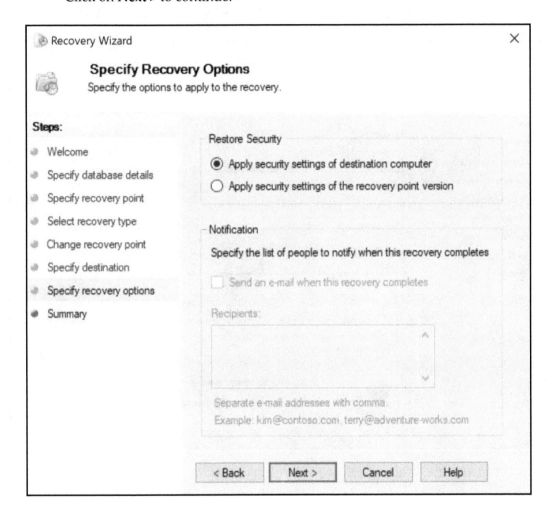

23. In the **Summary** page, you can see the results of your selections. Click on **Recover**. After a moment, you can see the message that **A recovery job with the specified settings was started successfully**. You can also monitor the progress of the job from the DPM console under **Monitoring** workspace. Click **OK**:

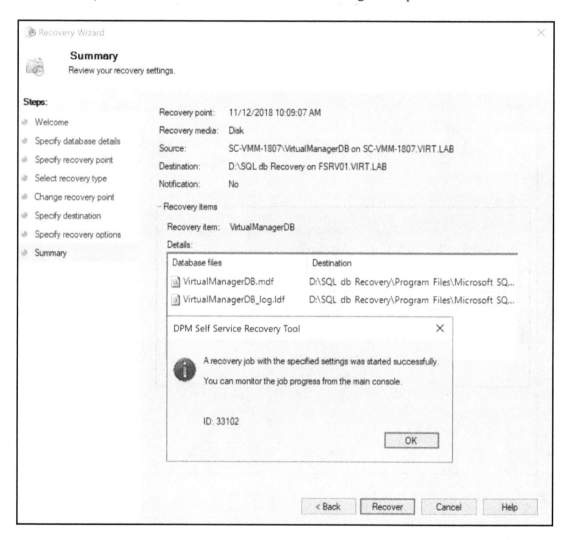

24. In the **DPM Self Service Recovery Tool**, you'll see that the database recovery job was completed successfully, including the amount of data transferred. Click **Close**:

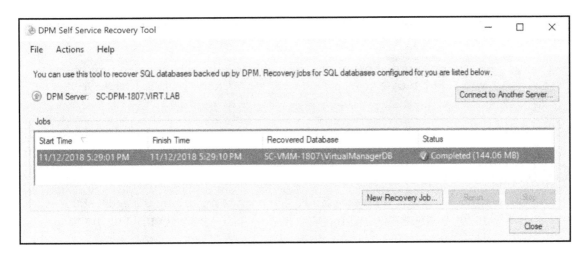

25. Open Windows Explorer on the destination server under D:\SQL db Recovery, and you will see that the database is restored successfully.

How it works...

Once you enable **Self-Service Recovery** in SCDPM, and install the SSRT on the SQL DBA's computer, you need to add the list of users that are allowed to perform self-service recovery to the security group in Active Directory, and then specify the set of databases that are permitted for self-service recovery to the DPM role. The target recovery SQL Server instances must also be added to the DPM role.

SSRT is a great feature that can be used in complex and large environments to assign non-administrators, such as SQL DBAs and developers, with sufficient permissions to recover SQL Server databases without requesting support from the backup administrator. You can be really granular with the permissions that you want to assign.

Recovering a failed server using bare-metal recovery

In this recipe, we'll show you how to recover a failed server using **bare-metal recovery** (**BMR**).

 For more information on how to enable Windows bare-metal protection with DPM, please `Chapter 5`, *Protecting Microsoft Workloads with DPM*.

Getting ready

Before you recover a failed server using BMR, you need to make sure the agent status is reporting **OK** in the **Management** workspace, as well as the protection status in the **Protection** workspace.

How to do it...

1. Open your DPM Administrator Console, and click on the **Recovery** workspace. You can see a calendar related to the selection in the left-hand navigator, where you can drill down under the domain, select the appropriate server, then **All DPM Protected Data**, and then **System Protection**. The calendar then lights up in bold. On those days when you've got restore points that you can recover from, you can see the recovery date and time. Over in the detail panel, toward the bottom-right corner, you can see **Bare Metal Recovery**, as demonstrated in the following screenshot:

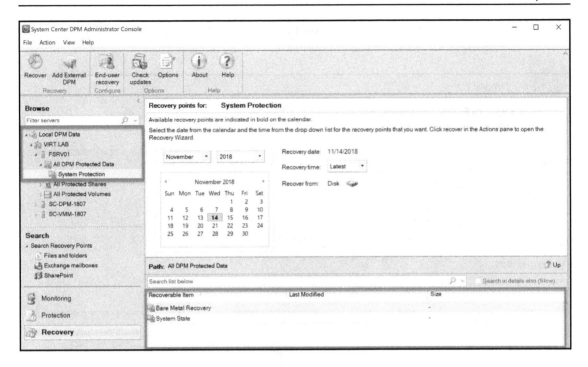

2. Next, right-click on **Bare Metal Recovery**, and then click **Recover...**

3. In the **Review Recovery Selection** page, you can review your recovery selections. Click on **Next >** to continue:

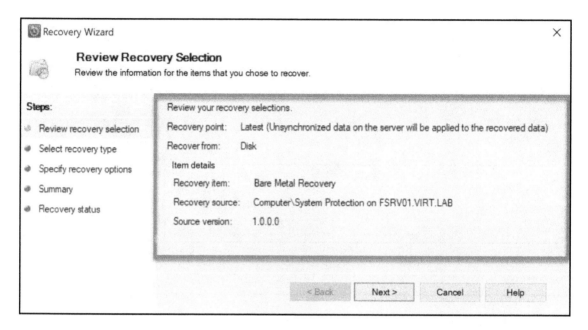

4. In the **Select Recovery Type**, select the type of recovery you want to perform. Since we are not using tapes, we will choose the **Copy to a network folder** here, and then click on **Next >** to continue:

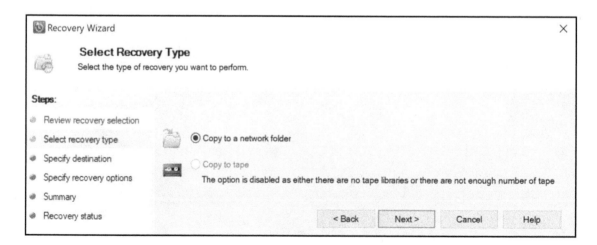

5. Next, you have to click **Browse...** to select a destination. In this example, we've already got a shared folder prepared to store this information on another server named WS2016-WDS. Specify the alternate recovery destination and click **OK**:

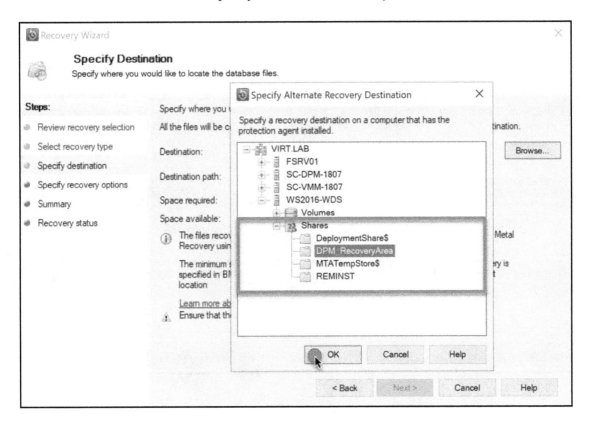

6. The information will be automatically filled in with the space required: for this particular example, **24.41** gigabytes, and we've got **39.86** gigabytes available, so everything looks good. Then click on **Next >** to continue:

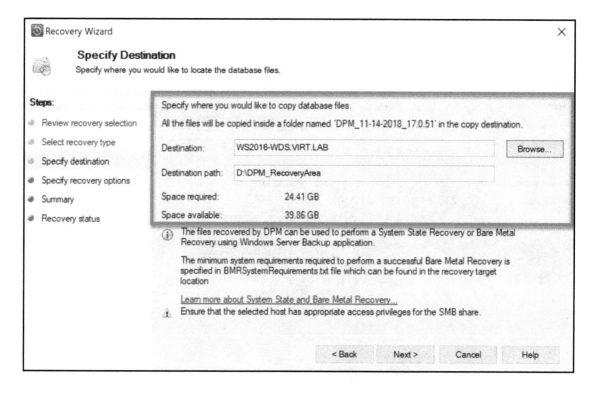

7. You're then asked whether you want to restore the security settings of the destination computer, or the security settings of the recovery point version that you're recovering from. In this example, we will choose **Apply the security settings of the recovery point** version. You have the option of enabling network bandwidth throttling; where this is kind of a larger deployment over the network, you could click the **Modify...** link, and throttle the bandwidth for work and non-work hours. However, we're not going to do this, assuming that this will take place when it's not going to affect anyone working on the network. Click on **Next >** to continue:

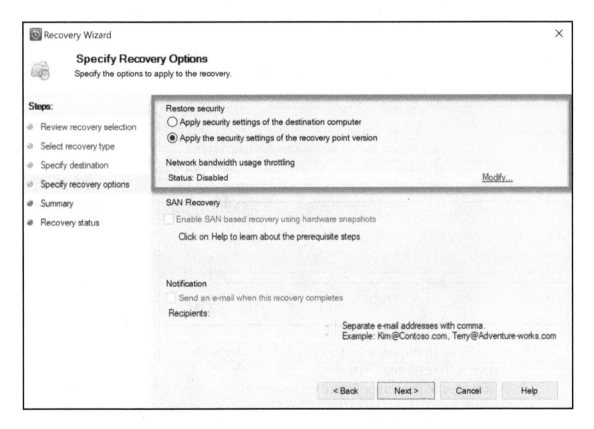

8. In the **Summary** page, you can see the results of your selections. Click on **Recover**. The recovery will take some time to push the BMR files to that network shared folder. Click **Close**:

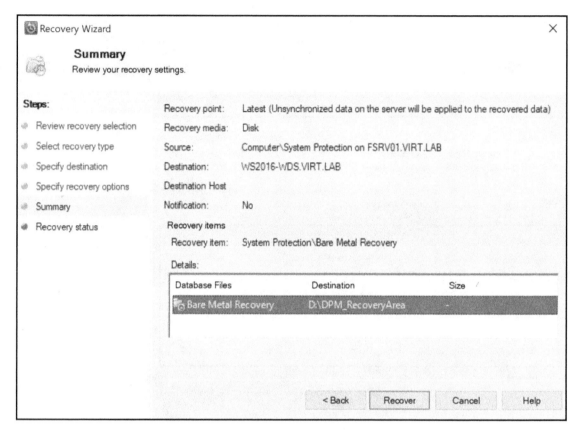

9. In the DPM admin console, you can switch over to the **Monitoring** workspace, and view the informational alerts.

10. Switch over to the server where you essentially copied the BMR files to a network share. If you go to the path on that server, under the recovery area folder and share, you will see the DPM folder with the date and time information, then the second-level DPM folder, then WindowsImageBackup, then your server name, and then, in there, you can see all the details, including the backup folder itself with all of the core files, as demonstrated in the following screenshot:

Name	Date modified	Type	Size
Backup 2018-11-14 144905	11/14/2018 5:00 PM	File folder	
Catalog	11/14/2018 5:00 PM	File folder	
SPPMetadataCache	11/14/2018 5:00 PM	File folder	
Mediald	11/14/2018 3:49 PM	File	1 KB

11. Now, it's this second-level DPM folder that you want to share. The reason is the recovery process needs to see the `WindowsImageBackup` folder at the root. So, right-click on the `DPM_Recovered_At_(Date_Time)` folder, go into **Properties**, then choose **Sharing**, and then click the **Advanced Sharing...** button, give the share name, and read permissions will be sufficient for this to work with bare-metal recovery.

12. The next step to perform is to boot up the server that won't boot normally. From the installation media for Server 2016, click on **Repair your computer**, as shown in the following screenshot:

13. Next, click **Troubleshoot**, and then select the **System Image Recovery** mechanism. You will see a message stating that it can't find a local system image on this computer, which is correct, because it's out on the network on another server. So, simply click **Cancel** and then **Next >**, and then click the **Advanced** button, as shown in the following screenshot:

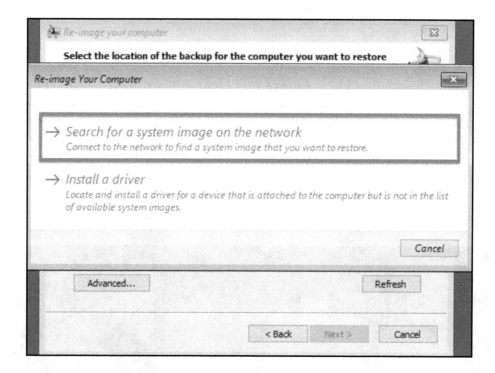

14. Select **Search for a system image on the network**, and then confirm that you want to connect to the network by clicking **Yes**. The network folder will start with a double backslash; then insert the IP address of the server, followed by the share name on that host for bare-metal recovery, and then click **OK**:

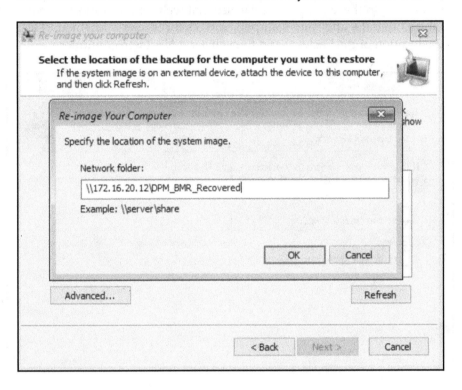

15. You need to authenticate with a domain's admin credentials, but any credentials that have read access to the contents of that share would do the trick in this case. Enter your credentials and then click **OK**. It may take a minute or two for it to give you a list of images that are date- and time-stamped on the remote server, so be patient. In this example, we can see that we've got our most-recent system image, it's date- and time-stamped, and it's for the server named `FSRV01`. Select the location of the backup, and then click on **Next >** to continue:

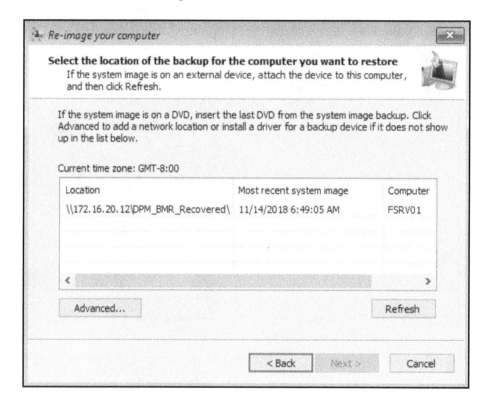

16. Select the date and time of the system image to restore, and then click **Next >**. You can choose the **Format and repartition disks** option, and when you do that, you can even **Exclude disks...** that might contain data. So, in this case, we are not going to format and repartition disks, and we don't need to utilize the **Install drivers...** option. If you were to click on **Advanced...**, you could automatically have the computer restarted, or not, depending on the state you select. However, we are going to leave that as it is, and then click **Next >**:

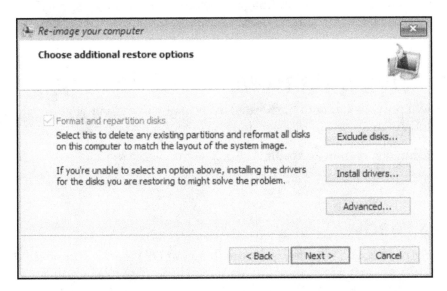

17. Last, but not least, you will see the date and time of the restore point, including the drive to restore, so, at this point, you would just continue by clicking **Finish**, and then you could view the results in the **Monitoring** workspace in the DPM administrator console, as demonstrated in the following screenshot:

How it works...

The way that this works is for you to have a network-shared folder available, essentially to place the recovery files for BMR, and then you need to boot up the failed server using an alternative method, assuming it won't boot at all. For example, if it's Windows Server 2019 that is having trouble booting up, then you should boot from the Server 2019 installation media, not performing an installation, but rather choosing **Repair**. Then you can go to **Troubleshoot**, and select the **System Image Recovery** mechanism by specifying the location of the system image on the network share and pulling down the BMR option.

Recovering data from Azure Backup

This recipe will provide you with the needed information to recover your production data from Microsoft Azure in case of disaster or data corruption.

For more information on how to enable Azure Backup, please see `Chapter 10`, *Integrating DPM with Azure Backup*.

Getting ready

Before you get started, you need to make sure that your DPM server is connected to Microsoft Azure and that it is in an online state. You can verify this by going to the **Management** workspace within the DPM console and browsing to the **Online** section:

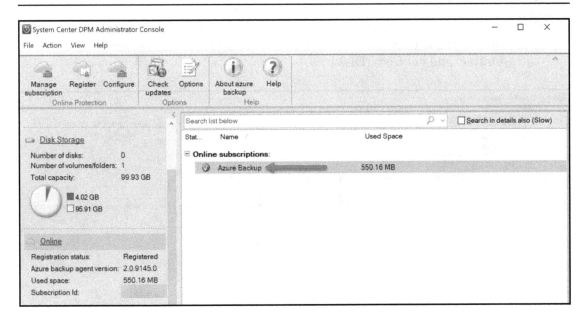

How to do it...

1. To restore your production data from Azure, open your DPM Administrator Console, and click on **Recovery** workspace.

2. On the left-hand side, you will find your protected data sources in both an active and inactive state. Start by browsing the tree so that your data source will be visible; in my case, this is the D:\ drive of my file server.

3. Next, you need to choose the right date, followed by choosing the right **Recovery time** from the drop-down list. In this example, we need to recover from Azure (**Online**) and not from (**Disk**):

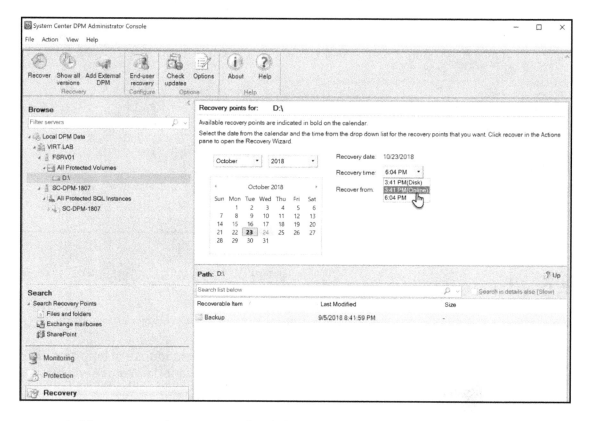

4. Next, to start the restore, right-click on the data source under the **Recoverable Item** and choose **Recover...**:

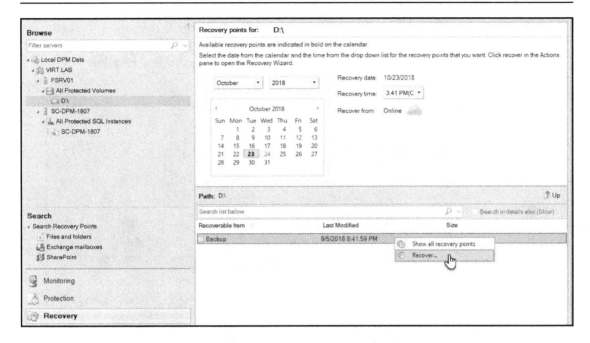

5. The **Recovery Wizard** will open and present you with the actual restore process. Click on **Next >** to continue:

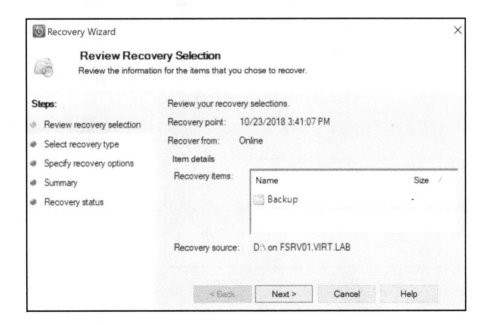

6. Next, you need to choose the recovery type for the restore operation. You can choose to recover the data to the original location, or to an alternate location. In this example, we will choose to recover the data to its original location. Click on **Next** to continue:

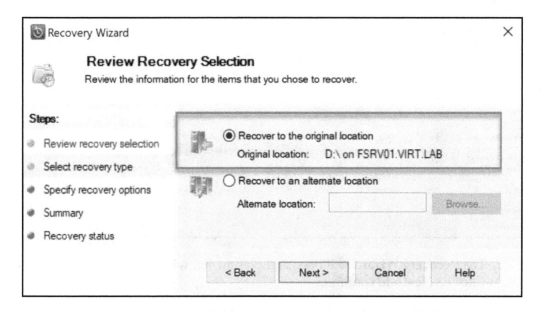

7. Finally, you need to select **Specify recovery options**, which will manage your **Existing version recovery behavior**, **Restore security** settings, **Network bandwidth usage throttling**, **SAN Recovery**, and email **Notification**. In this example, we will overwrite the exiting version. Click on **Next** to get to the **Summary** page:

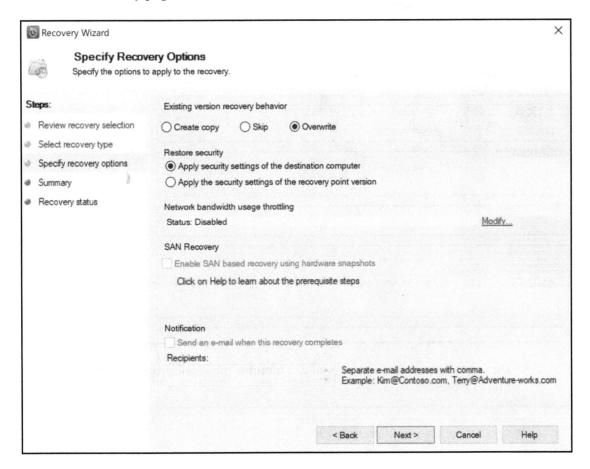

8. On the **Summary** page, you can verify the restore operation. If it fits your needs, click on the **Recover** button to start the recovery process:

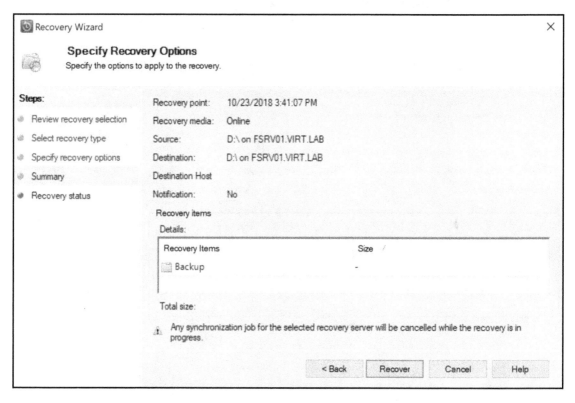

9. During the recovery process, you can monitor the work progress in the **Recovery Status** window:

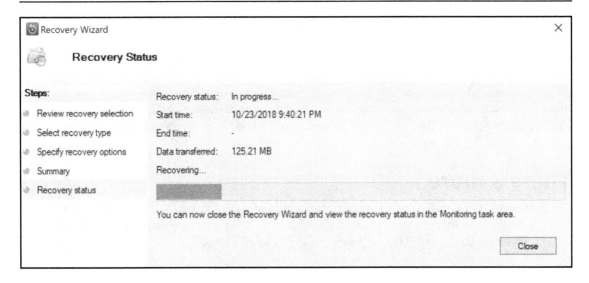

10. You can also monitor the recovery process and its status under the **Monitoring** workspace, **Alerts**, and **Jobs** section. In this case, the restore was completed successfully:

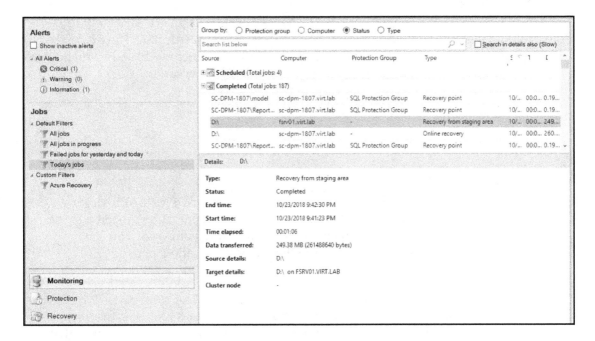

How it works...

The restore process from Microsoft Azure is a two-step process for DPM. During the Azure Backup registration phase, we pointed out something called **Recovery Folder Settings** (staging area); this folder comes into play during the restore process before the data is restored back to its original location. So, make sure you have enough free space in that folder before you start the recovery process, as otherwise the restore will fail.

There's more...

Keep in mind that Azure is applicable for all kinds of workload sizes. You can perform a daily, weekly, monthly, or yearly backup and restore of any data; this is a great example of what a **Disaster Recovery** (**DR**) scenario for DPM would look like.

Recovering data from an external DPM server

You can recover the data you've backed up to Azure Backup (Recovery Services Vault) from another DPM or MABS server in case of disaster or data corruption. The **external DPM server** feature can be used for this type of scenario. This recipe will show you how to recover your data from Azure Backup using an external DPM server.

For more information on how to enable Azure Backup, please see `Chapter 10`, *Integrating DPM with Azure Backup*.

Getting ready

Before you get started, you need to make sure you have another DPM/MABS server connected to Microsoft Azure, with the latest Azure Backup agent, and registered to the same Recovery Services Vault from which you want to restore your data. You can download the latest Azure Backup agent from the following location: `https://go.microsoft.com/fwLink/?LinkID=288905`.

 Please note that you cannot add an external DPM for recovery as long as you don't have another DPM/MABS server registered to the same Recovery Services Vault. In other words, only DPM or MABS servers that are associated with the same Recovery Services Vault in Azure can recover each other's data.

How to do it...

The following steps were followed to recover data to another DPM/MABS server from Microsoft Azure:

1. Open your **DPM Administrator Console** and click on **Recovery** workspace.
2. Click **Add External DPM** in the top-left corner:

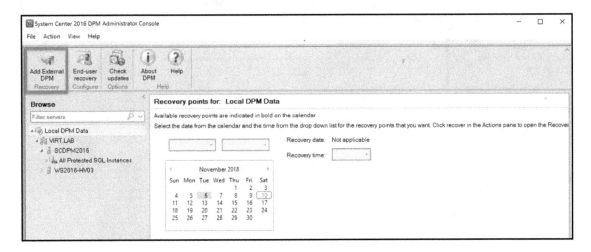

3. Download new vault credentials from the Recovery Services Vault associated with the DPM server where the data is being stored.
4. Select the DPM server from the drop-down list of DPM servers registered with the backup vault, and then provide the encryption passphrase key that you set when you registered the DPM server with Azure. You own the encryption passphrase, and Microsoft does not have the ability to see the passphrase used by you. If you lose this passphrase, you cannot recover your data.

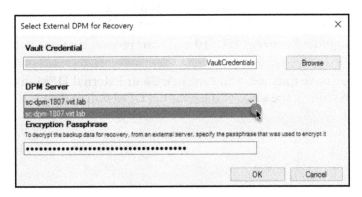

5. Once the external DPM server is successfully added, you can browse the data from the **External DPM Online Data** and **Local DPM Data**:

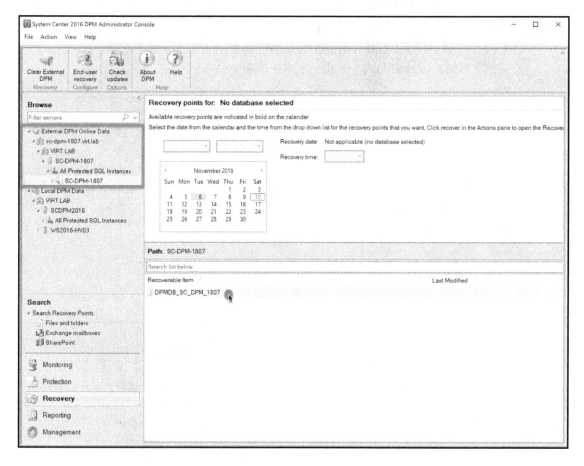

6. Select the date from the **Recovery points** drop-down list and then select the desired **Recovery time**. Right-click the appropriate item and click **Recover**.

7. Go through the **Recovery Wizard** and start recovering your data as described in this recipe.

8. When you have finished, you can click **Clear External DPM** in the top-left hand corner to remove the view of the external DPM online data.

How it works...

The restore process from Microsoft Azure is a two-step process for DPM. During the Azure Backup registration phase, we pointed out something called **Recovery Folder Settings** (staging area); this folder comes into play during the restore process before the data is restored back to its original location. So, make sure you have enough free space in that folder before you start the recovery process, as otherwise the restore will fail.

There's more...

An external DPM server can also be used to recover the data during the entire datacenter failure. DPM or Azure Backup Server has to be deployed and registered to the same Recovery Services Vault, and then External DPM server has to be added by providing appropriate Recovery Services vault credentials including the encryption passphrase key to restore the data saved on Azure's public cloud.

Recovering data from a secondary DPM server

In the scenario where you have a traditional DPM-DPM-DR implementation in your datacenter (known as Chaining or Cyclic protection) to provide additional offsite protection from a disaster recovery scenario, where you have a secondary DPM server in one location backing up a primary DPM server that is deployed in another location. This scenario is known as a classic approach compared to the modern Azure Backup solution, which is considered a light version of implementing a disaster recovery.

In this recipe, we will show you how to recover your data based on the DPM-DPM-DR scenario.

Getting ready

Before you get started, you need to have a second DPM server installed and connected to the primary DPM server. To do so, open **DPM Administrator Console** and go the **Management** workspace, click on **Add** under **Production Servers**, select the production server type as **Windows Servers**, then in **Select agent deployment method**, choose **Attach agents** and then select **Computer on trusted domain** if the DPM servers are domain joined. Then continue the wizard by selecting the primary DPM server and enter the necessary credentials:

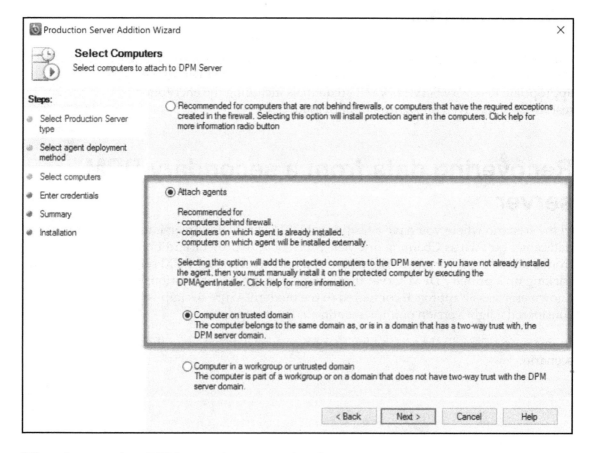

When the secondary DPM server is connected to the primary DPM server, you can go ahead and start creating protection groups by expanding your primary DPM server as shown in the following screenshot. Your primary protected data sources will be listed under the **Protected Servers** node.

Please note that when you have chosen to protect replicas on the primary DPM server, make sure that you protect the DPM database of the primary DPM server along with the replicas, because without protecting the DPM database you will not be able to recover the replicas of the primary DPM server in case of a disaster where the DPM database and the replicas are lost.

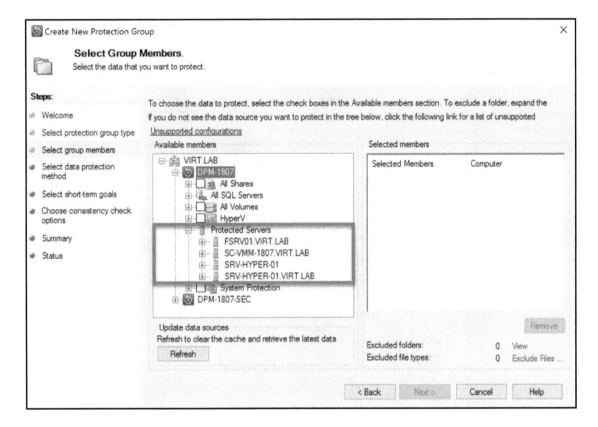

In the **Specify short-term goals**, there is no option to choose when to back up the data from the primary DPM server. You can only specify the **Synchronization frequency**, which you can offset starting at 12 a.m. by clicking on **Modify synchronization start time**:

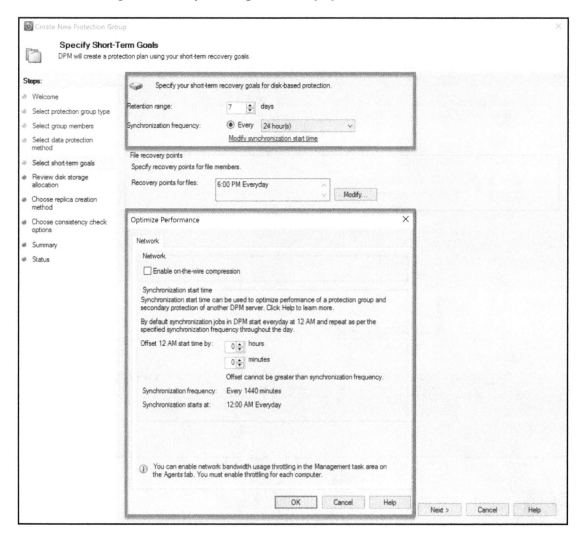

How to do it...

The following steps were followed to recover data from a secondary DPM server:

1. Open your **DPM Administrator Console** on the secondary DPM server, and click on the **Recovery** workspace. You can see a calendar related to the selection in the left-hand navigator, where you can drill down under the domain, select the appropriate server, and then **All Protected Data**. The calendar then lights up in bold. On those days when you've got restore points that you can recover from, you can see the recovery date and time. Over in the detail panel, toward the bottom-right corner, you can see the **Recoverable Item**, as demonstrated in the following screenshot:

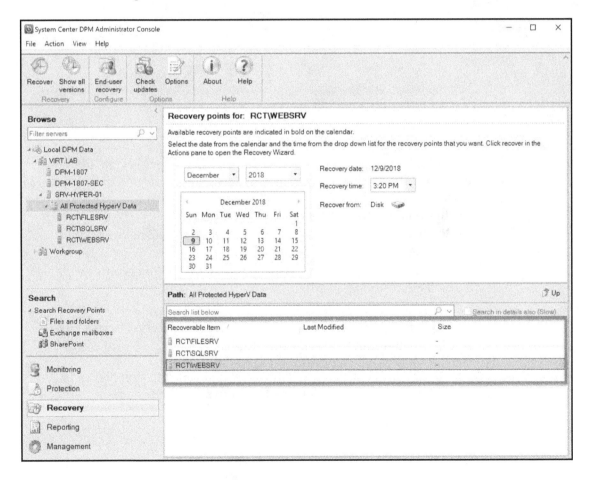

2. Next, right-click on the desired recoverable item, and then click **Recover...**

3. In the **Review Recovery Selection** page, you can review your recovery selections. Click on **Next >** to continue:

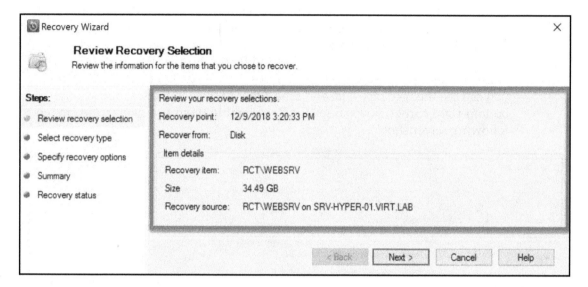

4. In the **Select Recovery Type** page, you will see that you have several options for the restore job. You can choose to restore the secondary protected data source to the following:

   - **Recover replica to primary DPM server**
   - **Recover to original instance** (the current files will be overwritten during recovery)
   - **Recover as virtual machine to any host** (this option is only available if you are restoring a VM)
   - **Copy to a network folder**
   - **Copy to tape** (this option is grayed out since we don't have a tape library attached to the DPM server)

5. Choose the option that will apply to your restore job and click on **Next >** to continue. In this example, we will **Copy to a network folder**:

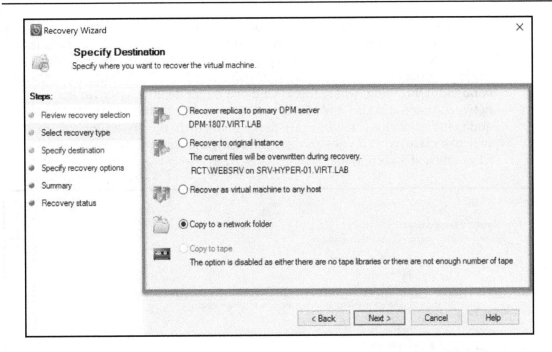

6. In the **Specify Destination** page, click **Browse...** and then specify where you want to recover the virtual machine. Click on **Next >** to continue:

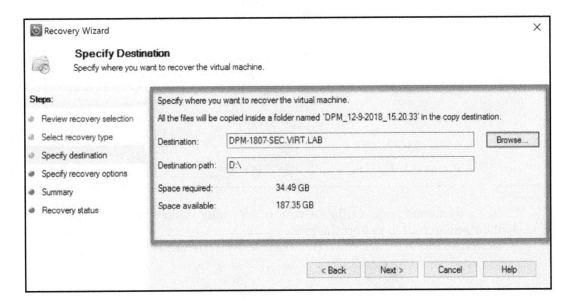

7. You're then asked whether you want to restore the security settings of the destination computer, or the security settings of the recovery point version that you're recovering from. In this example, we will choose **Apply the security settings of the recovery point version**. You have the option of enabling network bandwidth throttling; where this is kind of a larger deployment over the network, you could click the **Modify...** link, and throttle the bandwidth for work and non-work hours. However, we're not going to do this, assuming that this will take place when it's not going to affect anyone working on the network. Click on **Next >** to continue:

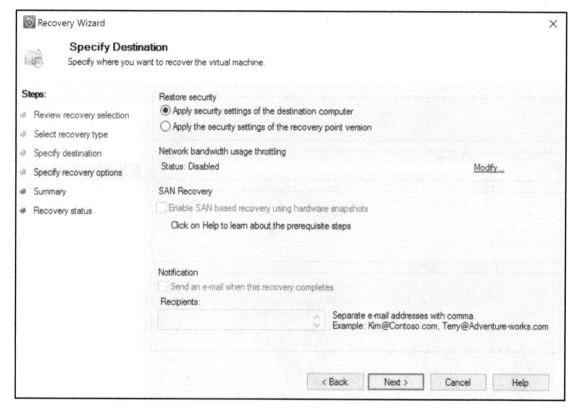

8. In the **Summary** page, verify the restore job configuration and click on the **Recover** button to start the recovery job:

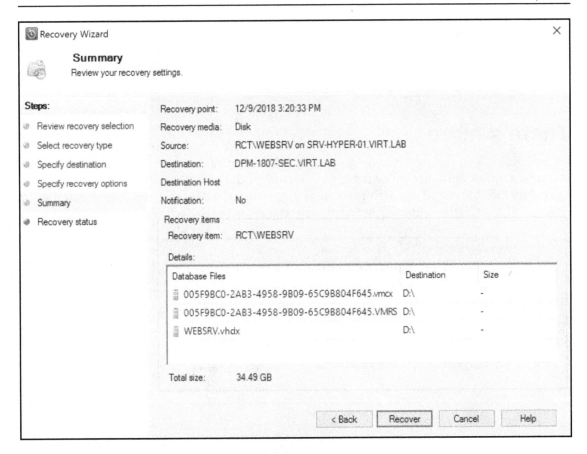

9. You can keep track of the progress via the **All jobs in progress** filter located in the **Monitoring** workspace of the DPM console.

How it works...

When you protect a data source that resides on a primary DPM server, the secondary DPM server will query the primary DPM server VSS writer called DPM writer, which will create the replication process from the primary DPM server to the secondary, and finally store the recovery points on the backup storage volume on the secondary DPM sever. When you recover the protected data source from a secondary DPM server, the data will be recovered from its storage volume.

Additionally, one or more primary DPM servers can be protected by the secondary DPM server. This is important while implementing the offsite backup scenario. A DPM server could also be enabled for chaining, which means that it is both a primary and a secondary DPM server at the same time.

There's more...

Please note that you cannot recover data to its **original instance** or **original location** from a secondary server without first switching protection of the protected computer to the secondary DPM server. To switch protection, right-click the data source in the protection group as shown in the following screenshot, and then select **Switch disaster protection**:

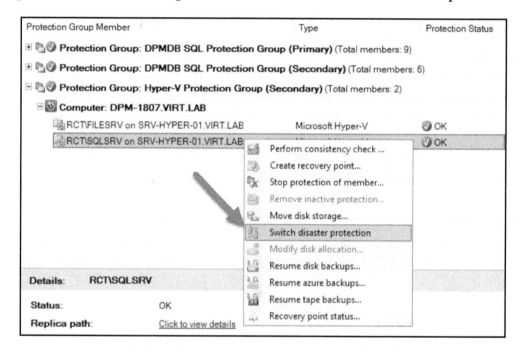

When you perform a switch operation on a protected data source that resides on a primary DPM server, the secondary DPM server reaches out to the DCOM object managing the DPMRA services on the protected server hosting the DPM agent and provides the information that the previous secondary DPM server is now the new primary DPM server. The secondary DPM server must have network access to the primary protected data source to be able to verify access to the DCOM object.

If you forget to perform the switch operation, you will receive the following error message during the recovery process as a friendly reminder:

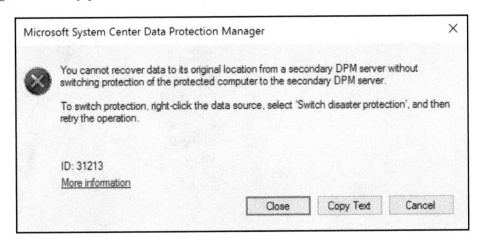

Keep in mind that the DPM-DPM-DR scenario is applicable for all kinds of workload sizes. You can perform a daily backup based on the synchronization frequency that you choose and restore any data; this is a great example of what a **Disaster Recovery** (**DR**) scenario for DPM would look like in.

10
Integrating DPM with Azure Backup

In this chapter, we will cover the following topics:

- Integrating DPM with Azure Backup
- Protecting data with Azure Backup
- Creating online recovery points
- Monitoring and centralized reporting

Introduction

Azure Backup makes a great case for moving on-premises tape and disk infrastructure to the cloud. As with all cloud solutions, it is cost-effective, with a pay-as-you-go model and no upfront costs. But unlike other cloud-connect strategies, Azure Backup is built as a cloud-first platform as a service with a single management pane, no backup infrastructure to maintain (other than the on-premises footprint), and no storage egress cost.

This model has several advantages. The Azure Backup service comes with 99.9 percent availability time. As you create Recovery Services Vaults in Azure to store data, the data is stored in geo-replicated storage, protecting it from disasters. Even if there is an outage of one of the Azure data centers, the data will still be accessible. With Azure Backup, backed-up data is always encrypted on both the wire and at rest on Azure such that it is always secure before it leaves your data center (on-premises).

Azure Backup is a good choice when it comes to maintaining backups for small and large organizations. Azure Backup provides an easy-to-use interface to back up Windows-based servers from on-premises to Azure. By integrating **System Center Data Protection Manager** (**SCDPM**) with Azure Backup, you can embrace Azure Backup as a viable, short-term and long-term retention target. The Azure Backup service also maintains backup metadata that enables you to restore data anywhere from Azure to an alternate DPM server. Please read `Chapter 12`, *Implementing Disaster Recovery with DPM*.

This chapter describes how Azure Backup and DPM provide a compelling, hybrid cloud backup solution for your organization.

Integrating DPM with Azure Backup

This recipe will cover how to integrate and configure your DPM server with Azure Backup.

Getting ready

To integrate and configure your DPM server with Azure Backup, all you need is an Azure subscription. With a subscription, you can sign in to the Azure Portal at `https://portal.azure.com` and create a Recovery Services Vault, then download the vault credentials, install the Azure Backup agent on each DPM server, and finally register the DPM server with the Recovery Services Vault.

How to do it...

Now take the following steps:

1. Open your **DPM Administrator Console**, click on the **Management** workspace, and then click on **Online** followed by the **Manage subscription** button, as shown in the following screenshot:

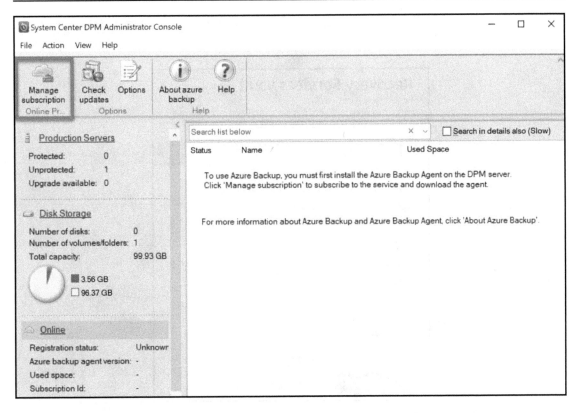

The Azure portal web page will open; sign in to your subscription.

2. Select **All services** from the left menu, and then type `Recovery Services Vaults`. On the **Recovery Services vaults** page, click **+Add**:

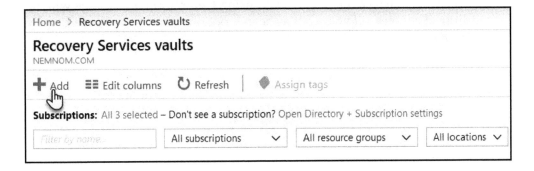

3. Enter the **Name**, **Subscription**, **Resource group** name, and Azure data center **Location**. Click **Create**:

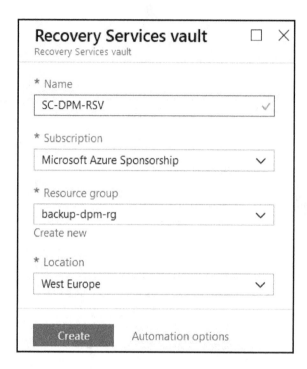

By default, when the vault is created, the storage replication is set to **Geo-redundant** storage, which means that the data you backed up to Azure will be automatically replicated to another adjacent Azure data center for extra protection, so the data is resilient if a regional outage occurs, or if the primary region cannot be recovered. However, using **Geo-redundant** storage will incur additional charges—if you want a cheaper option, you can configure **Locally-redundant** storage.

4. To do that, open your vault and browse to the **Manage** section. Click on **Backup Infrastructure**, and then select **Backup Configuration**. Choose the storage replication option for your vault, and finally, click on **Save**:

 Please note that one copy of your data is stored locally on disks on-premises, three copies of the same data is stored in Azure with **Locally-Redundant Storage** (**LRS**), and in the case of **Geo-Redundant Storage** (**GRS**), you will have three more copies in another Azure region. Please be aware that after choosing the storage option for your vault and starting to protect your data with Azure, you cannot change the storage option afterwards—it's a one-time decision, so plan carefully.

5. Next, you need to download the **vault credentials** file, which is a certificate generated by the Azure Portal and valid only for two days. From the Azure Portal, open your vault and browse to the **Settings** section. Click on **Properties**, and under **Backup Credentials**, select **Already using the latest Recovery Services Agent**, and then click the **Download** button. Make sure that the vault credentials file is saved in a location that can be accessed from your DPM machine:

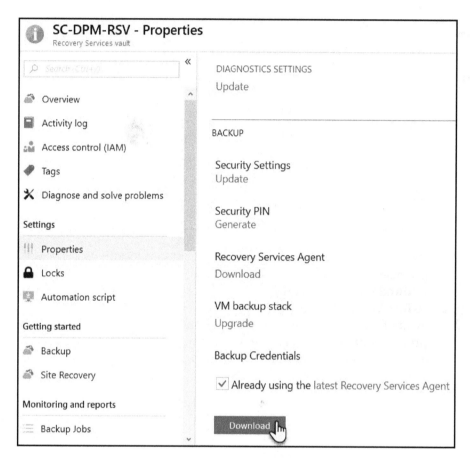

6. Within the same blade, under **Recovery Services Agent**, click **Download** to download the latest **Microsoft Azure Recovery Services** (**MARS**) agent. Copy the MARSAgentInstaller.exe file to your DPM machine and launch the installation.

7. On the **Installation Settings** page, choose the installation folder and scratch folder required for the agent. The cache location specified must have free space of at least 5 percent of the backup data. Click **Next** to continue:

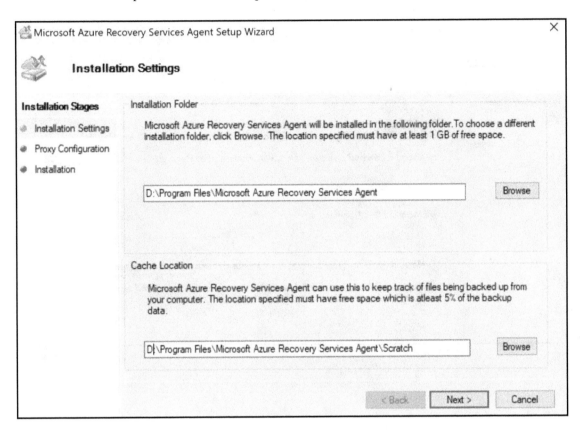

8. If you are using a proxy server in your environment, then set the custom proxy settings. Click **Next** to continue, and then click **Install.** Once the agent is installed, **Close** the window:

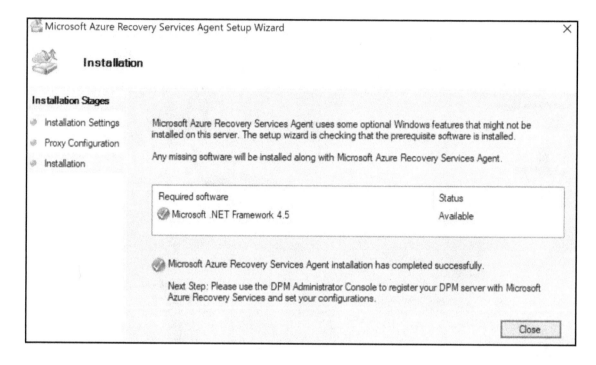

9. Now switch to the **DPM Administrator Console**, click on the **Management** workspace, and then click on **Online**, followed by the **Register** button, to begin the registration process, as shown in the following screenshot:

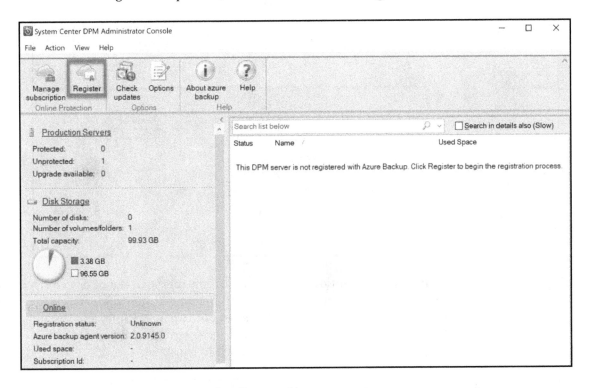

The registration wizard will open. If you are using a proxy server in your environment, then set the custom proxy server for Azure Backup. Click **Next** to continue.

10. In the **Backup Vault** window, browse to and select the vault credentials file you previously downloaded. Click **Next** to continue:

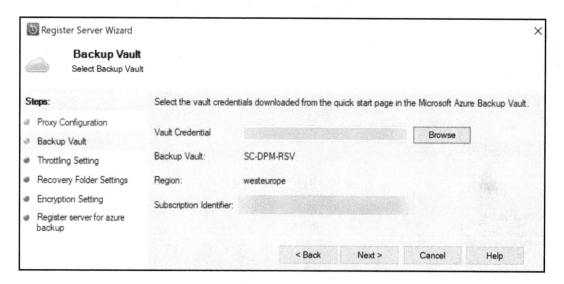

11. In the **Throttling Setting** window, if you want to control the usage of network bandwidth during working hours and non-working hours, then you can select **Enable internet bandwidth usage throttling for backup operations** and define the work and non-work hours. Please note that these settings can be changed later from the DPM console if needed. Click **Next** to continue:

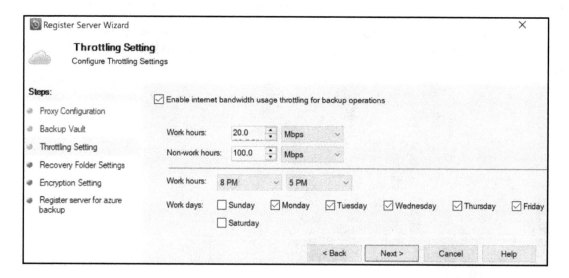

12. In the **Recovery Folder Settings** window, specify a staging area folder with sufficient space to hold the recoverable items in parallel. For example, if you want to recover 10 virtual machines from online protection in parallel and the size of each VM backed up is 100 GB, then you need to make sure the selected volume can hold 10 x 100 GB = 1 TB of data. The `StagingArea` folder location can be changed later from the DPM console if needed. Click **Next** to continue:

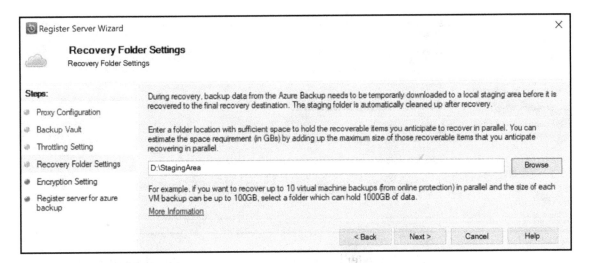

13. In the **Encryption Setting** window, you can either generate a passphrase or provide a passphrase (a minimum of 16 characters).

 Please note that if the passphrase is lost or forgotten, Microsoft cannot help you in recovering the backup data. You own the encryption passphrase, and Microsoft does not have the ability to see the passphrase used by you. Please make sure to store the passphrase (encryption key) in a safe place, such as in **Azure Key Vaults**. Otherwise, configuring subscription settings in DPM and online cloud recovery is kind of, well, impossible later.

If you lose this passphrase key, you cannot recover it later or make changes to online protection.

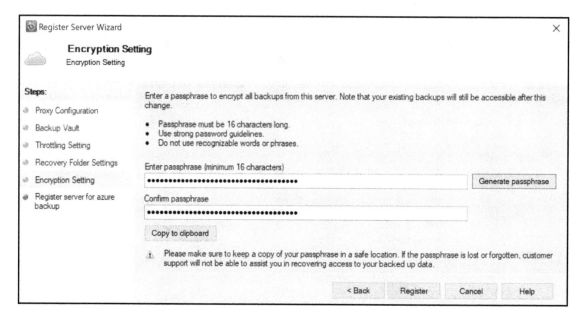

14. Once you click the **Register** button, the machine is registered successfully to the Azure Recovery Services vault, and you are now ready to start backing up your data to Microsoft Azure:

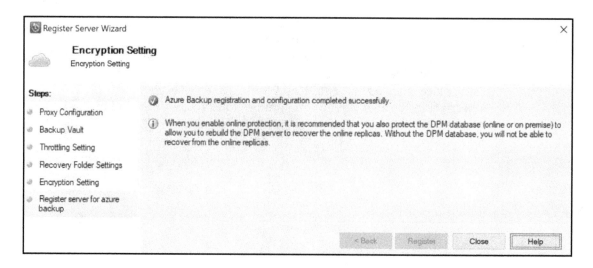

15. Please note that you can modify the settings that you specified during the registration workflow by clicking the **Configure** option by selecting **Online** under the **Management** workspace:

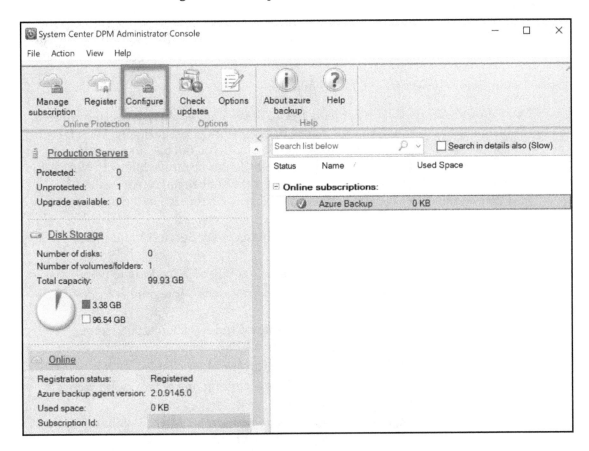

How it works...

For the SC DPM, Azure Backup acts as a secondary backup target. The primary backup target for SC DPM is locally mounted disks, but Azure Backup can be used for off-site backup, and even longer retention options. A single MARS agent and encryption key will be installed on the DPM server.

There's more...

Microsoft's free Azure Backup Server (**MABS**) is free on-premises backup software that will protect Microsoft workloads, such as Hyper-V, SQL Server, SharePoint, Windows clients, and more, by performing **disk-to-disk-to-cloud** (**D2D2C**) backup. MABS inherits the same functionality of DPM for workload backup. If you are familiar with DPM, MABS looks the same.

Azure Backup Server differs from DPM as follows:

- Microsoft Azure Backup Server is free to download; you pay for each **protected instance**, and you just pay for **Azure backup storage** usage, if any. With DPM you won't pay **protected instance** as long as you are not backing up to Azure, since you have already paid for the System Center license, while with MABS you will pay for **protected instance** even if you are not backing up to Azure. **Protected instance** is a fixed monthly fee based on the size of the data you want to protect.
- The installation requires an Azure Backup Recovery Services vault to be configured.
- It's the latest version of DPM that does not require any licensing to be purchased.
- It does not provide protection on tape, and nor does it integrate with System Center suite.
- It supports Hyper-V, Windows servers and Windows clients, SQL Server, SharePoint, Exchange Server, and VMware VM backup.
- It is designed for D2D2C restore from the local disk or cloud.
- It has continuous local protection to disk, including one or two cloud recovery points per day from the latest backup.
- It includes a free SQL Server license just to be used for MABS database locally.
- DPM **Update Rollups** (**UR**) do not apply to MABS.

> At the time of this writing, the free Azure Backup Server version 3 does NOT protect any workloads running on Windows Server 2019. However, you can install MABS version 3 on Windows Server 2019. SCDPM 2019 (LTSC) or SCDPM 1901 (SAC) can be used as alternative options to use Azure as a backup target and protects key Microsoft workloads such as SQL Server, SharePoint, and Exchange, as well as virtual machines running on Windows Server 2019 Hyper-V.
> The Azure Backup Team are actively working on allowing Azure Backup Server to support Windows Server 2019 workloads, and they will publish a release date soon.

See also

- Read this article to learn more on how to install Microsoft Azure Backup Server (MABS) version 3: `https://charbelnemnom.com/2018/11/microsoft-azure-backup-server-v3-is-now-generally-available-mabs-azure-scdpm-azurebackup/`
- Read this article to learn more about how to automate DPM integration with Azure Backup: `https://charbelnemnom.com/2018/09/automate-cloud-backup-integration-in-dpm-with-azurebackup-and-powershell-scdpm-azurebackup/`
- Read this white paper to learn more about Azure Backup: `https://charbelnemnom.com/2018/07/free-whitepaper-azure-backup-deep-dive-azurebackup-azure-azurebackup/`
- Read this article to learn more about Azure Backup pricing: `https://azure.microsoft.com/en-us/pricing/details/backup`

Protecting data with Azure Backup

This recipe will cover how to start protecting the workloads in your datacenter and enabling online protection.

Getting ready

After you have registered your DPM server with your Azure Backup Vault, you are ready now to configure your protected data. You can either create a new protection group or modify an existing protection group for online protection.

In this example, we already have a SQL protection group; we will modify and add the online protection for **DPMDB**, which is a SQL database that is supported for online protection, because to recover from DPM database corruption, you must ensure that the data is also protected at a second location, which is, in this case, Azure.

How to do it...

To modify the wizard for an existing protection group, there are few steps that are specific to online protection:

1. The first one is the **Select data protection method** step. To enable the online protection for your protected data, just select the checkbox next to **I want online protection**. Click on **Next** to continue:

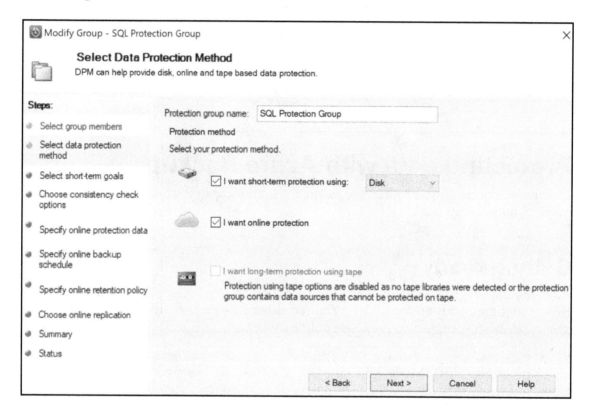

2. Next, you need to review the **Short-Term Goals** and update the retention range if needed. Click on **Next** to continue:

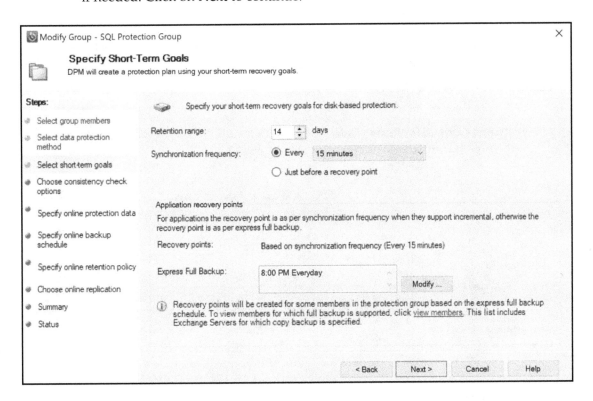

3. The next step is to **Specify Online Protection Data**. In this step, the workloads are chosen for enabling online protection. You can select **Protect auto protected SQL DBs, VMs to disk to cloud automatically**. With this option, all current and future DBs attached to this SQL instance will be protected to Azure automatically. This feature is not available for files and folders. Select the checkbox for your production data, and then click on **Next** to continue:

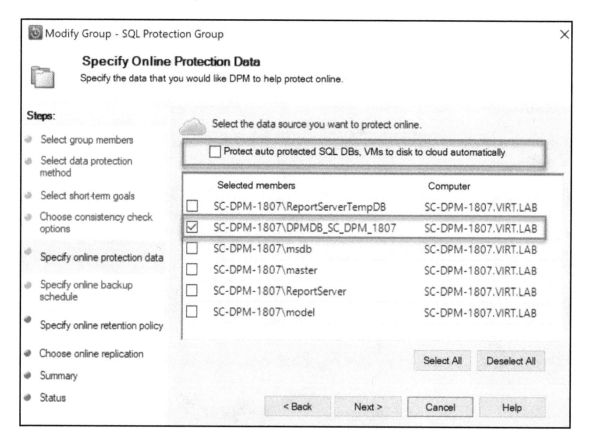

4. The next step is to **Specify Online Backup Schedule**. In this step, you will see how often incremental backups to Azure should occur. Backups can be scheduled to run every **Day**, **Week**, **Month**, or **Year**, along with the time and date at which they should run. Backups can occur up to maximum twice a day. A data recovery point is created in Azure from the copy of the backed up data stored on the DPM disk each time when the back up is run. Click on **Next** to continue:

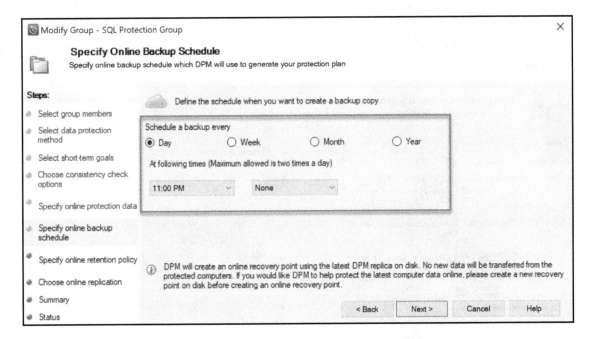

5. The next step is to **Specify Online Retention Policy**. As mentioned previously, you can use Azure Backup as a tape replacement strategy for your organization. The integral part of this strategy is the ability to store data for many years. With Azure Backup, you can technically store data for up to 99 years. However, if you take a monthly recovery point to Azure, you can retain recovery points up to 833 years before you run out, but in practice, most businesses need a solution that retains data for about 7 to 10 years. You can choose the backup frequency to be daily, weekly, monthly, or yearly, and the retention policy is based on the backup frequency you set in the previous step. Click on **Next** to continue:

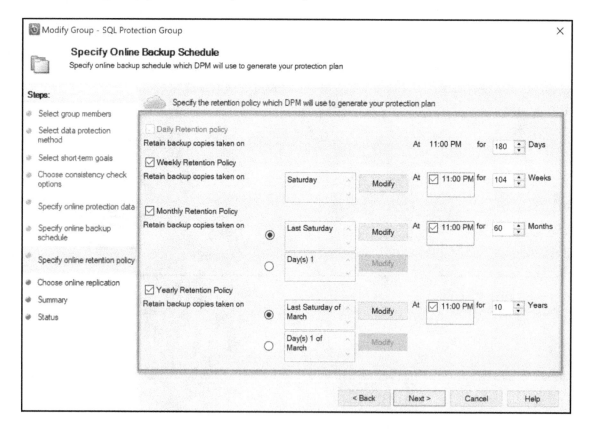

6. Last but not least, select how you want to create the initial backup. In this example, we will select **Automatically over the network**. Click on **Next** to continue:

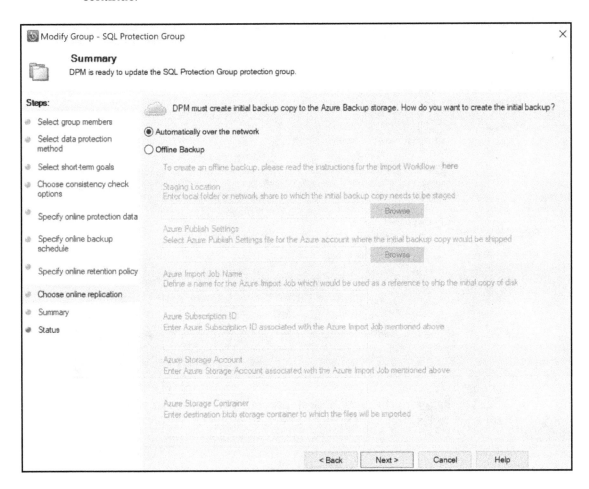

7. Finally, review the summary, click **Update Group**, and then click **Close**:

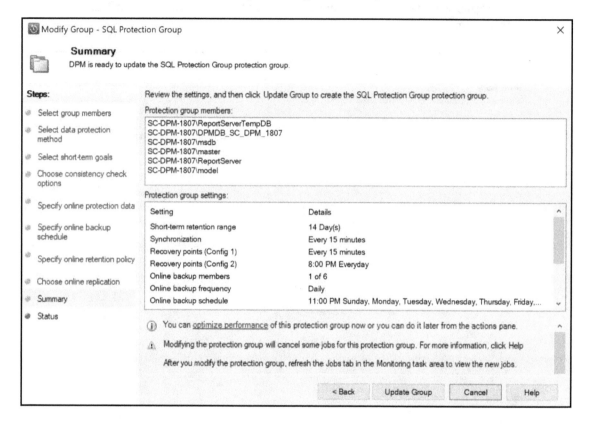

8. After you have run through these steps, you will notice that your production data is set to **Enabled** for **Online Protection** in the DPM console:

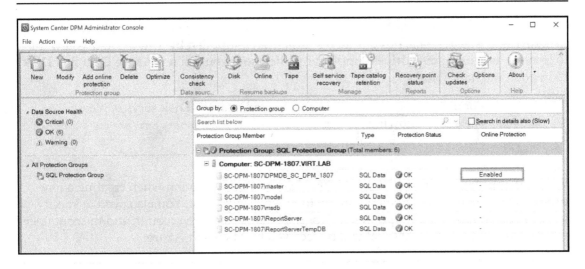

How it works...

Just as Microsoft SQL Server, Hyper-V VMs, and file/folders have been supported for backup to the cloud, you can also back up Exchange servers, SharePoint servers, and Windows client systems from on-premises environments to Microsoft Azure.

The backup and restore experiences for these scenarios are consistent with the backup and restore of data to on-premises disk media with just one exception: for SharePoint farms, the granularity of restore is a content database. This is unlike restore from disk replica where users can restore individual items from their SharePoint content databases. A cloud replica can be used if there is a disaster at the primary data center or if the local disk replica copy is broken. In this case, after the content database is downloaded, it can be attached to an existing on-premises SharePoint farm to allow for retrieval of the items.

There's more...

If you have a large amount of data to back up to Azure, you can use the Offline Backup option known as the Azure Import/Export service to store the initial seeding on disks during the protection group creation, and then send it via courier to a Microsoft Azure region of your choice. In this case, the incremental backups are smaller and require lesser bandwidth. This service is used to securely import large amounts of data to Azure Blob storage and Azure Files by shipping disk drives to an Azure data center.

With the Azure Import/Export service, you have two options—you can supply your own disk drives to transfer data, or you can use disk drives supplied by Microsoft. If you want to transfer data using disk drives supplied by Microsoft, you can use **Azure Data Box Disk** to import data into Azure.

 For more information about the **Azure Data Box Disk** service, please check the following article: `https://docs.microsoft.com/en-us/azure/databox/data-box-disk-overview`.

With this approach, you need to specify the **Offline Backup** option when creating a new protection group in DPM, as shown in the following screenshot. You also need to specify your Microsoft Azure subscription ID, import job name, storage account, and the container where you will place the data that will be received by Microsoft Azure:

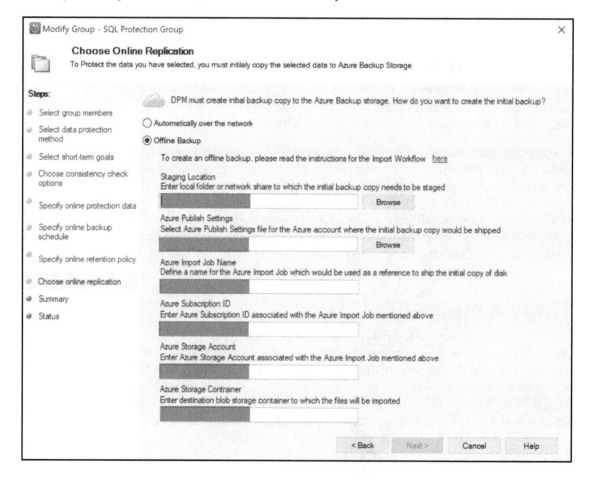

The data is copied to the set of specified removable SATA disks as soon as the backup begins, and when the backup is complete, your disks can be shipped to Microsoft Azure. For the arrival of contents in Azure, an Azure import job is created and tracked by the Azure Backup client.

See also

Microsoft has published step-by-step documentation about how to use the Import/Export service. You can read it here: `https://docs.microsoft.com/en-us/azure/storage/common/storage-import-export-service`.

Creating online recovery points

This recipe will cover how to create an on-demand recovery point for backup and archive purposes, and how to automatically replicate it to Azure Recovery Services Vault.

Getting ready

In some scenarios such as updating and patching your server or your application, you want to manually create recovery points for your data. The prerequisites are that you have the online protection enabled for the data source(s) present in your protection group. Please refer to the previous section if you have not yet done so.

How to do it...

1. To create a recovery point manually for your protected data, open your DPM Administrator Console, click on the **Protection** workspace, and then right-click on the data source and choose **Create recovery point...**:

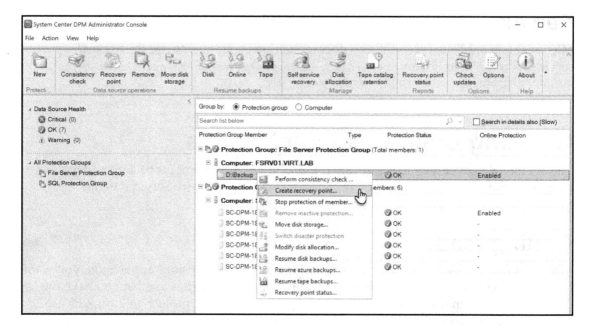

2. You will be prompted with the **Create recovery point** wizard. Select **Online protection** from the drop-down menu, and then click on the **OK** button:

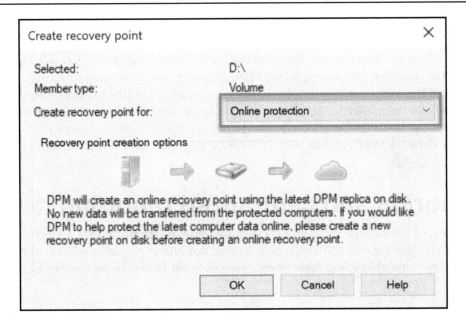

Create recovery point   ✕

Selected: D:\

Member type: Volume

Create recovery point for: Online protection ⌄

Recovery point creation options

DPM will create an online recovery point using the latest DPM replica on disk.
No new data will be transferred from the protected computers. If you would like
DPM to help protect the latest computer data online, please create a new
recovery point on disk before creating an online recovery point.

         OK   Cancel   Help

3. The DPM server will start creating a backup and then transfer it to Azure; you
   can follow its progress in the **Create Recovery Point** task window:

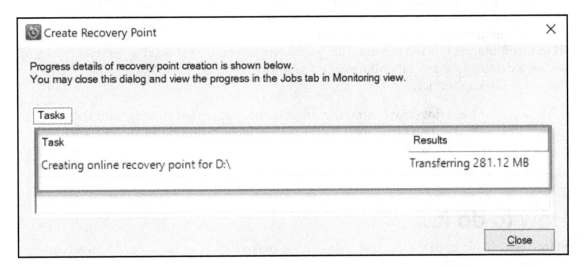

Create Recovery Point   ✕

Progress details of recovery point creation is shown below.
You may close this dialog and view the progress in the Jobs tab in Monitoring view.

Tasks

Task	Results
Creating online recovery point for D:\	Transferring 281.12 MB

        Close

How it works...

When you create an online recovery point, the DPM server will start creating a backup and store it on the disk first (on-premises) and then transfer it immediately to Azure. Always keep in mind that network bandwidth is very important for online backup. You can verify your network performance from on-premises to Azure via your **Internet Service Provider** (**ISP**), or you can use a tool available from Microsoft (`http://www.azurespeed.com/`) to verify your network latency from your IP location to Azure data centers around the world.

Monitoring and centralized reporting

Monitoring and centralized reporting is crucial when you are protecting a large amount of data. In this recipe, we will show you how to monitor and configure centralized reporting to gain business insights using Azure Log Analytics and Power BI reports for SC DPM and MABS.

Getting ready

To monitor and configure centralized reporting, all you need is an Azure subscription. With a subscription, you can sign in to the Azure Portal and create a storage account for reports, then turn on diagnostics, and finally add the **Azure Backup** content pack in **Power BI** to monitor and view the reports. The good news is, you do not need to set up a reporting server, a database, or any other infrastructure since everything is completely managed by the Azure Backup service.

> Please note that central reporting is only supported starting with DPM version 1801, 1807, 1901, DPM 2019 or later, including MABS version 3 onward, with the latest MARS agent. DPM 2016 or earlier versions are not supported.

How to do it...

Before you enable central reporting, you need to make sure your DPM or MABS server is already registered and connected to Microsoft Azure.

Configuring Azure Storage Account

Now take the following steps:

1. Log in to the Azure Portal at `https://portal.azure.com`, and on the left-hand side choose **All services**. Then scroll down to **Storage accounts**. On the **Storage accounts** window that appears, choose **Add**. Select the desired Azure subscription and resource group in which to create the storage account. Click **Review + create** to validate, and then click **Create**:

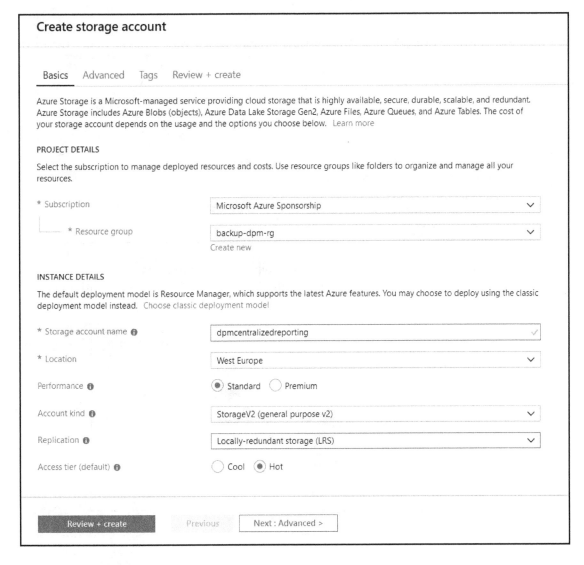

2. Next, browse to **Recovery Services Vaults** in the Azure Portal and select a vault you used to register your DPM server.

3. From the list of items that appears under the vault, under the **Manage** section select **Backup Reports** to configure the storage account for reports. On the **Backup Reports** blade, click on the **Diagnostics Settings** link:

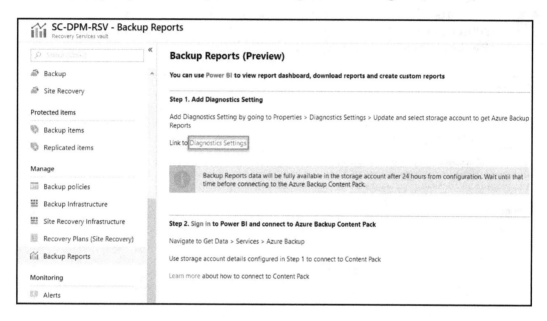

4. The **Diagnostics settings** UI will open, which is used to push data to your storage account. Select **Turn on diagnostics** to open a UI to use to configure a storage account:

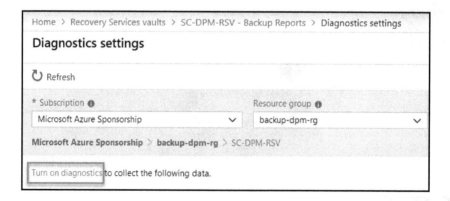

5. In the **Name** field, enter a desired name. Select the **Archive to a storage account** checkbox so that reporting data can start flowing into the storage account. Select the **Storage account** that you created in the previous step by selecting the relevant Azure subscription and the storage account from the list, and then click **OK**.

6. Under the **Log** section, select the **AzureBackupReport** checkbox, then move the slider to the desired retention (0–365 day period for this reporting data). Review all the changes, and then select **Save**:

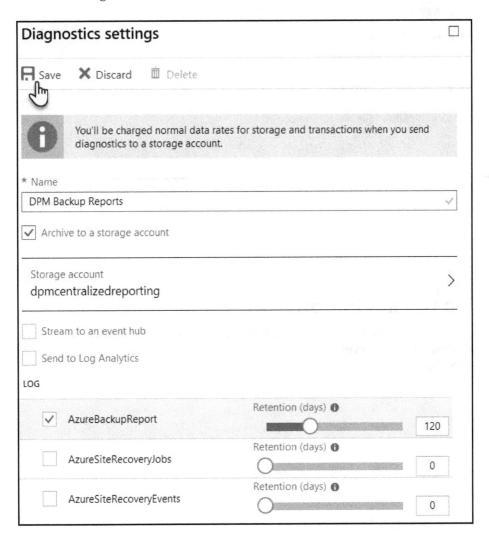

7. Refresh the table now to see the updated setting in the **Diagnostic settings** enabled for the vault:

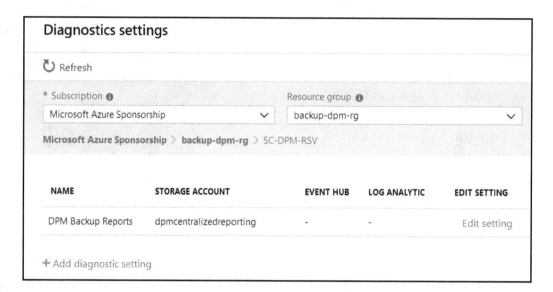

 After you have configured the storage account to store the reports, please wait for 24 hours for the initial data push to finish.

Viewing reports in Power BI

After 24 hours have passed since setting up the storage account, you can import the Azure Backup content pack in Power BI. Please note that it takes around 24 hours for reporting data to start showing in Power BI.

Follow these steps to view the reports in Power BI:

1. Sign in to Power BI at `https://powerbi.microsoft.com/landing/signin/`. On the left-hand side, select **Get Data**. In **Discover content** under **Services**, select **Get.**

> Please note that you can use a free Power BI subscription, but it is limited to 1 GB of data only. If you need more data, then you need to switch to a paid version.

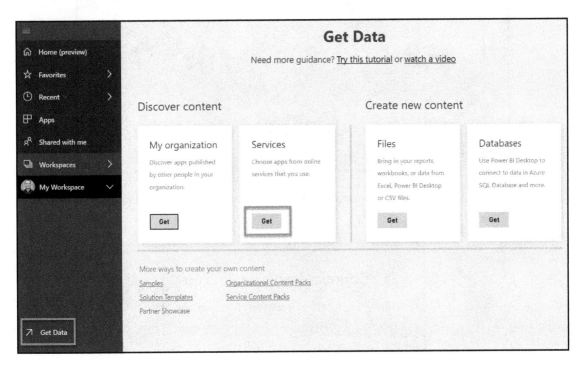

2. In the search bar, type `Azure Backup` and then select **Get it now**:

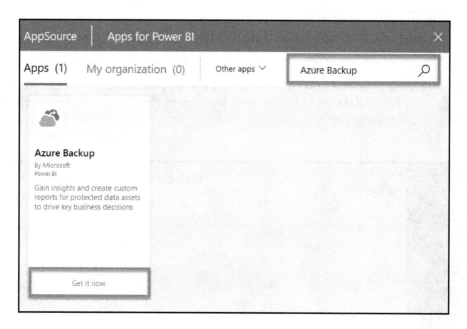

3. Enter the name of the storage account that you configured previously, and select **Next** to continue:

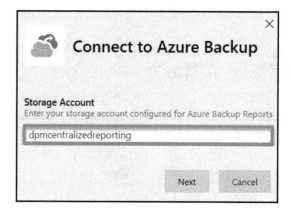

4. Enter the storage account key for this storage account. You can get the storage access keys by going to your storage account in the Azure Portal. Select **Sign in** to verify you can sign in successfully:

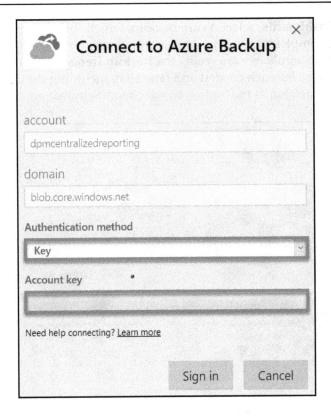

5. After signing in successfully, the **Azure Backup** content pack is visible in **Apps** in the navigation pane:

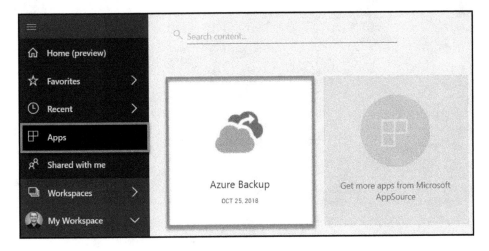

6. Under **Dashboards**, select **Azure Backup**, which shows a set of key reports. To view the complete set of reports, select any report in the dashboard. In the following example, we are seeing the **Backup Items** tab that shows the top five backup items for each created and failed job, including the alerts created. You can select each tab at the bottom to view reports in that area:

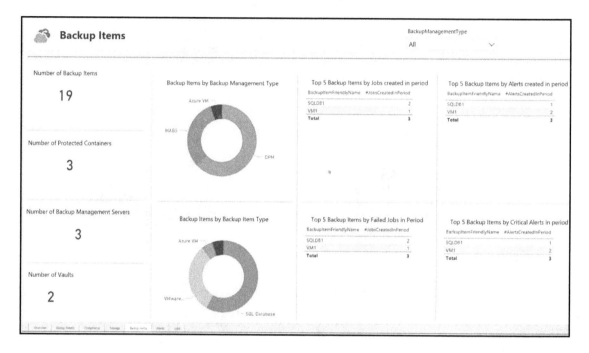

How it works...

The data will be pushed from DPM and MABS and exported as JSON files into a container in the storage account named `insights-logs-azurebackupreport`, and Power BI will consume/process that data. The timing of this varies depending on the data, but as we mentioned earlier, Microsoft confirms that it can take up to 24 hours for the first datasets to be visible:

The Azure Backup content pack can be used to monitor and view reports from multiple DPM/MABS servers in a central view. The content pack is updated regularly in Power BI to add more features.

There's more...

When you enable central reporting, you can also configure a Log Analytics (LA) workspace to send the same data to, which is part of Azure Monitor. You need to create first a Log Analytics workspace, or if you have already configured Log Analytics you can select it in the **Diagnostics settings** blade as shown in the following screenshot, and then click **Save**.

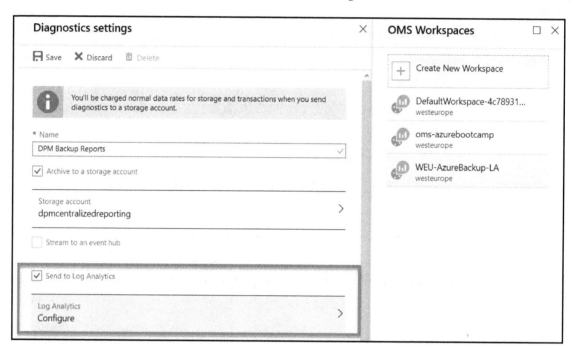

 If you have multiple Recovery Services Vaults, then make sure to choose the same workspace for all the vaults so that you get a centralized view in the workspace. After completing the configuration, allow 24 hours for initial data push to complete.

Once the data is in the workspace, you need a set of graphs to visualize the monitoring data. You need to deploy Azure Backup monitoring solution template to the workspace that you configured above. Make sure you give the same **Resource group**, **Workspace name**, and **Workspace location** to properly identify the workspace and then install this template on it as shown in the next screenshot, and then click **Purchase**.

You can deploy this template from the following location: `https://azure.microsoft.com/en-us/resources/templates/101-backup-oms-monitoring/`

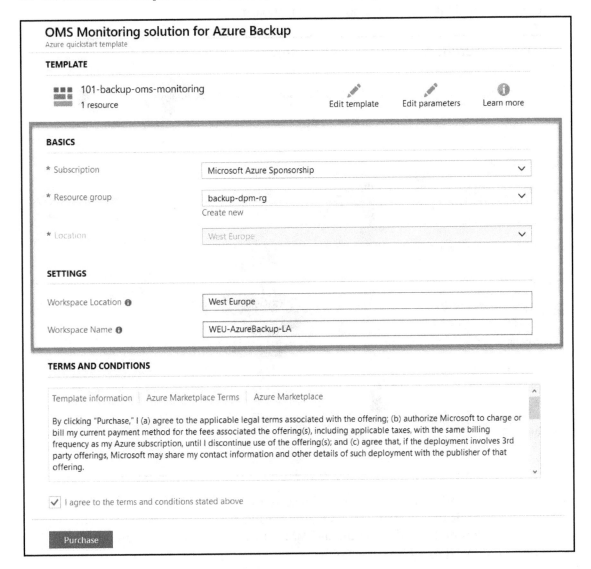

Once deployed, you will get an overview tile for Azure Backup in the workspace dashboard as shown in the next screenshot. If you click on the **Azure Backup Monitoring Solution** tile, it will take you to the solution dashboard.

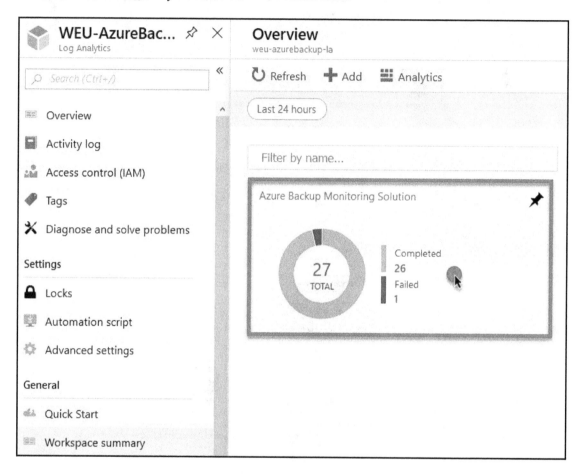

You can start monitoring daily backups and restore for all Azure Backup protected workloads. With this update, you can even monitor log backups for your SQL Databases whether they are running within Azure IaaS VMs or being run locally on-premises and being protected by DPM, or MABS server.

 Please make sure to select the relevant time range to monitor, by choosing the proper start and end dates.

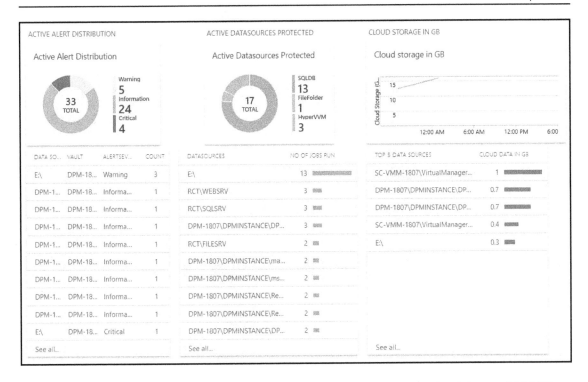

ACTIVE ALERT DISTRIBUTION				ACTIVE DATASOURCES PROTECTED		CLOUD STORAGE IN GB	

Active Alert Distribution

33 TOTAL

Warning 5
Information 24
Critical 4

Active Datasources Protected

17 TOTAL

SQLDB 13
FileFolder 1
HyperVVM 3

Cloud storage in GB

DATA SO...	VAULT	ALERTSEV...	COUNT	DATASOURCES	NO OF JOBS RUN	TOP 5 DATA SOURCES	CLOUD DATA IN GB
E:\	DPM-18...	Warning	3	E:\	13	SC-VMM-1807\VirtualManager...	1
DPM-1...	DPM-18...	Informa...	1	RCT\WEBSRV	3	DPM-1807\DPMINSTANCE\DP...	0.7
DPM-1...	DPM-18...	Informa...	1	RCT\SQLSRV	3	DPM-1807\DPMINSTANCE\DP...	0.7
DPM-1...	DPM-18...	Informa...	1	DPM-1807\DPMINSTANCE\DP...	3	SC-VMM-1807\VirtualManager...	0.4
DPM-1...	DPM-18...	Informa...	1	RCT\FILESRV	2	E:\	0.3
DPM-1...	DPM-18...	Informa...	1	DPM-1807\DPMINSTANCE\ma...	2		
DPM-1...	DPM-18...	Informa...	1	DPM-1807\DPMINSTANCE\ms...	2		
DPM-1...	DPM-18...	Informa...	1	DPM-1807\DPMINSTANCE\Re...	2		
DPM-1...	DPM-18...	Informa...	1	DPM-1807\DPMINSTANCE\Re...	2		
E:\	DPM-18...	Critical	1	DPM-1807\DPMINSTANCE\DP...	2		
See all...				See all...		See all...	

Last but not least, you can also create custom alerts for it to monitor the DPM and MABS servers and send you notification when something goes wrong. This solution is key for any organization to keep an eye over their backups and ensure that all actions are taken for successful backups and restore.

See also

Check this article to learn more about how to configure alerts for Log Analytics with Azure Monitor: https://docs.microsoft.com/en-us/azure/azure-monitor/learn/tutorial-response

Other Books You May Enjoy

If you enjoyed this book, you may be interested in these other books by Packt:

System Center 2016 Virtual Machine Manager Cookbook - Third Edition
Roman Levchenko, Edvaldo Alessandro Cardoso

ISBN: 978-1-78588-148-0

- Plan and design a VMM architecture for real-world deployment
- Configure fabric resources, including compute, networking, and storage
- Create and manage Storage Spaces Direct clusters in VMM
- Configure Guarded Fabric with Shielded VMs
- Create and deploy virtual machine templates and multi-tier services
- Manage Hyper-V and VMware environments from VMM
- Enhance monitoring and management capabilities
- Upgrade to VMM 2016 from previous versions

Deploying Microsoft System Center Configuration Manager

Jacek Doktor, Pawel Jarosz

ISBN: 978-1-78588-101-5

- Install ConfigMgr servers and the necessary roles
- Design and scale ConfigMgr environments
- Configure and administrate essential ConfigMgr roles and features
- Create software packages using .msi and .exe files
- Deliver detailed reports with an automatic patching process
- Apply proper hardening on your deployment and secure workstations
- Deploy operating systems and updates leveraging ConfigMgr mechanisms
- Create high-availability components using the built-in mechanism for backup and recovery

Leave a review - let other readers know what you think

Please share your thoughts on this book with others by leaving a review on the site that you bought it from. If you purchased the book from Amazon, please leave us an honest review on this book's Amazon page. This is vital so that other potential readers can see and use your unbiased opinion to make purchasing decisions, we can understand what our customers think about our products, and our authors can see your feedback on the title that they have worked with Packt to create. It will only take a few minutes of your time, but is valuable to other potential customers, our authors, and Packt. Thank you!

Index

CPSIA information can be obtained
at www.ICGtesting.com
Printed in the USA
LVHW100353151220
674148LV00008B/962

9 781787 289284